Forced Marriage Law and Practice

Forced Marriage Law and Practice

Joshua Hitchens, Barrister
4-5 Gray's Inn Square

Niamh Daly, Barrister
New Court Chambers

Bloomsbury Professional
LONDON • DUBLIN • EDINBURGH • NEW YORK • NEW DELHI • SYDNEY

BLOOMSBURY PROFESSIONAL
Bloomsbury Publishing Plc

50 Bedford Square, London, WC1B 3DP, UK
1385 Broadway, New York, NY 10018, USA
29 Earlsfort Terrace, Dublin 2, Ireland

BLOOMSBURY and the Diana logo are trademarks of Bloomsbury Publishing Plc

British Library Cataloguing-in-Publication Data

A catalogue record for this book is available from the British Library.

ISBN: PB: 978 1 52651 595 7
Epdf: 978 1 52651 597 1
Epub: 978 1 52651 596 4

Typeset by Evolution Design & Digital Ltd (Kent)

Foreword

This is an impressive book addressing an important issue. It also has the considerable advantage of being a pleasurable and, at times, compelling read, never easy to achieve in a legal textbook.

As the authors identify, whilst the insidious nature of forced marriage is internationally recognised, it remains the case that there is no internationally agreed definition. Achieving an accurate and comprehensive definition is more challenging than might, at first, appear given that it essentially involves a marriage where one or both parties either do not or cannot consent. Though these marriages are commonly characterised by physical or emotional abuse (frequently both) and though they will often involve pressure on one or both of the people involved, this is not universally the case. Arranged marriages are variously motivated, this includes financial greed; they may involve collusion in sexual exploitation or be driven by a perceived need to vindicate a misconceived perception of family honour.

In the United Kingdom forced marriage is recognised as a form of domestic or child abuse and identified as a serious violation of human rights. It is a criminal offence by virtue of the Anti-Social Behaviour Crime and Policing Act 2014, which creates a freestanding offence of forcing somebody to marry. However, as is pointed out in the book, there have been disturbingly few prosecutions, particularly when contrasted with the number of cases reported annually to the Forced Marriage Unit.

Sometimes a forced marriage may be rooted in more complex objectives and beliefs. It may, for example, be driven by a desire to provide a stable and financially secure future for a daughter who is loved or, as in *Re RS, (Forced Marriage Protection Order)* [2015] EWHC 3534 (Fam), represent a utilitarian attempt to provide a carer for a son who is unable to navigate life alone. Whilst such arrangements are no less exploitative, experience indicates that they are often most effectively addressed by education and dialogue.

The authors approach their subject by surveying the variety of remedies available across the whole spectrum of English law particularly including the criminal law, family law and the Court of Protection but also incorporating civil and public international law. It is an ambitious project, but it is one that has been skilfully realised. At the end of this odyssey the authors successfully demonstrate the benefit of a multi-disciplinary approach and the efficacy of a combination of remedies achieving the most effective outcomes.

The book unfolds a broad canvas of case law, it examines an extensive legal framework. In each discipline of law, the authors demonstrate not only that they have thoroughly mastered their subject matter but reveal an ability, on page after page, to focus on the key passages of the judgments they analyse. This spare and accessible style gives the book an energy which I am confident will make it of interest to a wide range of professionals and to anybody concerned with repression of personal autonomy.

The Honourable Mr Justice Hayden
Vice President of the Court of Protection
26 January 2021

Preface

Forced marriage is an age-old evil which affects all sections, religions, ethnicities and classes of society. It is a problem which requires a response both from all arms of the state and all disciplines of the law. The purpose of this book is to encourage practitioners to approach cases holistically, considering remedies across all practice areas and the full array of statutory services available in cases concerning forced marriage.

The book is divided into five parts. **Part 1** is intended to provide an accessible route into the book and contains chapters defining forced marriage, setting out the legal avenues to prevent, punish and remedy a forced marriage as well as chapters setting out the main causes and categories of forced marriage. **Part 2** sets out the law and procedure in the family courts, **Part 3,** the criminal courts, **Part 4** concerns the Court of Protection and **Part 5** provides guidance on best practice for a range of professionals.

We thank everyone at Bloomsbury, particularly Kiran Goss, Jane Bradford and Jenny Lank for their patience and making this book possible.

The law is stated as at January 2021. Any errors are our own.

Joshua Hitchens
Niamh Daly
January 2021

Acknowledgements

There are many people I ought to thank. Firstly, my unfailingly supportive and wonderful parents, Gary and Susannah, my sister, Lily, my grandparents and my partner and co-author Niamh, without whom this book would not have been possible.

Thank you also to Anand Beharrylal QC for his mentorship, advice, support and for leading me in some of the most interesting cases of my career and HH Crawford Lindsay QC for his kindness, generosity and guidance.

Finally, thank you to the Adult Services and Human Rights Law Team, Legal & Governance Department at Birmingham City Council for introducing me to Court of Protection work, briefing me in my first Forced Marriage case and making this book possible

Josh Hitchens
4-5 Gray's Inn Square

Thank you to my mother, HHJ Gargan for her inspiration, support and kindness and my sister, Kirsty. I am endlessly grateful to my colleagues and clerks from New Court Chambers and my past pupil supervisors for making this book possible. Thank you also to Kiran Goss and the rest of the team at Bloomsbury for giving us the opportunity to write this book and supporting us through the process of getting it to its completed state.

Niamh Daly
New Court Chambers

Contents

Table of Cases

[All references are to paragraph numbers.]

D

E

Table of Statutes

[All references are to paragraph numbers.]

Table of Statutory Instruments

[All references are to paragraph numbers.]

Table of International Material

[All references are to paragraph numbers.]

Part I

Types and stages of forced marriages

CHAPTER 1

Introduction

1.1 Forced Marriage is recognised as a global criminal and humanitarian crisis. In 2016, the International Labour Organisation estimated that 15.4 million people were in a forced marriage. Ninety per cent of those marriages took place in Africa and Asia.[1]

1.2 Forced marriage is a gendered crime which affects women and girls at a far higher rate than men and boys.[2] However, it is not a crime which exclusively victimises women. In 2019, 19 per cent of the cases dealt with by the Forced Marriage Unit related to male victims.[3] In 2016, the International Labour Organisation estimated that 0.6 per cent of forced marriage cases globally involved males.[4] Some academic research suggests that male forced marriage may be under-recognised and under-reported.[5]

1.3 There is a significant proportion of victims who are children, in 2016 it was estimated that female children accounted for 37 per cent of victims, with 44 per cent of those being forced to marry before the age of fifteen.[6] The proportion of victims of forced marriage generally who are female is twice that of other forms of modern slavery.

1.4 In a domestic context, during 2019 the Forced Marriage Unit[7] dealt with 1,355 possible cases of forced marriage.[8] It is likely that once cases dealt with exclusively by local authorities or police services are factored in, the number of annual forced marriage cases in the UK is significantly higher. Sixty one percent of these cases related to Pakistan, Bangladesh, India or Afghanistan. Just five per cent of cases dealt with by the Forced Marriage Unit in 2019 had no overseas

1 Global Estimate of Modern Slavery, International Labour Organization and Walk Free Foundation, 2017, page 10.
2 Forced Marriage Unit Statistics 2019, Home Office and Foreign and Commonwealth Office, 25 June 2020, page 9.
3 Forced Marriage Unit Statistics 2019, Home Office and Foreign and Commonwealth Office, 25 June 2020, page 9.
4 Global Estimate of Modern Slavery, International Labour Organization and Walk Free Foundation, 2017, page 43.
5 Samad, Forced Marriage among men: An unrecognised problem, journal of Critical Social Policy 2010 30: 189.
6 Global Estimate of Modern Slavery, International Labour Organization and Walk Free Foundation, 2017, page 11.
7 A joint Home Office and Foreign and Commonwealth Office Unit which leads HMG's efforts to combat Forced Marriage.
8 Forced Marriage Unit Statistics 2019, Home Office and Foreign and Commonwealth Office, 25 June 2020, page 9.

element.[9] This strong international element to the United Kingdom's response to forced marriage means that court disputes are likely to involve elements of international law and enforcement.

1.5 It is now universally recognised that forced marriage is a gross abuse of the human rights of the victim, a form of domestic abuse and, where children are concerned, child abuse.[10] The Statutory Guidance issued by the Secretary of State sets out the 'one chance' principle:

> 'All [public sector leaders] providing services to victims of forced marriage and honour-based violence need to be aware of the "one chance" rule. That is, their staff may only have one chance to speak to a potential victim and thus their staff may only have one chance to save a life'[11]

1.6 The 'one chance rule' underlines why it is critical for all practitioners involved in matters of forced marriage to take the right steps at the right time. The purpose of this book is to provide an easy to use and comprehensive guide to help inform the difficult and complex judgements those involved in the field shall inevitably have to take.

1.7 Twenty-seven per cent of those supported by the Forced Marriage Unit in 2019 were under the age of 18. Thus, a very significant proportion of victims are children. Ten per cent of those supported had learning difficulties.[12] There are therefore strong crossovers both with the law governing adults lacking capacity and public children law.

1.8 Forced marriage is also a specific criminal offence and therefore engages the criminal law. There are also civil law aspects of forced marriage and the potential liability of public bodies who fail to properly protect individuals or investigate reports relating to forced marriage. The purpose of this book is to approach forced marriage as a multidisciplinary subject matter highlighting the variety of remedies available across the whole spectrum of English Law jurisdictions.

1.9 In adopting this approach, we hope to advocate for a cross-practice area approach to issues of forced marriage. Often a combination of remedies may be required to achieve the most satisfactory outcome.

9 Forced Marriage Unit Statistics 2019, Home Office and Foreign and Commonwealth Office, 25 June 2020, page 13.

10 The Right to Choose: Multi-agency statutory guidance for dealing with forced marriage, HM Government, 2008, page 4

11 The Right to Choose: Multi-Agency Statutory Guidance for dealing with forced marriage, HM Government, page 1.

12 Forced Marriage Unit Statistics 2019, Home Office and Foreign and Commonwealth Office, 25 June 2020, page 13.

CHAPTER 2

What is a Forced Marriage?

Content at a Glance:

Introduction

Family law definition

Criminal law definition

Marriages where parties lack capacity and the Court of Protection

Arranged marriages and the 'grey area 'Civil law definition

Public international law

INTRODUCTION

2.1 Whilst the pernicious nature of forced marriage is universally recognised; there is no internationally agreed definition[1]. In *R (on the application of Quila and another) v Secretary of State for the Home Department*,[2] Lord Brown described how: 'Forced marriages are an appalling evil. Most commonly the victims are young women and all too often such marriages occur within the immigrant community'. This case demonstrates the politically charged and contentious nature of policy surrounding forced marriage. It was a judicial review of the Immigration Rules designed to deter forced marriage and the Home Secretary's application of those rules. The case also demonstrates the inter-disciplinary, cross practice area approach required to deter, prevent, punish and resolve forced marriages. Unfortunately, there has not been a single, uniform definition of forced marriage adopted across all disciplines.

2.2 Instead, each jurisdiction in the courts of England and Wales have subtly different criteria and/or definitions.

2.3 Within the United Kingdom, and at domestic governmental level, the following definition has been implemented by the Forced Marriage Unit[3]:

> 'A forced marriage is where one or both people do not (or in cases of people with learning disabilities or reduced capacity, cannot) consent to

1 European Union Agency for Fundamental Human Rights, *Addressing Forced Marriage in the EU: legal provisions and promising practices* (European Union, 2014) 9.

2 [2011] UKSC 45.

3 Central Government correct as of September 2020

> the marriage as they are pressurised, or abuse is used, to force them to do so. It is recognised in the UK as a form of domestic or child abuse and a serious abuse of human rights.'

2.4 Whilst subtly varied definitions are used, this has broadly been adopted across all government departments.

2.5 The government definition goes on to recognise that physical, psychological, emotional and financial abuse may all contribute to a forced marriage. In reality, this broad-brush approach is reflected in the approaches adopted by the civil, family and criminal courts as well as the Court of Protection. However, it is necessary to examine the definition adopted by each jurisdiction.

FAMILY LAW DEFINITION

2.6 The concept of a forced marriage under English Law was originally based upon the principle of the duress. In *Szechter v Szechter*,[4] a case in which the wife had married the husband solely to escape from a repressive regime in Poland, Jocelyn Simon P held that in order to establish duress as a basis for a decree of nullity, a party must prove:

> 'That the will of one of the parties thereto had been overborne by the genuine and reasonably held fear caused by threat of immediate danger to life, limb or liberty, so that the constraint destroys the reality of consent to ordinary wedlock'.

2.7 The landscape has significantly changed since 1970, the Family Law Act 1996, s 63A, (as amended by the Forced Marriage (Civil Protection) Act 2007, s 1), having created a statutory definition of the term 'forced marriage'.

> **'63A. Forced Marriage Protection Orders**
>
> (4) For the purposes of this Part a person ("A") is forced into a marriage if another person ("B") forces A to enter into a marriage (whether with B or another person) without A's free and full consent.
>
> (5) For the purposes of subsection (4) it does not matter whether the conduct of B which forces A to enter into a marriage is directed against A, B or another person.
>
> (6) In this Part—
>
> "force" includes coerce by threats or other psychological means (and related expressions are to be read accordingly); and
>
> "forced marriage protection order" means an order under this section.'

4 [1970] 3 All ER 905.

2.8 What is clear is that the courts have adopted a wide interpretation of what constitutes 'force' or 'coercion'. The applicant must show that 'the threats, pressure or whatever it is, is such to destroy the reality of consent and overbears the will of the individual.[5] Undue emotional pressure is capable of amounting to force or coercion for the purposes of s 63A.[6] So too is violence or the threat of violence, financial abuse and psychological abuse.

2.9 Where a party lacks capacity to marry at the time the marriage is contracted, the marriage will necessarily be a forced marriage (see **21.15** et seq for the test for capacity to marry).

2.10 The Family Division of the High Court has repeatedly underlined the need to distinguish forced marriages from arranged marriages (see **10.4** et seq).

CRIMINAL LAW DEFINITION

2.11 There are two routes to committing a criminal offence relating to a forced marriage. The first, is breaching a Forced Marriage Protection Order made pursuant to the Family Law Act 1996, s 63A. Breach of a Forced Marriage Protection Order is made a criminal offence by the Anti-social Behaviour Crime and Policing Act 2014, s 120, punishable by up to five years' imprisonment.

2.12 Further, the Anti-social Behaviour Crime and Policing Act 2014, s 121 creates a freestanding offence of forcing someone to marry which is not dependent on the existence of a civil order:

> **'121. Offence of a forced marriage: England and Wales**
>
> (1) A person commits and offence under the law of England and Wales if he or she-
>
> (a) uses violence, threats or any other form of coercion for the purpose of causing another person to enter into a marriage, and
>
> (b) believes, or ought reasonably to believe, that the conduct may cause the other person to enter into the marriage without free and full consent.
>
> (2) In relation to a victim who lacks capacity to consent to marriage, the offence under subsection (1) is capable of being committed by any conduct carried out for the purpose of causing the victim to enter into a marriage (whether or not the conduct amounts to violence, threats or any other form of coercion).
>
> (3) A person commits an offence under the law of England and Wales if he or she-

5 *Re P (Forced Marriage)* [2011] 1 FLR 2060.

6 *Re SK (An Adult) Forced Marriage; Appropriate Relief)* [2004] EWHC 3202 (Fam).

(a) Practises any form of deception with the intention of causing another person to leave the United Kingdom, and

(b) intends the other person to be subjected to conduct outside the United Kingdom that is an offence under subsection (1) or would be an offence under that subsection if the victim were in England or Wales.

(4) "Marriage" means any religious or civil ceremony of marriage (whether or not legally binding).

(5) "Lacks Capacity" means lacks capacity within the meaning of the Mental Capacity Act 2005.

(6) It is irrelevant whether the conduct mentioned in paragraph (1) of subsection (1) is directed at the victim of the offence under that subsection or another person.

(7) A person commits an offence under subsection (1) or (3) only if, at the time of the conduct or deception—

(a) the person or the victim of both of them are in England or Wales,

(b) neither the person nor the victim is in England or Wales but at least one of them is habitually resident in England and Wales, or

(c) neither the person nor the victim is in the United Kingdom but at least one of them is a UK national.

...'

2.13 In the four years between the enactment of the Anti-social Behaviour Crime and Policing Act 2014 and November 2018, there were just four convictions under s 121.[7] The result of this dearth of convictions is that there is no appellate case law supplementing the above statutory definition. In particular, it remains unclear what amounts to coercion under s 121(1)(a). Whether the criminal courts shall ultimately adopt the broad definition of 'coerce' used in the courts in include varying degrees of emotional, financial and psychological abuse is unclear.

MARRIAGES WHERE PARTIES LACK CAPACITY AND THE COURT OF PROTECTION

Mental Capacity Checklist:

A Capacity must be assumed unless it is established P lacks it

B Capacity is to be decided on the balance of probabilities

C The court must first consider the diagnostic test: does the person have an impairment or disturbance in the functioning of the mind or brain; and

7 Home Office, Preventing and tackling forced marriage: a consultation, November 2018.

D Then the decision-making test: is P unable to do any of the following:
- i Understand information relevant to the decision;
- ii Retain that information;
- iii Use or weigh that information as part of the process of making the decision
- iv Communicate their decision

E Have all practical steps to help P make the decision been taken?

F Remember, capacity is decision specific, P may have capacity to make some decisions but not others.

2.14 The Mental Capacity Act 2005, s 1 creates a statutory presumption that a person has capacity to make decisions. Capacity is decision specific, meaning that a person may have capacity to make certain decisions but lack capacity in respect of others. In order to establish that a person lacks capacity in any relevant domain, it must be shown on the balance of probabilities that at the material time they are unable to make a decision for themselves in relation to the matter because of an impairment of, or a disturbance in the functioning of, the mind or brain. It does not matter whether the impairment or disturbance is permanent or temporary.[8]

2.15 A person is unable to make a decision if they are unable to do any of the following:[9]

(a) To understand the information relevant to the decision,

(b) To retain that information,

(c) To use or weigh that information as part of the process of making the decision, or

(d) To communicate his decision (whether by talking, using sign language or any other means).

2.16 A marriage which is contracted when one or both of the spouses lack capacity to consent to marriage is necessarily a forced marriage (*YLA v PM & MX*[10]). The test for capacity to marry is considered at **Chapter 8** whilst the remedies following an marriage where the parties lack capacity are explored at **Chapters 14** and **15**.

The relevance of capacity to consent to sexual relations

2.17 In *London Borough of Southwark v KA and Others* ,[11] Parker J held that in order to have capacity to marry, one must not lack capacity to consent to sexual relations.

8 Mental Capacity Act 2005, s 2.
9 Mental Capacity Act 2005, s 3.
10 [2013] EWHC 4020 (COP).
11 [2016] EWCOP 20 at [37].

2.18 The basis for this rule was set out by Munby J in *X City Council v MB, NB & MAB*[12] which is a case concerning a man with severe autistic spectrum disorder whose parents had allegedly arranged for him to be married to his cousin. The ratio can be summarised as:

(a) Sexual relations are implicit in, although not a requisite of, marriage as part of a man and woman living together and loving each other as man and wife.

(b) Whilst a marriage contract does not require a sexual element and does not oblige either spouse to engage in sexual activity, it does grant each party the right to choose whether to engage in sexual activity within the union.

(c) In circumstances where one party cannot consent to sexual relations, there is a risk of sexual offences being committed within the marriage.

2.19 In *D Borough Council v B*,[13] which concerned to man with moderate learning difficulties who had developed a homosexual relationship with a fellow service user, Mostyn J made the additional point that consenting to marriage is a more complex decision than consenting to sex.

2.20 The consistency of *X City Council* and *D Borough Council* with more recent authority is unclear. It has been recognised since 1868 that a valid marriage does not require sexual relations.[14] The judgment of Munby J (as he was then) in *X City Council* was heavily predicated on the principles he had set out in *Sheffield City Council v E and S* [15]. In *Mundell v Name 1*,[16] Mostyn J considered *Sheffield City Council:*

> 'That was written in 2004 interpreting a body of jurisprudence that stretched back centuries. However, in 2019, it is questionable whether the duties and responsibilities as stated by Munby J in 2004 apply as fully as he then believed. I do not believe that it is the essence of a marriage contract that the parties should live together, let alone that they should love one another. There are plenty of examples, both in the distant past and more recently, of marriages being created where the parties like each other but could not be said to love each other: where their relationship is one of platonic friendship rather than one of passion. Moreover, there are plenty of examples in this modern age of parties marrying where they do not share a common home or a common domestic life but, nonetheless, their marriage is well and truly a marriage.'

2.21 Thus, the basis that sexual relations are an implicit part of living together and loving each other does not appear to be sustainable in circumstances whereby living together and loving each other is not an implicit part of marriage. Similarly,

12 [2006] EWHC 168 (Fam).
13 [2011] EWHC 101 (Fam).
14 *A v B* (1868) LR 1 P & D 559, 562, more recently affirmed by Mostyn J in *Mundell v Name 1* [2019] EWCOP 50.
15 [2005] 2 WLR 953.
16 [2019] EWCOP 50.

the presumption that the marriage contract entitles the parties to a degree of choice to engage in sexual relations also does not appear to be sustainable.

2.22 Finally, the risk of sexual offences taking place is a welfare, not a capacity consideration. In any event, in circumstances where the settled law is that platonic friendship can sustain a valid marriage,[17] it does not follow that a risk of sexual assault automatically arises where a party lacks capacity to consent to sexual relations.

2.23 It is also self-evident that the nature of the decision as to whether to have sexual relations is wholly different to that of whether to get married. It is conceivable, for example that a person with learning difficulties who is sexually disinhibited may be unable to use or weigh information relating to the risks of sexual intercourse, but would be capable of understanding, retaining, weighing the 'rudimentary' level of information necessary to make the decision to get married.[18]

2.24 Whilst the issue of capacity to consent to marriage is fully considered at **Chapter 8**, the essential broad-brush rule has remained unchanged since *Durham v Durham*,[19] namely that parties to a marriage must be able to understand the nature of the marriage contract. If sexual relations are not an essential part of marriage, then it is conceivable that someone may be deemed to have capacity to marry, but not to consent to sexual relations. In such circumstances, consideration ought to be given to applications to the Court of Protection for declaratory relief and injunctive protection for the spouse unable to consent to sexual relations.

ARRANGED MARRIAGES AND THE 'GREY AREA'

2.25 The distinction between forced and arranged marriage is of central importance. An arranged marriage is one in which the bride and the groom are selected by third parties, often family members with each spouse having consented to the union and being free to refuse to wed should they wish.

2.26 In *West Sussex County Council and Anor v F & Ors*,[20] Williams J underlined the importance of distinguishing 'a loosely arranged engagement' or arranged marriage from a forced marriage.

2.27 In *Chief Constable & Anor v YK & Ors*[21] the President of the Family Division, Sir Nicholas Wall, gave helpful guidance on distinguishing arranged and forced marriages, His Lordship held:

17 See *A v B* (1868) LR 1 P & D 559, 562, more recently affirmed by Mostyn J in *Mundell v Name 1* [2019] EWCOP 50.
18 *London Borough of Southwark v KA and Others* [2016] EWCOP 20 at [37].
19 [1885] 10 PD 80.
20 [2018] EWHC 1702 (Fam).
21 [2010] EWHC 2438 (Fam).

> 'Nonetheless forced marriage cases are likely to throw up issues which are profound in the extreme. The subject matter itself is highly sensitive. In every case, as it seems to me, a clear distinction needs to be drawn between, on the one hand, forced marriage as a form of domestic violence and a serious abuse of human rights, and, on the other, the concept of the consensual arranged marriage which is rightly perceived as a cultural norm in certain societies and thus wholly acceptable'.

2.28 In *Re SK*,[22] Singer J underlined the difference between forced marriages and 'marriages arranged traditionally which are in no way to be condemned, but rather supported as a conventional concept in many societies'. However, His Lordship also highlighted the risk of an arranged marriage 'slipping into' a forced marriage and described the 'grey area' that separates the two categories.

2.29 Cases in the 'grey area' are likely to include arranged marriage cases where the emotional, financial and familial pressure is so great that the ability of a spouse to consent is called into question. Another scenario likely to be difficult to categorise are cases where a spouse's capacity to consent to marriage is borderline or fluctuating. Such cases are likely to give rise to a duty on the part of local authorities under the Care Act 2014, s 42 to make any enquiries they think necessary to determine whether there is a risk of forced marriage in each individual case.

CIVIL LAW DEFINITION

2.30 Beyond the definitions found in the Family Law Act 1996, s 63A and the Anti-social Behaviour Crime and Policing Act 2014, s 121 there is no separate definition of forced marriage for use in the civil courts. However, there are a number of remedies available in the civil courts which supplement the criminal and family law provisions outlined above.

Public nuisance

2.31 The Local Government Act 1972, s 222 permits local authorities to bring proceedings where they consider it expedient for the promotion or protection of the interests of the inhabitants of their area.

2.32 Public nuisance is a crime, for which a person is guilty when he or she:

> '(a) Does an act not warranted by law, or
>
> (b) Omits to discharge a legal duty, if the effect of the act or omission is to endanger the life, health, property, morals or comfort of the public, or to obstruct the public in the exercise or enjoyment of rights common to all Her Majesty's subjects.'[23]

22 [2004] EWHC 3202 (Fam).

23 *Clerk and Lindsell on Torts*, 22nd edn (Sweet & Maxwell, 2017) 20 – 02.

2.33 Thus, it appears that forced marriage as defined by either the criminal or family provisions amounts to a public nuisance. The ability to seek injunctive relief for public nuisance is subject to a number of provisos and limitations is considered in **Chapter 3**.

Harassment and tortious claims

2.34 Claims in Tort and under the Protection from Harassment Act 1997 are specifically preserved as potential remedies and protections against forced marriage by the Family Law Act 1996, s 63R. These potential remedies are again considered fully at **Chapter 3**.

PUBLIC INTERNATIONAL LAW

2.35 Forced marriage is a matter which has been extensively discussed on the international level and has been subject to a number of international conventions. In spite of this, there has been no single internationally adopted definition of forced marriage. However, an approach broadly taken by international organisations and agreements is that a forced marriage is one entered into without the free and full consent of both spouses.

International conventions

2.36 The issue of forced marriage has been prohibited by international law provisions long before a statutory definition existed within the United Kingdom.

2.37 Article 37(1) of the 2011 Council of Europe Convention on preventing and combatting violence against women and domestic violence ('Istanbul Convention') requires signatories to take the necessary legislative or other measures to ensure that forcing an adult or child into marriage is criminalised. Article 37(2) requires that measures are taken to ensure that the luring of a child or adult to another territory or state in order to force them to marry is criminalised.

2.38 Regrettably, the Istanbul Convention does not define the term 'forced marriage' and doesn't stipulate the type of conduct which can amount to forcing a spouse to marry.

2.39 Article 16(2) of the Universal Declaration of Human Rights provides: 'Marriage shall be entered into only with the free and full consent of the intending spouses'. The issue of child marriage was further dealt with in Article 16 of the New York Convention on the Elimination of All Forms of Discrimination Against Women, 1979 which states: 'the betrothal and the marriage of a child shall have no legal effect, and all necessary action, including legislation, shall be taken to specify a minimum age for marriage and to make the registration of marriages in an official registry compulsory'.

2.40 The United Kingdom is a signatory to the 1962 Convention on Consent to Marriage, Minimum Age for Marriage and Registration of Marriages ('Convention on Consent to Marriage'). The Convention requires states to impose a number of practical requirements in order to eradicate forced marriages.

2.41 The United Kingdom ratified the 1991 Convention on the Rights of the Child which requires that member states enforce a minimum age of 18 for marriage. It has also committed to eliminate child, early and forced marriage by 2030 in accordance with target 5.3 of the Sustainable Development Goals.

2.42 Article 23 (1) of the Convention on the Rights of Persons with Disabilities also stipulates the right of persons with disabilities to marry on the basis of full and free consent. Whereas Article 23(3) of the International Covenant on Civil and Political Rights requires that no marriage be entered into without the full and free consent of the intended spouses.

Human rights

2.43 Applying Article 16 of the Universal Declaration of Human Rights, forced marriage has been an express violation of International Human Rights Law since at least 1948. It is also the case that a forced marriage is a serious interference with the rights guaranteed under Articles 3, 4 and 8 of the 1953 European Convention on Human Rights. The Convention gained direct legal effect in the UK in 2000 with the Human Rights Act 1998 coming into force. Both the Convention and the Human Rights Act 1998 are only capable of vertical application – that is against public bodies. However, a number of positive obligations have been developed by the Strasbourg and domestic courts which require public bodies to prevent or investigate acts by private citizens which amount to interferences with another's Convention rights.

2.44 As such, certain positive obligations arise on the part of public authorities when put on notice of potential forced marriages (see **Chapters 20** and **25**).

European Union and the United Kingdom's exit

2.45 The European Union has not adopted a single definition of forced marriage; however, The European Union Agency for Fundamental Rights describes a forced marriage 'as a marriage concluded without the consent of one or both partners, and therefore against the will of at least one of them.'[24]

2.46 There does not appear to be any express provision relating to forced marriage in the European Union Treaties with Article 9 of the EU Charter of Fundamental Rights simply stating: 'The right to marry and the right to found a

24 European Union Agency for Fundamental Human Rights, *Addressing Forced Marriage in the EU: legal provisions and promising practices* (European Union, 2014) 9.

family shall be guaranteed in accordance with the national laws governing the exercise of these rights'.

2.47 Whilst there have been a number of reports by EU agencies and resolutions of the EU Parliament, it appears that the EU has largely deferred to the Council of Europe, of which all EU member states are a member, in driving policy and conventions on forced marriage. The UK's International Law obligations in respect of Forced Marriage are therefore unlikely to be substantially changed following the UK's exit from the EU.

CHAPTER 3

Prevention

Contents at a Glance:

POSITIVE OBLIGATION TO PREVENT AND PROTECT UNDER THE CONVENTION

3.1 It is established law that a forced marriage offends the human rights of the victim.[1] A forced marriage is likely to include behaviour sufficient to breach the prohibition on torture and inhuman and degrading treatment under Article 3 of the European Convention on Human Rights.[2] Forced marriages are also likely to offend the right to marry under Article 12 of the Convention, the right to a family life under Article 8 and a breach of a person's Article 5 right to liberty. It follows that Public Authorities within the meaning of the Human Rights Act 1998, s 6 shall fall under positive obligation to take reasonable effective steps to protect forced marriages when they become aware of a real risk of one occurring.[3]

3.2 The means by which a public authority discharges its positive obligations shall be dependent on the circumstances of the individual case. However, the most appropriate remedy shall often be the seeking of a Forced Marriage Protection Order.

FORCED MARRIAGE PROTECTION ORDERS

Forced Marriage Protection Orders, which are fully considered in **Chapter 10** were created by the Forced Marriage (Civil Protection) Act 2007. The Act

1 See *Re SK (An Adult) (Forced Marriage: Appropriate Relief)* [2004] EWHC 3202 (Fam).
2 *Re K (Forced Marriage: Passport Order)* [2020] EWCA Civ 190.
3 See **Chapter 6** at **6.30** *et seq.*

inserted s 63A into the Family Law Act 1996 which in turn empowers the court to make an order for the purposes of protecting:

(a) A person from being forced into marriage or from any attempt to be forced into marriage; or

(b) A person who has been forced into marriage.

3.3 Once the statutory test for the imposition of a Forced Marriage Protection Order is met, the court has a wide discretion as to what terms it is necessary to impose. Common terms of Forced Marriage Protection Order s include orders confiscating the protected person's passport, a prohibition on applying for further travel documents, a travel ban, a prohibition on any marriage ceremonies and a prohibition on contact with a prospective spouse.

3.4 Breaching a Forced Marriage Protection Order is a freestanding criminal offence punishable by up to five years' imprisonment.

Parties

3.5 The procedure for applying for a Forced Marriage Protection Order is set out in full at **Chapter 10**. The key point is that an order can be applied for as of right either by the person to be protected or by a local authority.[4] All other prospective applicants must obtain the leave of the Court to bring an application. A common third party in applying for leave to bring an application are police forces.

Ex-parte applications

3.6 The Family Law Act 1996, s 63D grants the court the power to make a Forced Marriage Protection Order in circumstances where the respondent has not been given notice. When deciding whether to make an ex-parte order, s 63D(2) requires the court to have regard to all the circumstances including:

> '(a) any risk of significant harm to the person to be protected or another person if the order is not made immediately;
>
> (b) whether it is likely that an applicant will be deterred or prevented from pursuing an application if an order is not made immediately; and
>
> (c) whether there is reason to believe that—
>
> > (i) the respondent is aware of the proceedings but is deliberately evading service; and

4 As a relevant third party under the Family Law Act 1996 (Forced Marriage) (Relevant Third Party) Order 2009, art 3.

(ii) the delay involved in effecting substituted service will cause serious prejudice to the person to be protected or (if a different person) an applicant.'

3.7 Following the making of an ex-parte order, the respondent must be given an opportunity to make representations as soon as is just and convenient at a hearing of which proper notice has been given to all the parties.

3.8 The decision as to whether to make an ex-parte application is an important one which applicants shall want to consider in each case. Circumstances where there is reason to believe that there is an immediate risk of forced marriage or the person to be protected being removed from the jurisdiction shall often justify an urgent ex-parte application.

INTERNATIONAL PREVENTION

3.9 A party to be protected shall have been removed from the jurisdiction either before a Forced Marriage Protection Order is made, or be in breach of it. In such cases, cooperation with the Foreign Office's Forced Marriage Unit shall be essential.

3.10 The appropriate remedy to prevent a forced marriage when the person requiring protection has been removed overseas is likely to be a return order pursuant to the High Court's inherent jurisdiction if in relation to an adult lacking capacity or a child. In the event of an adult lacking capacity, an application for an injunction requiring P's return to the Court of Protection is likely to be the appropriate remedy.

The inherent jurisdiction and wardship

3.11 The origins of the inherent jurisdiction and wardship lay in the Sovereign's duty as *parens patriae;* to protect those unable to protect themselves. Since 1971, this duty has been administered by the Family Division.

3.12 The Family Procedure Rules 2010,[5] r 2.3 states:

> 'inherent jurisdiction' means the High Court's power to make any order or determine any issue in respect of a child, including in wardship proceedings, where it would be just and equitable to do so unless restricted by legislation or case law'.

3.13 The ongoing justification for the inherent jurisdiction is best articulated by Lord Donaldson of Lymington MR *Re F (Mental patient: sterilisation)*:[6]

5 SI 2010/2955.
6 [1990] 2 AC 1.

> '[13] … the common law is the great safety net which lies behind all statute law, and is capable of filling gaps left by that law, if and insofar as those gaps have to be filled in the interests of society as a whole. This process of using the common law to fill the gaps is one of the most important duties of the judges.'

3.14 In *JK v KC*,[7] Parker J sought to explain the wardship jurisdiction in a judgment likely to be sent to the United States. Her Ladyship explained:

> 'Wardship is a way in which the inherent jurisdiction with respect to children (ie the *parens patriae* jurisdiction) may be exercised. Once a child is a ward of court, that child is under the continuous protection of the court, even after a final order has been made determining the issues in respect of that child. Once a child is a ward of court that child's place or country of residence or school cannot be changed without court order. The court can make various orders providing for the care of the child and access/ contact and orders for the protection of the child. The court can order the return of the child to this jurisdiction.'

3.15 In *Re Y (risk of young person travelling to join IS) (No 1)*,[8] Hayden J suggested that use of the warship jurisdiction would be particularly useful in forced marriage cases.

3.16 Wardship may only be exercised over children whereas the inherent jurisdiction other than wardship can be utilised to protect vulnerable adults. In *Re SA (Vulnerable adult with capacity: marriage)*,[9] Munby J (as he then was) set out that there is no practical difference or distinction in the exercise of the power of the inherent jurisdiction between cases involving children and those involving vulnerable adults with capacity.

3.17 For the inherent jurisdiction of the court to arise, the child or vulnerable adult must either be habitually resident in the jurisdiction or following the Supreme Court's judgments in *Re A (Jurisdiction: return of child)*[10] and *Re B (A child) (Habitual residence: inherent jurisdiction)*,[11] a British national.

3.18 The rationale of affording British nationals the protection of the inherent jurisdiction irrespective of residence was set out by Pearson LJ in *In re P (GE) (An Infant)* ,[12] in which His Lordship held 'an infant of British nationality, whether he is in or outside this country, owes a duty of allegiance to the Sovereign and so is entitled to protection.'

7 [2011] EWHC 1284 (Fam).
8 [2015] EWHC 2098 (Fam).
9 [2015] EWHC 2942 (Fam).
10 [2013] UKSC 60.
11 [2016] UKSC 4.
12 [1965] Ch 568, at 587.

3.19 In respect of adults, the court's jurisdiction is available where there is a serious justiciable issue requiring the court's adjudication.

3.20 Munby J set out the principles governing the exercise of the inherent jurisdiction in respect of adults in *Re SA (Vulnerable adult with capacity: marriage)*.[13] His Lordship made the following observations:

(a) The inherent jurisdiction can be exercised in relation to a vulnerable adult who, even if not incapacitated by mental disorder or mental illness, is, or is reasonably believed to be, either under constraint or subject to coercion or undue influence;

(b) It does not matter whether the constraint amounts to actual incarceration. The jurisdiction is exercisable whenever a vulnerable adult is confined, controlled or under restraint. It is enough that there is some significant curtailment of the freedom to do those thing which in this country free men and women are entitled to do.

(c) The court exercises what is, in substance and reality, a jurisdiction in relation to incompetent adults which is for all practical purposes indistinguishable from its well-established jurisdiction in relation to children. There is little, if any, practical difference between the types of orders that can be made in exercise of the two jurisdictions.

3.21 In *DL v A Local Authority*[14] the Court of Appeal held that the inherent jurisdiction does not extend to matters falling within the scope of the Mental Capacity Act 2005.

Exercise of discretion

3.22 In *A v A (Children: Habitual Residence)*,[15] the Supreme Court held at paragraph 65 that there should be "extreme circumspection" in the High Court deciding to exercise the inherent jurisdiction in an international context given the potential conflict of laws issues which may arise.

3.23 This approach is seen as early as Lord Denning's judgment in *Re P (GE) (an infant)*[16] in which His Lordship said that the court will only exercise the jurisdiction abroad '... where the circumstances clearly warrant it'.

3.24 In *Al-Jefferey v Al Jefferey (vulnerable adult; British citizen)*,[17] the court was concerned with a 21-year-old woman who had been taken to Saudi Arabia aged 16 and was reportedly being constrained and mistreated by her father. An

13 [2005] EWHC 2942 (Fam).
14 [2012] EWCA Civ 253.
15 [2013] UKSC 60.
16 [1965] Ch 568.
17 [2016] EWHC 2151 (Fam).

application for an order under the inherent jurisdiction returning the woman was applied for alongside a Forced Marriage Protection Order. The application for the FMPO was discontinued but Mr Justice Holman did order the father to procure the woman's return to the United Kingdom.

DECLARATIONS AND INJUNCTIONS UNDER THE MENTAL CAPACITY ACT 2005

3.25 In *Re: SF (Injunctive Relief)*,[18] Keehan J held:

> 'Having had the benefit of counsels' submissions and the time to reflect on the authorities cited to me, I am now persuaded that the Court of Protection does indeed have the power to grant injunctive relief in support of and to ensure compliance with its best interest's decisions and its orders.'

3.26 The Mental Capacity Act 2005, s 17(c) also empowers the court to prohibit contact between P and named persons.

3.27 It is an established principle that the inherent jurisdiction must not be invoked where there is an applicable statutory regime. It therefore appears that the appropriate avenue through which to seek injunctive relief obtaining the protection of an adult lacking capacity or their return to the jurisdiction may be through an application to the Court of Protection as opposed to the High Court.

3.28 A declaration that an adult lacks capacity to consent to marriage or sex may be appropriate in circumstances where a Forced Marriage Protection Order is not necessary, but P is expressing an interest in marriage or sex in circumstances where their capacity to make related decisions is in doubt.

3.29 Where an application for a Forced Marriage Protection Order relies upon a disputed fact that P lacks capacity, it may be necessary to instigate Court of Protection proceedings to obtain a declaration of a lack of capacity. Such an application could be heard alongside the family proceedings as long as the matter has been allocated to the Family Division of the High Court.

CIVIL INJUNCTIONS

3.30 There is no freestanding civil remedy specifically targeting forced marriage other than those provided for by the Family Law Act 1996. However, there are a number of civil remedies that may be applicable to cases involving forced marriage.

18 [2020] EWCOP 19.

Public nuisance

3.31 Under the Local Government Act 1972, s 222 local authorities are empowered to bring proceedings where they consider it expedient for the promotion or protection of the interests of the inhabitants of their area.

3.32 Public nuisance is a crime, for which a person is guilty when he or she: '(a) does an act not warranted by law; or (b) omits to discharge a legal duty, if the effect of the act or omission is to endanger the life, health, property, morals or comfort of the public, or to obstruct the public in the exercise or enjoyment of rights common to all Her Majesty's subjects'.[19] Thus, forced marriage is likely to amount to a public nuisance.

3.33 Where a private individual suffers particular damage beyond that suffered by the public at large, public nuisance also becomes a tortious act giving rise to an entitlement to damages. Recent years have seen the tort deployed alongside the Local Government Act 1972, s 222 by local authorities in applications for injunctive relief to deal with matters such as car cruising,[20] gang violence[21] and begging.[22]

3.34 The Police and Justice Act 2006, s 27 enables the court to attach a power of arrest without warrant to any injunction made pursuant to an application under the Local Government Act 1972, s 222 including those for public nuisance. The conditions for a power of arrest being attached is that the nuisance injuncted involves the use or threat of violence or a significant risk of harm to a person being protected by the injunction.

3.35 The ability of local authorities to seek injunctive relief for public nuisance is subject to a number of provisos and limitations. However, it does appear that it is prima facie possible to injunct the sexual exploitation or any attempts to forcible marry a person within a local authority's area. In respect of forced marriage, this power would only be useful, or appropriate where the identity of those seeking to marry the victim are unclear or there is no obvious person to bring proceedings against under the Family Law Act 1996, s 63A.

3.36 In these circumstances it may be necessary or appropriate to seek to bring a public nuisance injunction against persons unknown.

3.37 In the case of sexual exploitation of an adult lacking capacity where the perpetrators are known, it is open to the local authority to seek declarations and injunctions in the Court of Protection.

19 *Clerk and Lindsell on Torts* 22nd edn, (Sweet & Maxwell, 2017) 20 – 02.

20 *Birmingham City Council v Persons Unknown* [2018] EWHC 1601 (QB).

21 Birmingham City Council was unsuccessful in seeking injunctive relief to combat gang crime in *Birmingham City Council v Shafi* [2008] EWCA Civ 1186.

22 Leeds City Council successfully applied for an injunction preventing begging ahead of the Tour De France, but later conceded that the injunction ought not to have been made: *Leeds City Council –v-Persons Unknown & Scott* 2015 unreported.

Harassment and tortious claims

3.38 Claims in tort and under the Protection from Harassment Act 1997 are specifically preserved as potential remedies and protections against forced marriage by the Family Law Act 1996, s 63R.

3.39 The Protection from Harassment Act 1997, s 1(1) prohibits someone from pursuing a course of conduct which amounts to harassment of another which he knows or ought to know amounts to harassment.

3.40 Of particular relevance to forced marriage s 1(1A) provides:

> '(1A) A person must not pursue a course of conduct —
>
> (a) which involves harassment of two or more persons, and
>
> (b) which he knows or ought to know involves harassment of those persons, and
>
> (c) by which he intends to persuade any person (whether or not one of those mentioned above)—
>
> (i) not to do something that he is entitled or required to do, or
>
> (ii) to do something that he is not under any obligation to do.'

3.41 Thus, harassing someone in the hope of causing them to marry another person is likely to be an unlawful act under the Protection from Harassment Act 1997, s 1. The Protection from Harassment Act 1997, s 3A allows the person being harassed to marry to make an application to the High Court or county court for an injunction to prohibit the conduct complained of. Should the Defendant breach the injunction, then s 3(3) allows the protected party to seek a warrant for their arrest.

THE MODERN SLAVERY ACT 2015

3.42 The International Labour Organisation defines forced marriage as a form of modern slavery.[23] It follows that forced marriage is likely to be defined as a form of slavery or servitude within the meaning of the Modern Slavery Act 2015, s 1 which creates the offence of holding another person in slavery or servitude. Under the Modern Slavery Act 2015, the police, National Crime Agency, Border Force and the Gangmasters and Labour Abuse Authority may apply for injunctive relief to prevent and deter modern slavery offences.

3.43 Under the Modern Slavery Act 2015, s 2 a person commits an offence if they arrange or facilitate the travel of another person with a view to that person

23 International Labour Organisation, Global Estimates of Modern Slavery: Forced Labour and Forced Marriage, September 2017.

being exploited. It does not matter whether the victim consents to the travel. Travel includes arriving in or entering any country, departing any country and travelling within any country. The offence is extraterritorial insomuch as a British National may commit it anywhere in the world. A foreign national commits the office if the arranging or facilitating of the travel takes part into the United Kingdom or the travel consists of entry into or departure from the UK or travel within the country.

3.44 Exploitation is defined by the Modern Slavery Act 2015, s 3 as anything which would constitute an offence under the Protection of Children Act 1978, the Sexual Offences Act 2003, Part 1 or the Modern Slavery Act 2015, s 1.

3.45 The Modern Slavery Act 201, s 15 provides a power for a Chief Police Officer, immigration officer, the Director General of the NCA or the Gangmasters and Labour Abuse Authority to apply for slavery and trafficking prevention orders in respect of relevant offenders, as defined by s 16, who have acted in such a way that there is a real risk they may commit a slavery or human trafficking offence.

3.46 Such an order may contain any prohibitions which the court is satisfied are necessary for the purpose of protecting persons generally or particular persons from physical or psychological harm should the Defendant commit slavery or human trafficking offences.

3.47 The Modern Slavery Act 2015, s 23 provides a power for a Chief Police Officer, immigration officer, the Director General of the NCA or the Gangmasters and Labour Abuse Authority to apply to the Magistrate's Court for Slavery and trafficking risk orders.

3.48 These orders do not require a previous conviction but simply that the defendant has acted in a way which means that there is a risk they will commit a slavery or human trafficking offence and that it is necessary to make the order for the purpose of protecting persons generally, or particular persons, from the physical or psychological harm which would likely to be occur if the defendant committed such an offence.

3.49 Such an order may impose any terms necessary for the protection of persons generally or particular persons and may include a prohibition on foreign travel for up to five years, the surrender of the defendant's passports and a requirement to notify the authorities of any changes in the defendant's name and address.

CHAPTER 4

Punishment

Content at a Glance:

INTRODUCTION

4.1 The UK Government's guidance on forced marriage describes forced marriage as 'a criminal offence. It is child abuse, domestic abuse and a form of violence against women and men'.[1] Yet since 2014, when forced marriage was criminalised, there have been only a handful of convictions.[2] There are increasing efforts to increase the number of convictions for forced marriage offences, each CPS area has a lead forced marriage prosecutor, prosecution guidance was revised in 2019 and a CPS working group has developed a training package for prosecutors and an investigation and prosecution protocol.[3]

4.2 In November 2016, the CPS and National Police Chiefs' Council published a joint honour-based violence, abuse and forced marriage protocol[4]. The protocol provides detailed guidance on the roles of police and prosecutors in forced marriage cases and establishes a roadmap from initial complain to steps to be taken post-conviction. The protocol emphasises that crimes including common assault, grievous bodily harm, harassment, kidnap, rape, threats to kill and murder can all be committed in a forced marriage context. The full spectrum of violent offences occurring in a forced marriage context is beyond the scope of this chapter. As such, we concentrate on the specific forced marriage offences created by the Anti-Social Behaviour Crime and Policing Act 2014 as well as kidnap and child abduction. A fuller consideration of offences which may arise in a forced marriage context is found in **Chapter 20**.

4.3 In circumstances where the very small number of convictions is contrasted with the 1,359 cases per year the Forced Marriage Unit dealt with

1 HM Government, Multi-agency practice guidelines: Handling cases of Forced Marriage, 2014.

2 Home Office, Preventing and tackling forced marriage: a consultation, November 2018.

3 Hansard, Forced Marriage: Prosecutions: Written question – 2607, 13 January 2020.

4 Crown Prosecution Service, National Police Chief's Council, Protocol on the handling of 'so-called' Honour Based Violence/Abuse and Forced Marriage Offences between the National Police Chiefs' Council and the Crown Prosecution Service

between 2011 and 2018, it is clear that the effective prosecution and punishment of forced marriage offences remains a challenge.[5]

CRIMINAL OFFENCES

4.4 Forced marriage has constituted a specific criminal offence since 2014, however in the vast majority of forced marriage cases other criminal offences shall have been committed to bring about the marriage. The criminal aspects of forced marriage are fully considered in Part IV of the book. Here, the most relevant offences are considered in a forced marriage context.

Anti-social Behaviour Crime and Policing Act 2014

4.5 The Anti-social Behaviour Crime and Policing Act 2014, s 121 creates a freestanding offence of forcing someone to marry.

> **'121. Offence of a forced marriage: England and Wales**
>
> (1) A person commits and offence under the law of England and Wales if he or she-
>
> (a) uses violence, threats or any other form of coercion for the purpose of causing another person to enter into a marriage, and
>
> (b) believes, or ought reasonably to believe, that the conduct may cause the other person to enter into the marriage without free and full consent.
>
> (2) In relation to a victim who lacks capacity to consent to marriage, the offence under subsection (1) is capable of being committed by any conduct carried out for the purpose of causing the victim to enter into a marriage (whether or not the conduct amounts to violence, threats or any other form of coercion).
>
> (3) A person commits an offence under the law of England and Wales if he or she-
>
> (a) Practises any form of deception with the intention of causing another person to leave the United Kingdom, and
>
> (b) intends the other person to be subjected to conduct outside the United Kingdom that is an offence under subsection (1) or would be an offence under that subsection if the victim were in England or Wales.
>
> (4) "Marriage" means any religious or civil ceremony of marriage (whether or not legally binding).

5 Joint publication between the Home Office and the Foreign and Commonwealth Office, Forced Marriage Unit Statistics 2019, 25 June 2020.

(5) "Lacks Capacity" means lacks capacity within the meaning of the Mental Capacity Act 2005.

(6) It is irrelevant whether the conduct mentioned in paragraph (1) of subsection (1) is directed at the victim of the offence under that subsection or another person.

(7) A person commits an offence under subsection (1) or (3) only if, at the time of the conduct or deception-

(a) the person or the victim of both of them are in England or Wales,

(b) neither the person nor the victim is in England or Wales but at least one of them is habitually resident in England and Wales, or

(c) neither the person nor the victim is in the United Kingdom but at least one of them is a UK national.

...'

One consequence of the very few forced marriage convictions achieved under the Act is that there is no appellate case law supplementing the above statutory definition.

In particular, it remains unclear what amounts to coercion under the Anti-social Behaviour Crime and Policing Act 2014, s 121(1)(a). Whether the criminal courts shall ultimately adopt the broad definition of 'coerce' used in the family courts in include varying degrees of emotional, financial and psychological abuse is unclear.

4.6 There are no specific sentencing guidelines for forced marriage. However, it is likely that the Sentencing Council's Overarching Principles – Domestic abuse: Definitive guidelines are likely to be applicable. In *R v Kayani*,[6] the Court of Appeal suggested that two years' imprisonment would likely be an utterly inadequate punishment for a forced marriage and made clear that child abduction for the purposes of a forced marriage would be an aggravating factor.

4.7 In January 2020, a sentence of four years was imposed on a man who attempted to force his niece into marriage having imprisoned and mistreated her for a period of years in Pakistan.[7] A sentence of four years for forced marriage was imposed to run concurrently with a 12-year sentence for rape in the first forced marriage conviction in 2015 imposed by Merthyr Tydfil Crown Court.[8]

4.8 In 2018, a mother was sentenced to four and a half years imprisonment for taking her daughter to Pakistan on what she told her was a family holiday and then forcing her into marriage.[9]

6 [2011] EWCA Crim 2871.
7 Birmingham Crown Court, unreported, 24 January 2020.
8 Merthyr Tydfil Crown Court, unreported, 11 June 2015.
9 Birmingham Crown Court, unreported, 23 May 2018.

4.9 Finally, in the same year, HHJ Simon Phillips QC passed sentence in a case where a couple had tricked their teenage daughter into travelling to Bangladesh with the intention of forcing her to marry her cousin. The father was sentenced to four and a half years whilst the mother was sentenced to three and a half years imprisonment.[10]

4.10 Thus, it appears that a sentence for an offence under the Anti-social Behaviour Crime and Policing Act 2014, s 121 at the upper end of the seriousness bracket is likely to attract a sentence in excess of four years imprisonment.

False imprisonment

4.11 False imprisonment is a common-law offence which is also a civil law Tort. The offence was defined by the House of Lords in *R v Rahman*[11] as 'the unlawful and intentional or reckless restraint of a victim's freedom of movement from a particular place'.

4.12 The *actus reus* of the offence is preventing the victim's freedom of movement whether by physical restraint or by intimidation (*R v James*[12]). In a civil context, it does not matter whether the victim realises they are being imprisoned without lawful excuse.[13] It is highly unlikely that the position is any different in a criminal context.

4.13 In *Rahman,* their Lordships held that the *mens rea* of the offence is either recklessness as to consent or intent.

4.14 False Imprisonment, being a common law offence has a penalty at large. The sentencing council has not produced sentencing guidelines for the offence. However, in the *A-G's Ref (Nos 92 and 93 of 2014)*,[14] the Court of Appeal held that the following factors are relevant sentencing considerations:

(a) The length of the detention;

(b) The circumstances of the detention;

(c) The location and method of restraint;

(d) The extent of any violence used;

(e) The involvement of weapons;

(f) Whether demands were made of others;

(g) Whether threats were made to others;

(h) The effect on the victim and others;

10 Leeds Crown Court, Indictment number T20197741, unreported, 30 July 2018.
11 (1985) 81 Cr App R 349.
12 (1997) The Times, 2 October 1997.
13 *Meering v Grahame White Aviation Co. Ltd* (1919) 122 LT 44.
14 [2015] 1 Cr App R (S) 44 (323).

(i) The extent of the planning;

(j) The number of offenders involved;

(k) The use of torture or humiliation;

(l) Whether what was done arose from or was in furtherance of previous criminal behaviour; and

(m) Any particular vulnerability of the victim whether by reason of age or otherwise.

Kidnap

4.15 The common law offence of kidnapping consists of the taking or carrying away of one person by another by force or fraud, without the consent of that person and without lawful excuse.[15] In *R v Archer*,[16] the Court of Appeal confirmed that 'force' includes the threat of force.

4.16 In *R v D*,[17] the House of Lords considered the case of a parent who took their child in contravention of a Court order. Their Lordships held that even where a parent is not breaching a court order, they could still be acting unlawfully in taking their child. In each case, it shall be a question of fact whether the parent has lawful excuse to exercise such physical control over the child.

4.17 Whilst kidnapping must be committed without the consent of the victim, consent procured by fear or forced does not amount to valid consent (*R v Greenhalgh*[18]).

4.18 It was thought that it was inappropriate to pursue a prosecution for kidnap, a common law offence when the elements of the statutory offence of child abduction are made out. Following *R v Kayani*[19] it is permissible to bring a prosecution for kidnap in circumstances where child abduction is an appropriate alternative charge.

4.19 The sentencing considerations set out in **4.14** also apply to sentencing exercises following a conviction for kidnapping.

Child abduction

4.20 The Child Abduction Act 1984 creates three offences of child abduction. In *R v Kayani*,[20] the Court of Appeal specifically envisaged prosecutions for child abduction being brought in the context of a forced marriage.

15 *Blackstone's Criminal Practice 2019* (Oxford University Press), B.98.
16 [2011] EWCA Crim 2252.
17 [1984] AC 778.
18 [2001] EWCA Crim 1367.
19 [2011] EWCA Crim 2871.
20 [2011] EWCA Crim 2871.

The Child Abduction Act, s 1

4.21 The Child Abduction Act, s 1 creates the offence of abduction of a child by a parent, guardian or other person with custody of the child whereas s 2 creates the offence of child abduction by other persons.

> **'1 Offence of abduction of child by parent, etc.**
>
> (1) Subject to subsections (5) and (8) below, a person connected with a child under the age of sixteen commits an offence if he takes or sends the child out of the United Kingdom without the appropriate consent.
>
> (2) A person is connected with a child for the purposes of this section if—
>
> (a) he is a parent of the child; or
>
> (b) in the case of a child whose parents were not married to, or civil partners of, each other at the time of his birth, there are reasonable grounds for believing that he is the father of the child; or
>
> (c) he is a guardian of the child; or
>
> (ca) he is a special guardian of the child; or]
>
> (d) he is a person named in a child arrangements order as a person with whom the child is to live; or
>
> (e) he has custody of the child.
>
> (3) In this section 'the appropriate consent', in relation to a child, means—
>
> (a) the consent of each of the following—
>
> (i) The child's mother;
>
> (ii) the child's father, if he has parental responsibility for him;
>
> (iii) any guardian of the child;
>
> (iiia) any special guardian of the child;
>
> (iv) any person named in a child arrangements order as a person with whom the child is to live;
>
> (v) any person who has custody of the child; or
>
> (b) the leave of the court granted under or by virtue of any provision of Part II of the Children Act 1989; or
>
> (c) if any person has custody of the child, the leave of the court which awarded custody to him.
>
> (4) A person does not commit an offence under this section by taking or sending a child out of the United Kingdom without obtaining the appropriate consent if—

(a) he is a person named in a child arrangements order as a person with whom the child is to live and he takes or sends the child out of the United Kingdom for a period of less than one month; or

(b) he is a special guardian of the child and he takes or sends the child out of the United Kingdom for a period of less than three months.

(4A) Subsection (4) above does not apply if the person taking or sending the child out of the United Kingdom does so in breach of an order under Part II of the Children Act 1989.

(5) A person does not commit an offence under this section by doing anything without the consent of another person whose consent is required under the foregoing provisions if—

(a) he does it in the belief that the other person—

(i) has consented; or

(ii) would consent if he was aware of all the relevant circumstances; or

(b) he has taken all reasonable steps to communicate with the other person but has been unable to communicate with him; or

(c) the other person has unreasonably refused to consent,

(5A) Subsection (5)(c) above does not apply if—

(a) the person who refused to consent is a person—

(i) named in a child arrangements order as a person with whom the child is to live;]

(ia) who is a special guardian of the child; or

(ii) who has custody of the child; or

(b) the person taking or sending the child out of the United Kingdom is, by so acting, in breach of an order made by a court in the United Kingdom.

(6) Where, in proceedings for an offence under this section, there is sufficient evidence to raise an issue as to the application of subsection (5) above, it shall be for the prosecution to prove that that subsection does not apply.

(7) For the purposes of this section—

(a) "guardian of a child", "special guardian", "child arrangements] order" and "parental responsibility" have the same meaning as in the Children Act 1989; and

(b) a person shall be treated as having custody of a child if there is in force an order of a court in the United Kingdom awarding him (whether solely or jointly with another person) custody, legal custody or care and control of the child.

(8) This section shall have effect subject to the provisions of the Schedule to this Act in relation to a child who is in the care of a local authority detained in a place of safety, remanded otherwise than on bail] or the subject of] proceedings or an order relating to adoption.'

4.22 Unlike kidnapping, child abduction may take place even where the child consents to the taking.[21]

4.23 The Child Abduction Act 1984, s 4(2) requires that the consent of the Director for Public Prosecutions is obtained before a prosecution under s 1 can be brought. Section 1 creates an either way offence. The maximum sentence on indictment is seven years' imprisonment. If tried summarily, the court may impose up to six months' imprisonment or an unlimited fine or both.

4.24 Their Lordships held in *R v RH*[22] that it is an aggravating factor to remove the child to a non-Hague Convention country, such as Pakistan which accounted for 41 per cent of forced marriage enquiries in 2019.[23] The Court of Appeal also held that in cases of child abduction for the purposes of forced marriage, a custodial sentence of five to seven years following trial can be expected.

Offence of abduction of child by other persons

4.25 The Child Abduction Act 1984, s 2(1) creates two further offences of child abduction.

'(1) Subject to subsection (3) below, a person, other than one mentioned in subsection (2) below. commits an offence if, without lawful authority or reasonable excuse, he takes or detains a child under the age of sixteen—

(a) so as to remove him from the lawful control of any person having lawful control of the child; or

(b) so as to keep him out of the lawful control of any person entitled to lawful control of the child.

(2) The persons are—

(a) where the father and mother of the child in question were married to, or civil partners of, each other at the time of his birth, the child's father and mother;

(b) where the father and mother of the child in question were not married to, or civil partners of, each other at the time of his birth, the child's mother; and

(c) any other person mentioned in section 1(2)(c) to (e) above.

21 *Blackstone's Criminal Practice 2019* (Oxford University Press), B.2.109.

22 [2017] 1 Cr App R (S) 23.

23 Joint publication, Home Office and Foreign Office, Forced Marriage Unit Statistics 2019, 25 June 2020.

(3) In proceedings against any person for an offence under this section, it shall be a defence for that person to prove—

(a) where the father and mother of the child in question were not married to, or civil partners of, each other at the time of his birth—

(i) that he is the child's father; or

(ii) that, at the time of the alleged offence, he believed, on reasonable grounds, that he was the child's father; or

(b) that, at the time of the alleged offence, he believed that the child had attained the age of sixteen.'

4.26 Unlike prosecutions brought under the Child Abduction Act 1984, s 1, charges brought under s 2 do not require the consent of the Director of Public Prosecutions. The maximum sentence on indictment is seven years' imprisonment or up to six months' imprisonment and/or an unlimited fine following trial on indictment.

BREACH OF INJUNCTIONS

4.27 The effectiveness of injunctive relief is underpinned by the severe consequences of breaching orders of the court. For regular civil and family orders with penal notices attached, the appropriate application is to have the party in breach of the order held in contempt.

4.28 Forced Marriage Protection Orders are governed by a specific regime and the Anti-Social Behaviour Crime and Policing Act 2014, s 120 creates a specific offence of breaching a Forced Marriage Protection Order. The offence is committed when a person without reasonable excuse does anything which he is prohibited from doing by a Forced Marriage Protection Order.

4.29 The offence is triable either way and is punishable by up to five years' imprisonment on indictment or up to six months' imprisonment and/or an unlimited fine is tried summarily.

4.30 The Family Law Act 1996, s 63J provides that an interested party may apply to the Court for the issue of an arrest warrant if a person has failed to comply with a Forced Marriage Protection Order or is otherwise in contempt in relation to the Order.

4.31 Such an application must be sustained on oath and the court must have reasonable grounds for believing that the person to be arrested has failed to comply with the order or is otherwise in contempt of court. These applications may be brought by the protected party, the applicant for the Forced Marriage Protection Order or any other person with the leave of the court.

CHAPTER 5

Remedies following a forced marriage

Content at a Glance:

INTRODUCTION

5.1 Sometimes forced marriage cases only comes to the attention of the authorities after the marriage has been contracted. Often such marriages shall have taken place overseas. Such situations require a consideration of the rules of English private international law. This chapter shall seek to set out an overview of the remedies available when a forced marriage is contracted overseas. The remedies are further considered in more detail within **Chapters 14** and **15**.

5.2 The Family Law Act 1996, s 63A(1)(b) empowers the court to make a Forced Marriage Protection Order to protect a person who has been forced into marriage. Following discovery of a forced marriage, it shall usually be appropriate to apply for protective orders under s 63A of the Act to protect the victim from further harm.

5.3 However, the issue that shall remain is which legal device best allows for the dissolution of the marriage. As we shall see, this is highly dependent on the circumstances in which the marriage was contracted.

FOREIGN MARRIAGES

5.4 English international law divides questions concerning the validity of overseas marriages into two categories:

(a) Questions concerning the formal validity of a marriage; and

(b) Questions affecting the 'essential validity' of a marriage.

5.5 This is considered in detail under **Chapter 15**, however, in summary, there are essentially two forms of 'validity'. First, 'formal validity' which is governed by the '*lex loci celebrationis*', the law of the country where the marriage was celebrated.

5.6 Secondly, is the 'essential validity', in particular capacity to marry. Essential validity is generally governed by the law of either party's domicile prior to the marriage. The capacity of the parties to marry is usually to be governed by the law of each party's ante-nuptial domicile.[1]

DECLARATION OF NON-RECOGNITION

5.7 A declaration of non-recognition is a declaration that while a marriage may be valid according to the law of where it was celebrated, is not recognised as a valid marriage in this jurisdiction.[2] The High Court shall exercise its power under the inherent jurisdiction to declare that a marriage should not be recognised where it considers the union 'is so offensive to the conscience of the English Court' that it shall not be recognised by the court.

5.8 In *Cheni v Cheni*,[3] Sir Jocelyn Simon P held that the power ought to be exercised with 'common sense, good manners and a reasonable tolerance'.

5.9 In *KC v City of Westminster Social and Community Services Department*,[4] a case concerning a vulnerable adult with severe learning difficulties, the Court of Appeal affirmed that in cases in marriages where parties lack capacity or forced marriages, the High Court had the jurisdiction to make a declaration of non-recognition even where no application for such an order had been made.

5.10 In *XCC v AA & Ors*,[5] Parker J considered the case of DD, a woman with very significant learning difficulties who had been married in Pakistan. The court held that she had been married for the purposes of obtaining her purported husband a spousal visa. Her Ladyship invited the local authority and the Official Solicitor to consider whether a declaration of non-recognition ought to be sought and in striking language described how the parties sought to 'duck' the issue of the recognition of the marriage under English law leading the court to express its disappointment both of the local authority and the Official Solicitor.

5.11 Having received no assistance from the parties, the court concluded it required the assistance of the Attorney General and an advocate to the court. Her Ladyship ultimately made a declaration of non-recognition emphasising:

1 See *Wilkinson v Kitzinger* [2006] EWHC 2022 (Fam), at [15], *Padolecchia v Padolecchia* [1968] P. 314 and Rule 74 at *Dicey, Morris & Collins on the Conflict of Laws* 15th Edn (Sweet and Maxwell, 2018), 17R-057.

2 *KC v City of Westminster Social and Community Services Department* [2008] EWCA Civ 198, at [103].

3 [1962] 3 All ER 873.

4 [2008] EWCA Civ 198.

5 [2012] EWCOP 2183 (COP).

'a public policy interest in the Court stating openly that such marriages should not be recognised[6]'.

5.12 In *Re RS (Forced Marriage Protection Order)*,[7] Hayden J set out what it is submitted is the strong presumption that marriages where parties lack capacity shall lead to the court making a declaration of non-recognition:

> '[52] In most cases an overseas marriage, entered into by an individual who lacks capacity to consent to either sexual relations or marriage, is likely to require the Court to make a declaration of non-recognition… However, it overstates the position to regard the discretionary exercise here as essentially "illusionary". Whilst I am not prepared to predict the circumstances in which the discretion might be exercised, neither am I prepared to say that a Court is never likely to do so. The interests of justice, fairness and respect for different aspects of individual autonomy may, in certain circumstances prevail. That said, those circumstances are likely to arise very rarely indeed'.

5.13 Interestingly, in *Re RS* (above) the question for the court was 'whether the court should exercise its power under the inherent jurisdiction to declare that the marriage is not recognised as valid in England and Wales as a precursor to the initiation of formal proceedings to annul the marriage'

5.14 It follows that a declaration of non-recognition and a petition for nullity are not mutually exclusive. On the contrary, it appears that a declaration of non-recognition in circumstances where annulment is not statute-barred may be applied for concurrently or preceding a nullity petition.

DECREE OF NULLITY

5.15 In *P v R (Forced Marriage: Annulment: procedure)*,[8] Coleridge J set out the following principles:

(a) where forced marriage is alleged, the proper course is a petition under the Matrimonial Causes Act 1973, s 12(c) is for a decree of nullity;

(b) this is in part because of the stigma that can be attached in certain communities to divorce;

(c) public funding ought to be available to spouses bringing nullity proceedings following an alleged forced marriage.

5.16 In *A Local Authority v X & Anor*,[9] Holman J considered circumstances where a 14-year-old girl had been forcibly married with the use of a firearm and

6 *XCC v AA & Ors* [2012] EWCOP 2183 at [72].
7 [2015] EWHC 3534 (Fam).
8 [2003] 1 FLR 661.
9 [2013] EWHC 3274 (Fam).

physical violence. His Lordship held that in circumstances where a marriage was void under the Matrimonial Causes Act 1973, s 11 as the bride was under the age of 16, the appropriate remedy was an application for a decree of nullity. Accordingly, his Lordship failed to grant a declaration of non-recognition.

5.17 In *B v I*,[10] Baron J considered the case of a young woman forced into marriage. Her Ladyship made clear that she would have granted a decree of nullity 'unhesitatingly' had such a decree not been time barred.

5.18 The Matrimonial Causes Act 1973, ss 11 and 12 set out the grounds for a decree of nullity. Section 11 sets out that the marriage shall be void if:

(a) the parties are within the prohibited degrees of relationship;

(b) either party is under the age of 16; or

(c) the parties have intermarried in disregard of certain requirements as to the formation of marriage;

(d) that at the time of the marriage, either party was already lawfully married; and

(e) in the case of a polygamous marriage entered into outside England, that either party was at the time of the marriage domiciled in England and Wales.

5.19 The ground contained in the Matrimonial Causes Act 1973, s 11(a)(ii), namely that a spouse was under the age of sixteen is likely to be the most relevant ground to the issue of forced marriage. The case of *Pugh v Pugh*[11] established that statutory provisions as to minimum age are extraterritorial in effect.

5.20 The Matrimonial Causes Act 1973, s 12 sets out the grounds upon which a marriage shall be voidable, these are:

(a) that the marriage has not been consummated owing to the incapacity of either party to consummate it;

(b) that the marriage has not been consummated owing to the wilful refusal of the respondent to consummate it;

(c) that either party to the marriage did not validly consent to it, whether in consequence of duress, mistake, unsoundness of mind or otherwise;

(d) that at the time of the marriage either party, though capable of giving a valid consent, was suffering (whether continuously or intermittently) from mental disorder within the meaning of the Mental Health Act 1983 of such a kind or to such an extent as to be unfitted for marriage;

(e) that at the time of the marriage the respondent was suffering from venereal disease in a communicable form;

10 [2010] 1 FLR 1721.
11 [1951] P 482.

(f) that at the time of the marriage the respondent was pregnant by some person other than the petitioner;

(g) that an interim gender recognition certificate under the Gender Recognition Act 2004 has, after the time of the marriage, been issued to either party to the marriage;

(h) that the respondent is a person whose gender at the time of the marriage had become the acquired gender under the Gender Recognition Act 2004.

5.21 The grounds in the Matrimonial Causes Act 1973, s 12(1)(c) and (d) are most relevant to the issue of forced marriage, namely the lack of valid consent or the presence of a mental disorder. Section 16 stipulates that a marriage shall be treated as subsisting up until the date of the granting of an annulment.

5.22 If it is averred that the formal requirements of marriage under the local law for the jurisdiction the marriage was celebrated were not complied with, then the court is likely to require expert evidence of the requirements for marriage in the jurisdiction concerned.

5.23 If, however, it is alleged that the marriage is voidable under the Matrimonial Causes Act 1973, s 12(1)(c) or (d), namely that there was an absent of valid consent or one of the parties suffered from a mental disorder at the time, then the issue shall be determined in accordance with English law.

Bars to nullity

5.24 Under the Matrimonial Causes Act 1973, s 13(2) the court must refuse an application for nullity based on lack of consent or mental disorder if proceedings were not started within three years of the marriage. The one relevant exception to this rule is where the court is satisfied that the petitioner has at some time during the period of three years from the date of marriage suffered from a mental disorder within the meaning of the Mental Health Act 1983 and the court considers that in all the circumstances of the case it would be just to grant permission to bring proceedings.[12]

5.25 There are two further general bars to relief in nullity and the court will refuse a decree if the respondent satisfies the court:[13]

(a) that the petitioner with knowledge that it was open to him to have the marriage avoided, so conducted himself in relation to the respondent as to lead the respondent reasonably to believe that he would not seek to do so; and

(b) that it would be unjust to the respondent to grant the decree.

12 MCA 1973, s 13(2).
13 MCA 1973, s 13(1).

5.26 In the case of marriages allegedly voidable under a foreign law, the bar will only apply so far as the rules of private international law require.[14]

Nullity and adults lacking capacity

5.27 In *Sandwell Metropolitan Borough Council v RG & Ors*,[15] the court was concerned with an application by the local authority for an order that it was in P's best interests for the Official Solicitor to petition for a decree of nullity.

5.28 All parties accepted that P lacked capacity in respect of marriage and sex. Colman J held that on an analysis undertaken in accordance with the Mental Capacity Act 2005, s 4 it was not in P's best interests for a petition for nullity to be made. The court held that the Mental Capacity Act 2005 left no room for considerations of broader public interest points. His Lordship expressly stated that the case turned on the particular facts of that case and ought not to be considered to set a general policy or presumption. It is notable that this case was decided before forced marriage was criminalised in 2014 and it is unclear whether the case would be approached in the same way today.

14 MCA 1973, s 14(1).
15 [2013] EWCOP 2373 (COP).

CHAPTER 6

Forced Marriage and Human Rights

Contents at a Glance:

THE EUROPEAN CONVENTION ON HUMAN RIGHTS

6.1 The European Convention on Human Rights (ECHR) is an international convention agreed between the member states of the Council of Europe in 1949. In 1959, the European Court of Human Rights (ECtHR) was established and in 1966, the United Kingdom accepted the right of individuals to appeal to the ECtHR.

6.2 It is established law that forced marriage engages and offends the human rights of the victim. In *Re SK (An Adult) (Forced Marriage: Appropriate Relief)*,[1] a case relating to a young woman taken to Bangladesh to be married, Singer J stated 'forced marriage is simply an abuse of human rights… it dehumanises people'.

6.3 Whilst the Convention only applies to the state, so that another individual cannot violate a citizen's Convention Rights, it is established law that positive obligations arise on the part of contracting states to protect citizens from conduct by individuals which would amount to an interference with their Convention Rights and in certain circumstances to carry out effective investigations into such conduct.

1 [2004] EWHC 3202 (Fam).

6.4 It is beyond the scope of this book to provide a comprehensive treatment of the Convention or the jurisprudence of the ECtHR and its interplay with domestic courts. As such, the focus shall be on Articles 3, 6, 8 and 14 of the Convention which have the greatest bearing on the law of forced marriage.

ARTICLE 3: PROHIBITION OF TORTURE

6.5 Article 3 of the Convention provides:

> 'No one shall be subject to torture or to inhuman or degrading treatment or punishment'

6.6 Article 3 is an absolute right meaning that there are no limitations or exceptions to it. A violation of Article 3 cannot be justified or lawful under any circumstances.

6.7 In *Re K (Forced Marriage: Passport Order)*,[2] the Court of Appeal considered a case where K had applied to discharge a Forced Marriage Protection Order which prevented her from attending her mother's funeral in Pakistan. The court held:

> '[25] Against that perspective it must be accepted that a forced marriage is likely to include behaviour sufficient to breach ECHR Article 3 which provides that "no one shall be subjected to torture or to inhuman or degrading treatment or punishment.'

6.8 It is also of note that forced marriage is defined as a form if domestic violence by Practice Direction 12J of the Family Procedure Rules 2010. In *Volodina v Russia*,[3] the ECtHR held that domestic abuse falls within the ambit of Article 3.

6.9 It is therefore clear that a forced marriage is likely to engage Article 3 of the Convention. It follows that public authorities, whether national or local, shall fall under certain positive obligations. Breach of these positive obligations can lead to liability for substantial damages.

ARTICLE 6: RIGHT TO A FAIR TRIAL

Article 6 and Forced Marriage

A Article 6 appears to be more acutely engaged in return hearings and applications to set-aside FMPOs than ex-parte applications.

2 [2020] EWCA Civ 190.
3 Application No 41261/17.

B The use of special advocates shall be 'rare in the extreme'[4]

C Article 6 does not impose an absolute and unqualified right to see all documents in proceedings.

D A refusal of legal aid for litigants that cannot afford representation may amount to a breach of Article 6.

E In criminal proceedings, special considerations apply.

6.10 Article 6, another absolute right of the Convention states:

> 'In the determination of his civil rights and obligations or of any criminal charge against him, everyone is entitled to a fair and public hearing within a reasonable time by an independent and impartial tribunal established by law. Judgment shall be pronounced publicly but the press and public may be excluded from all or part of the trial in the interest of morals, public order or national security in a democratic society, where the interests of juveniles or the protection of the private life of the parties so require, or the extent strictly necessary in the opinion of the court in special circumstances where publicity would prejudice the interests of justice.'

6.11 The issue of the applicability and relevance of Article 6 to a forced marriage application was considered by *A Chief Constable v YK & ors* ,[5] a case which concerned the use of special advocates in forced marriage proceedings. Sir Nicholas Wall P found that Article 6 did not demand the appointment of special advocates and held:

> 'Furthermore, when I come to analyse the ECHR Article 6 rights of the parties affected, I am tempted to the view that ECHR Article 6 is not engaged at all. Article 6 protects a party's right to a fair trial in the determination of his civil rights and obligations. To force a person into marriage is manifestly not a civil right, still less an obligation. In my view, accordingly, it is arguable that ECHR Article 6 is not engaged in an application for a FMPO. In any event, since the court permits the exercise of jurisdiction ex parte and on the basis of the applicant's belief, it does not seem to me that a respondent's right to apply to set the order aside entitles him or her to access to information which, if abused, will lead to serious breaches of the rights of the person to be protected.
>
> Any application to set aside a FMPO, however, is likely to engage ECHR Article 6. A person against whom the order has been made (A's parents in this instance) may well deny forcing A into marriage or any intention of doing so and may assert that the order represents a breach of their ECHR Article 8 right to respect for their family life in arranging a

4 *A Chief Constable v Yk & Ors* [2010]0 EWHC 2438 (Fam), at [109].

5 [2010] EWHC 2438 (Fam).

> marriage for their daughter. We are thus back to the dichotomy identified in paragraph 9 of this judgment. Assuming, therefore, that ECHR Art 6 is engaged, it nonetheless seems to me that the right to a fair trial manifestly does not entitle a party either to see all the documents in the case or to have all the information in the possession of the court'.

6.12 Article 6 shall not entitle a party to see all documents in proceedings. In *Re B (Disclosure to other parties)*,[6] a father alleged to have committed serious acts of domestic violence was added as a party to public children proceedings. He sought disclosure of all documents in proceedings, but the mother averred that this would violate her and her child's right to privacy. The case therefore concerned a conflict between the mother and the child's Article 8 right to privacy and the father's Article 6 right to a fair trial. Munby J (as he then was) devised three principles which can be summarised as follows:

(a) An entitlement to a fair trial under ECHR Article 6 is absolute, however this does not mean that a party has an absolute and unqualified right to see all the documents.

(b) The advent of the Human Rights Act 1998 means it is no longer the case that the only interests capable of denying a litigant access to documents are the interests of children involved in the litigation. Thus, the interests of anyone else who is involved, whether as victim, party or witness and who can demonstrate that their ECHR Article 8 rights are sufficiently engaged, can also have that effect.

(c) A limited qualification of the right to see the documents may be acceptable if directed towards a clear and proper objective. Non-disclosure must be limited to what the situation imperatively demands and is justified only when the case is compelling or strictly necessary, with the court being rigorous in its examination of the feared harm and any difficulty caused to the litigant counterbalanced by procedures designed to ensure a fair trial.

6.13 Article 6 may also become engaged in a forced marriage case through the Legal Aid Agency's decision to refuse legal aid. A refusal to provide free legal aid in a case relating to a 'civil right' does not establish a breach of Article 6 *per se* (*Airey v Ireland*[7]).

6.14 The question is whether in all the circumstances of the case, the lack of legal aid would deprive the applicant of a fair hearing (*Steel and Morris v the United Kingdom*,[8] *McVicar v The United Kingdom*[9]).

6.15 It is a regular feature of forced marriage that the person to be protected and other respondents may either have learning difficulties or limited capacity. Often there are also language barriers which make the prospect of them self-

6 [2001] 2 FLR 1017.
7 Application No 6289/73.
8 Application No 68416/01.
9 Application No 46311/99.

representing unrealistic. As such, it is submitted that a failure of the Legal Aid Agency to fund representation for litigants unable to pay for it themselves shall likely amount to a breach of Article 6.

6.16 In a criminal context, Article 6 shall be most acutely engaged. *Archbold: Criminal Pleading Evidence and Practice 2020*, 16-72–16-127 provides comprehensive commentary of how Article 6 applies to criminal law and procedure.

ARTICLE 8: RIGHT TO RESPECT FOR PRIVATE AND FAMILY LIFE

6.17 Article 8 of the Convention is a qualified right meaning that an interference may be lawful if it can be shown that the interference is a proportionate means of achieving a legitimate aim. The Article provides:

> 'Everyone has the right to respect for his private and family life, his home and his correspondence.
>
> There shall be no interference by a public authority with the exercise of this right except such as is in accordance with the law and is necessary in a democratic society in the interests of national security, public safety or the economic well-being of the country, for the prevention of disorder or crime, for the protection of health or morals, or for the protection of the rights and freedoms of others.'

6.18 Article 8 shall inevitably be engaged in cases of forced marriage. On the one hand, forcibly marrying a person shall be a violation of their Article 8 rights. Given that such an interference would be otherwise than in accordance with law, it is de facto an unlawful interference and a consideration of proportionality or legitimate aim is not necessary.

6.19 On the other hand, measures to prevent or combat forced marriage shall engage and potentially violate the Article 8 rights of Respondents. For example, in *R (on the application of Bibi and another) (FC) v Secretary of State for the Home Department*,[10] the Supreme Court considered the lawfulness of Paragraph 277 of the Immigration Rules which were designed to deter forced marriages. The provision prevented the entry for settlement of foreign spouses unless both parties to the marriage were over the age of 21.

6.20 The measure was one which had been adopted across several European states and had even been endorsed by way of a European Union Directive.[11] However, the Supreme Court by a majority of 5 to 1 that the measure was an unlawful interference with the Article 8 Rights of the respondent's Article 8 rights. Lord Brown was strongly critical of the majority in his dissenting judgment

10 [2015] UKSC 68.
11 The 'Family – Reunification' Directive 2003/86/EC.

which provides an interesting example of the debate as to judicial competence in policy making.

ARTICLE 14: PROTECTION FROM DISCRIMINATION

6.21 Article 14 is also a qualified right and provides the following:

> 'The enjoyment of the rights and freedoms set forth in this Convention shall be secured without discrimination on any ground such as sex, race, colour, language, religion, political or other opinion, national or social origin, association with a national minority, property, birth or other status.'

6.22 Article 14 is an ancillary right and does not create a freestanding right not to be subject to discrimination or prohibit discrimination in a general sense.

6.23 Instead, Article 14 functions to prevent discrimination in the application and enjoyment of other rights created by the Convention. As the Strasbourg Court held in *The Belgian Linguistic Case*:[12]

> 'It is as though [Article 14] formed an integral part of each of the Articles laying down rights and freedoms.'

6.24 However, whilst another Convention Right must be engaged in order for Article 14 to come into play, there is no requirement that the substantive right has been violated. For example, in *Carson v the United Kingdom*,[13] the appellant, who had spent several years living overseas, complained to the Strasbourg Court that her rights under Article 1 of Protocol 1[14] had been violated by a refusal of the UK Government to uprate her pension. The court held that this complaint was ill-founded.

6.25 Despite not finding a violation of a substantive right, the court did hold that the issue fell within the wide ambit of Article 1 of Protocol 1 and as such Article 14 was engaged. The court also held that country of residence is 'other status' under Article 14 albeit the court ultimately held on the facts that there had been no discrimination.

6.26 Thus, whether or not there has been a substantive violation of Articles 3 or 8, forced marriage cases and the state's response to them shall invariably fall within the ambit of Articles 3 and 8 of the Convention.

12 [1968] ECtHR 1474/62.

13 [2010] ECtHR 42184/05.

14 Every natural or legal person is entitled to the peaceful enjoyment of his possessions. No one shall be deprived of his possessions except in the public interest and subject to the conditions provided for by law and by the general principles of international law.

6.27 In order for discrimination in the application of a Convention Right to be lawful, the discrimination must be capable of being reasonably and objectively justified and it must be pursuant to a legitimate aim with a reasonable relationship of proportionality between the discrimination and the aim sought to be realised.

6.28 Both direct and indirect discrimination can amount to a violation of Article 14. Indirect discrimination arises in the context of Article 14 where a seemingly neutral provision has a disproportionately prejudicial effect on a particular group.

6.29 Forced marriage is a phenomenon which disproportionately affects both females and all people of South Asian descent. Sixty-one per cent of cases dealt with by the Forced Marriage Unit were from Pakistan, Bangladesh or India. Seventy-five per cent of victims were women.[15]

6.30 Given the disproportionate effect of forced marriage on South Asian women in particular, it is possible to envisage circumstances where a failure by a public authority to provide effective protection from and investigation of forced marriage could constitute indirect discrimination under Article 14 as well as breaches of Articles 3 and/or 8.

6.31 Further, if public authorities were to adopt heavy handed or discriminatory practices based on the assumption that a South Asian family are more likely to be engaged in forced marriage, this too could constitute a violation of Article 14.

6.32 Thus, public authorities must carefully consider the compatibility of their actions with both Article 14 and the Equality Act 2010.

POSITIVE OBLIGATIONS

6.33 Negative obligations under the Convention require the state not to do acts which would violate a citizen's Convention Rights. Police officers torturing somebody would be a violation of the state's negative obligation not to torture under Article 3.

6.34 By contrast, positive obligations require the public authorities to do positive acts. The ambit of the state's positive obligations is expanding, however, some of the key positive obligations relevant to forced marriage are:

(a) When the state is on notice of a specific and immediate threat to someone's life, it is bound to take effective protective steps (*Osman v United Kingdom*[16]);

(b) The law must provide effective and adequate protection against rape and sexual abuse (*MC v Bulgaria*[17]);

15 Foreign and Commonwealth Office, Forced Marriage Statistics 2018, April 2020.

16 (Application No 23452/94) (2000) 29 EHHR 245.

17 [2005] 40 EHRR 20.

(c) Conduct effective investigations into allegations of rape or other conduct which amounts to an interference with Article 3 (*Commissioner of Police of the Metropolis v DSD*[18]).

6.35 In *Re K (Forced Marriage: Passport Order)*,[19] the Secretary of State identified the following positive obligations in respect of forced marriage cases:

> '1) Preventing a breach of the right to marry under ECHR, Article 12 (see *R (Quila) v Secretary of State for the Home Department*[20]);
>
> 2) Discharging the UK's positive obligation under ECHR Article 8 with regard to the right to respect for private life and the protection of the moral and physical integrity of individuals by enhancing or liberating the autonomy of a vulnerable adult;
>
> 3) Discharging the UK's positive obligations under ECHR, Article 3 in cases where forced marriage may give rise to a real risk of behaviour sufficient to engage Article 3. In cases in which the Article 3 threshold has been crossed, the UK has an obligation to take reasonable steps to prevent a real risk of inhuman or degrading treatment at the hands of non-State actors, which includes treatment which may be imposed outside the jurisdiction;
>
> 4) Discharging the UK's positive obligation under ECHR Article 5 with respect to deprivation of liberty;
>
> 5) In particularly serious cases, discharging the UK's positive obligations under ECHR Article 2.'

BALANCING OF RIGHTS

6.36 Forced marriage cases shall invariably involve a conflict of rights. On the one hand, a forced marriage shall constitute a breach of Article 3 of the Convention. On the other hand, the measures put in place to protect the victim from being forced into marriage are likely to amount to interferences with both the victim and other family members' Article 8 rights. These measures may include restrictions on contact, movement, travel, seizing passports and preventing marriages from taking place. This conflict was addressed by the Court of Appeal in *Re K (Forced Marriage: Passport Order)*.[21]

6.37 The circumstances of *Re K* were that the police had first obtained a Forced Marriage Protection Order to protect K in 2015. In 2017, K was living separately from her family and had withdrawn the allegations made against her family. In December 2017, K's mother died. The Forced Marriage Protection

18 [2018] UKSC 11.
19 [2020] EWCA Civ 190.
20 [2011] 3 WLR 836.
21 [2020] EWCA Civ 190.

Order prevented her from going to her mother's funeral in Pakistan and so she applied to discharge it. The circuit judge hearing the application found there was a threat of violence that would amount to a violation of her Article 3 rights should the order be discharged; as such after giving K the opportunity to engage with the authorities to consider protective measures, the judge refused the application to discharge the Order.

6.38 The Court of Appeal when considering the obvious tension between K's Article 3 and 8 rights endorsed the submissions of an intervening charity that:

> 'Cases of forced marriage do not just involve private individuals, but they involve the State undertaking an active and positive role in the protecting of an individual from themselves and, normally their community. ...When considering what protection should be put in place for a victim in what is near-universally by definition a family setting, the Family Court has to undertake a sensitive and careful balancing exercise.
>
> The issue in such cases is not *whether* there should be State intervention, but rather *what* that intervention should be, taking into account human rights considerations (in particular Article 3) and the victim's standpoint and views. Where the court's obligation to protect a victim does not conform – as in the instant case – with the victim's expressed wishes – the court must be particularly careful as to how it evaluates the evidence and reaches a conclusion as to what, if any, protective orders should be put in place. ... Ultimately though, the court's primary focus is likely to be to prevent a victim being left unprotected and exposed to the risk of further harm, and a breach of their Article 3 rights'

6.39 This analysis reflects the differing statuses of Article 3, an absolute right and Article 8, a qualified right. Thus, where an irresolvable conflict between Articles 3 and 8 arise, Article 3 must prevail and the Court ought to put in the protection necessary to effectively safeguard the parties' Article 3 rights.

THE HUMAN RIGHTS ACT 1998

6.40 The Human Rights Act 1998 came into effect in October 2000. Before its enactment, parties could not rely on Convention Rights in the domestic courts. The Human Rights Act 1998, s 6 makes it unlawful for a public authority to act in a manner incompatible with a Convention Right. Section 6(3) defines a public body as either a court or tribunal or any person carrying out a public function.

6.41 This means that local authorities, police forces and courts all have a duty to give effect to the Convention when making decisions about forced marriage.

6.42 If a party is or would be a victim of an unlawful act under the Human Rights Act 1998, s 6; that is of a public body acting in a manner incompatible with the Convention, then s 7 comes into play. The Human Rights Act 1998, s 7 first provides a right to bring proceedings against the authority which has violated the victims Convention rights.

6.43 Secondly, s 7 allows the victim to rely on their violated Convention Rights in the course of any legal proceedings. It follows that if the applicant for a Forced Marriage Protection Order is the person to be protected, it is open to them to rely on Articles 3 and 8 during the course of those proceedings if they aver that they are at risk of those Rights being breached.

6.44 Similarly, a respondent who avers that measures imposed interfere with his Article 8 or other Convention Rights may rely on such arguments in the course of forced marriage proceedings.

6.45 Finally, should a public authority breach someone's Convention Rights in a forced marriage context by, for example failing effectively to investigate an allegation of forced marriage or fail to put into effect protective measures when put on notice of a forced marriage, the Human Rights Act 1998, s 7 allows the victim to bring proceedings against the public authority. It is likely such proceedings would include a claim for damages.

CHAPTER 7

Honour-based forced marriage

Contents at a Glance:

INTRODUCTION

7.1 The cross-government definition of honour-based violence is:

> 'an incident or crime involving violence, threats of violence, intimidation coercion or abuse (including psychological, physical, sexual, financial or emotional abuse) which has or may have been committed to protect or defend the honour of an individual, family and/ or community for alleged or perceived breaches of the family and/or community's code of behaviour'.

7.2 The Government's Multi-Agency Guidance provides that honour-based forced marriage and violence is to be distinguished from other forms of abuse as it 'is committed with some degree of approval and/or collusion from family and/ community members. Victims will have multiple perpetrators not only within the UK'.[1]

7.3 Preconceptions as to the likely ethnic or cultural identity of families prone to honour-based force marriage are unhelpful. In 2005, Professor Hester led a report on forced marriage in Birmingham for the Home Office.[2] Whilst there was evidence that forced marriage was a particular problem in the South Asian community, the research found that forced marriage was also an issue in a wide range of communities outside the South Asian diaspora. These groups include:

(a) Orthodox Christians;

(b) Irish traveller women;

1 HM Government, Multi-agency guidelines: Handling Cases of Forced Marriage.
2 Hester et al, Forced Marriage: the risk factors and the effect of raising the minimum age for a sponsor, and of leave to enter the UK as a spouse or fiancé, University of Bristol, 2007.

(c) Eastern European Communities;

(d) Eritrean communities;

(e) Sudanese Communities;

(f) Sierra Leonean Communities;

(g) Mozambican Communities;

(h) Armenian Communities;

(i) Turkish Communities;

(j) Some mainland Chinese communities; and

(k) Afro-Caribbean communities.

7.4 Similarly, a range of religious faiths were found to be affected by forced marriage, including orthodox Christians, Hindus, Sikhs, Muslims and a minority of atheists. Therefore, public bodies and professionals must be vigilant for forced marriages in all cases where warning signs arise and not make decisions that there is no risk on the basis of non-evidence-based preconceptions. The proposition that forced marriage is not exclusively an issue confined to the South Asian Community was further confirmed in a 2009 qualitative study of forced marriage in the UK.[3]

MOTIVATIONS FOR HONOUR-BASED FORCED MARRIAGES

7.5 It appears that the impact of honour-based forced marriage is even more acutely gendered than forced marriage generally. Studies appear to show not only that women are far more likely to be forced to marry for honour-based reasons, but also that such forced marriages are likely to have far more damaging effects on women than men.[4]

7.6 UK statistics, so far as they are available, appear to support this proposition. The Metropolitan Police data reports that between January 2015 and June 2017, 529 reported victims were female and 92 male, 15 victims were under the age of 12, 159 teenagers, 267 aged from 20–30, 115 aged from 30–40, 40 aged from 40–50, 14 aged from 50–60 and 11 over the age of 60.[5]

7.7 Motivations for honour-based forced marriage vary. There are few UK studies examining the causal link between pre-marital sex and forced

3 Chantler, K., Gangoli, G., & Hester, M. (2009). Forced Marriage in the UK: Religious, Cultural, Economic or State Violence. *Critical Social Policy*, *29*(4), 587– 612.

4 Els Leye 'Forced marriages in Belgium: an analysis of the current situation, 2014; Directorate General for Internal Policies, European Union, Forced Marriage from a gender perspective, 2016.

5 Metropolitan Police Information Rights Unit 20/10/2017 available at <https://www.met.police.uk/SysSiteAssets/foi-media/metropolitan-police/disclosure_2018/february_2018/information-rights-unit---honour-based-violence-and-forced-marriage-crime-statistics-from-january-2015-to-june-2017.

marriage, but it appears that one motivation of honour-based forced marriages can be to preserve a family member's honour or limit the potential community consequences of pre-marital sexual intimacy.[6]

7.8 More broadly, forced marriage is often used a means of controlling a woman's sexuality and reducing the risk of extra-marital sex or illegitimate pregnancies.[7] Some families consider that their reputations rely on the 'proper' sexual behaviour of women within the family unit. Thus, forced marriage is a means, in the context of patriarchal power structures, of controlling unwanted sexuality of women.

7.9 Protecting the perceived cultural or ethnic identity of the family is a further consideration which applies to both male and female forced marriages. In particular, ensuring that children marry within certain ethnic, cultural, caste or social groups.[8]

LGBTQ+ FORCED MARRIAGE

7.10 Both male and female victims are forced into marriage either to disguise their sexuality or due to their family or community's fears about their sexuality.[9] In 2019, two per cent of those seeking assistance from the Forced Marriage Unit identified themselves as LGBTQ+, however it is probable that there is significant underreporting.[10]

7.11 A German study suggests that same-sex relations are in some instances considered to be a serious illness that might be cured through marriage.[11] Other research has suggested that men, in particular, are forced into marriage for its 'therapeutic' effects.[12] The belief being that sense of responsibility bestowed by a marriage can somehow 'save' a person from being gay or prevent them from engaging in homosexual relations and drug addictions as well as helping resolve any psychiatric issues.

6 Stark, Motives and Agency in Forced Marriage among the Urban Poor in Tanzania, 2019.
7 HM Government, Chapter 3.9 Multi-Agency Practice Guidelines on handling cases of forced marriage.
8 Ibid.
9 Maastricht University, 'Femmes for Freedom en Verwey Jonker Instituur, Zo zijn we niet getrouwd. Een onderzoek naar omvang en aard van huwelijksdwang, achterlating en huwelijkse gevangenschap' (August 2014).
10 HM Government, Forced Marriage Unit Statistics 2019.
11 Federal Ministery, for families, senior citizen, women and youth 'Combating forced marriage – affected persons protecting effectively. A handbook for child and youth welfare services' (Bundesministerium für Familie, Seniorn, Frauen und Jugend, Zwangsverheiratung bekämpfen – Betroffene wirksam schützen. eine Handreichung für die Kinder- und Jugendhilfe) 3th edn, Silberdruck OHG, Niestetal, 2012) 42.
12 Timmerman C., Descheemaeker E., Heyse P., Clycq N., 'Choix de la conjointe et mariage des hommes allochtones : une analyse quantitative et qualitative du processus de choix de la conjointe et du mariage des homes marocains, Turcs et Sikhs', 2009 ; Bensaid, N. and Rea, A., 'Study on forced marriage in the BrusselsCapital Region (Étude relative aux mariages forcés en région de Bruxelles-Capitale)', ULB, 2012, pp.135-136.

7.12 Forced marriage has been described as a means of enforcing 'compulsory heterosexuality'.[13]

7.13 Marriages motivated by homophobia or transphobia give rise to a number of specific considerations. Police and prosecutors ought to have regard to the CPS Prosecution Guidance on homophobic, biphobic and transphobic hate crime and whether an uplift under the Criminal Justice Act 2003, s 146 ought to be applied for.

7.14 Further, social care professionals ought to consider what specialist services or support can be provided to LGBTQ+ individuals in these circumstances. There are a number of specialist charities which provide mental health services and therapy to members of the LGBTQ+ community. Many NHS Trusts also employ specialist trained mental health practitioners experienced in supporting LGBTQ+ people who have been subject to discrimination or rejection because of their sexuality or gender.

ISSUES WITH THE TERM 'HONOUR-BASED VIOLENCE'

7.15 There is no statutory definition of 'honour-based abuse' or 'honour-based forced marriage'. The use of the term 'honour-based' has been subject to some academic criticism in that the language 'is in the danger of supporting unwillingly the perpetrators because it might make them believe that they are truly acting in the name of honour'.[14] It has been suggested that when considering the most severe circumstances, the term 'shame killing' should be used instead'.[15]

7.16 The use of the term honour-based 'violence' may also be misleading in that the term violence often connotes imagery of physical force; however, the definition encompasses abuse that may involve, as well as violence, 'threats of violence, intimidation coercion or abuse (including psychological, physical, sexual, financial or emotional abuse) which has or may have been committed to protect or defend the honour of the family and/or community'.[16]

13 Chantler, K., Gangoli, G., & Hester, M. (2009). Forced Marriage in the UK: Religious, Cultural, Economic or State Violence. *Critical Social Policy*, *29*(4), 587 – 612.

14 Directorate General for Internal Policies, Policy Department C: Citizens' Rights and Constitutional Affairs, Justice Freedom and Security, Forced Marriage and Honour Killings Study.

15 Directorate General for Internal Policies, Policy Department C: Citizens' Rights and Constitutional Affairs, Justice Freedom and Security, Forced Marriage and Honour Killings Study.

16 Crown Prosecution Service, Honour Based Violence and Forced Marriage available at <https://www.cps.gov.uk/publication/honour-based-violence-and-forced-marriage> and Crown Prosecution Service, So-Called Honour-Based Abuse and Forced Marriage: Guidance on Identifying and Flagging Cases available at <https://www.cps.gov.uk/legal-guidance/so-called-honour-based-abuse-and-forced-marriage-guidance-identifying-and-flagging.

INTERPLAY OF CULTURAL AND RELIGIOUS RIGHTS

7.17 In 2000, Leti Vlopp undertook a powerful comparison of the approach taken by the US authorities and public in respect of two cases of forced marriage.[17] In the first case, a white 16-year-old called 911 reporting that her father, the leader of a polygamist sect had forced her to marry her 32-year old uncle as his 15th wife. The uncle received ten years' imprisonment. The father, who had beaten the girl unconscious when she tried to run away, received 28 weeks in prison, a $2,700 fine and was ordered to attend an anger management course.

7.18 Utah had a strong tradition of child marriages and polygamy. Until 1999, the age of consent to marry in Utah was 14. Proposals in 1997 to increase the age of consent were unsuccessful partially due to a belief that child marriage discouraged promiscuity.

7.19 Similarly, polygamy continued to persist amongst certain groups after the Mormon Church renounced the practice in 1890. In 1998, the Governor, a descendent of polygamists refused to condemn polygamy suggesting that it was a matter of religious freedom.

7.20 The case sparked a public discourse of condemnation about polygamy and child abuse in Utah. But there were no suggestions that those involved were un-American, had failed to Americanise or threatened American values. Nor did anybody characterise the issue as a clash between multiculturism and feminism.

7.21 The second case profiled by Vlopp related to a family called Al-Saidy. The Iraqi immigrant father of the family forced his 13 and 14-year-old daughters to marry 28 and 34-year-old men. Eventually, the older daughter ran away and the police became involved leading to the arrest of the parents and the husbands. Lawyers for the Al-Saidys suggested that the daughters were married for religious and cultural reasons and the case was 'a clash between cultural mores and U.S. Law'. The media immediately presented the case as the proper limits of multiculturalism.

7.22 Vlopp describes how the Dallas Morning News followed the rest of the media in depicting the incident as a threat to American values in reporting the case as 'a conflict shrouded in issues of multiculturalism and ignorance in the ways of a strange new world'. Whereas the Omaha World suggested that 'multiculturalism goes too far if it insists that all cultures are equally valid'.

7.23 As Vlopp writes 'In this view, "newcomers" import primitive and backward values threatening the Western cultural traditions'.

7.24 The case studies reveal a legal and policy dilemma at the heart of forced marriage in the UK. How does society effectively combat a heinous, universally

17 Vlopp, L (2000) 'Blaming Culture for Bad Behaviour, Yale Journal of Law and the Humanities 12(1): 89–116.

condemned practice which is disproportionately both perpetrated, and suffered, by minoritised communities without discriminating or reinforcing discriminatory narratives.

7.25 A failure to properly consider this question and the wider context of forced marriage can lead to the ostracism and vilification of communities. Conversely, an excessive or misplaced sensitivity to the issues has the potential to lead to statutory services failing to take appropriate action or vigorously protecting victims and pursuing perpetrators.

7.26 The starting point must be the aforementioned research which clearly demonstrates that forced marriage affects a wide range of racial and religious groups. Acknowledgement must also be made that all major faith groups reject and condemn the practice of forced marriage. Indeed, freely given consent to marriage is a pre-requisite for marriage in all major religions.[18] Similarly, even in the most impacted communities, only a very small minority of people consider forced marriage to be anything other than abhorrent.

7.27 The Multi-Agency Practice Guidelines makes clear that operational decisions should not be made on the basis of presumptions and an objective assessment of risk and the evidence available should always be carried out.

7.28 Simply put, the cultural, religious or traditional motivations for forced marriage are an irrelevance. It is a form of abuse which has been perpetrated in all racial, cultural, religious and ethnic groups. It is also a practice which causes unspeakable harm to its victims. It follows from this that no cultural, religious or other justifications should be accepted for forced marriage and that statutory services should not be deterred from taking every possible step to eradicate it and protect its victims.

18 HM Government, Multi-Agency Practice Guidelines on handling forced marriage, Chapter 3.9.

CHAPTER 8:

Vulnerable individuals and those lacking capacity

Contents at a Glance:

Introduction

Test for capacity

Before a marriage where parties lack capacity takes place

After a marriage where parties lack capacity takes place

Scope of the inherent jurisdiction

Test for vulnerability

Protections available

INTRODUCTION

8.1 Any marriage contracted with a spouse who lacks capacity to consent to marriage or sex shall necessarily be a forced marriage.[1] As is highlighted by the Government Multi-Agency Practice Guidelines, forced marriages can, on occasion be motivated by a desire to ensure that a disabled person has someone to care for them when their parents die.

8.2 However, situations can also arise where adults lacking capacity express strong and consistent wishes to be married. Sometimes, family members, unaware of the legal implications, seek to give effect to those wishes for entirely benevolent reasons. The use of the term 'forced marriage' in such circumstances can cause great distress. However, a marriage where parties lack capacity is a forced marriage irrespective of the absence of force or coercion.

8.3 In all cases where it is alleged that a spouse lacked capacity to consent to marriage at the material time, some form of expert evidence is likely to be required to rebut the presumption of capacity created by the Mental Capacity Act 2005, s 1. Capacity is act as opposed to person specific. A person either has capacity to marry or consent to sex or they do not, the test is not dependent on the identity of the spouse. Similarly, it is important not to adopt a wholesale approach to someone's capacity. Where someone is found to lack capacity to make one

1 *YLA v PM & MX* [2013] EWHC 4020 (COP).

decision, they must still be presumed to have capacity to make other decisions. Further, capacity is time specific and as such someone may lack capacity at one moment only to subsequently regain capacity.

8.4 Of particular importance in forced marriage cases is the requirement under the Mental Capacity Act 2005, s 1(3) that a person ought not to be treated as lacking capacity to make a decision until all reasonable steps have been taken without success. In the context of adults allegedly lacking capacity, this provision is likely to require the commission of educative work to maximise the person's capacity to make decisions about sex and marriage.

8.5 The wisdom of the proposed or contracted marriage is irrelevant when considering whether or not the person concerned had capacity to enter into it.[2]

8.6 When conducting mental capacity assessments in the context of suspected forced marriage cases, it is generally wise to also asses the person's capacity to conduct litigation as this shall expedite the appointment of a litigation friend should they lack capacity to litigate.

8.7 Where an adult has capacity under the Mental Capacity Act 2005 but is otherwise vulnerable, the High Court has broad common law powers under the inherent jurisdiction to protect them and their property from abuse. In the context of forced marriage, local authorities seeking to protect vulnerable adults should rely on the statutory remedies in the Family Law Act 1996, Part 4A for injunctive orders.

8.8 However, ancillary issues may remain unresolved even after the imposition of a Forced Marriage Protection Order. For example, those seeking to force the adult to marry may retain control of the vulnerable person's bank accounts or the vulnerable person may live in the same property as their abusers. Such issues may render the terms of the Order unenforceable, give rise to an unacceptable risk of the Order being breached or otherwise pose a risk to the adult concerned. Often such adults, although having capacity, may be overborne by their abusers and feel unwilling or unable to take steps to protect themselves. In circumstances such as these, an application under the High Court's inherent jurisdiction ought to be considered.

THE TEST FOR CAPACITY

Mental capacity checklist:

- Capacity must be assumed unless it is established P lacks it.
- Capacity is to be decided on the balance of probabilities.

2 *Southwark LBC v KA* [2016] EWCOP 20; Mental Capacity Act 2005, s 1(4).

- The Court must first consider the diagnostic test: does the person have an impairment or disturbance in the functioning of the mind or brain; and
- Then the decision-making test is P unable to do any of the following:
  - Understand information relevant to the decision;
  - Retain that information;
  - Use or weigh that information as part of the process of making the decision; or
  - Communicate his decision.
- Have all practical steps to help P make the decision been taken?
- Remember, capacity is decision specific, P may have capacity to make some decisions but not others.

8.9 The test for capacity to make decisions about sex and marriage is set out fully in **Chapter 21**. A person is unable to make a decision if they are unable to do any of the following due to an impairment of, or a disturbance in the functioning of, the mind or brain, whether permanent or temporary:

(a) to understand the information relevant to the decision;

(b) to retain that information;

(c) to use or weigh that information as part of the process of making the decision; or

(d) to communicate his decision (whether by talking, using sign language or any other means).

8.10 The current state of the law is that in order to have capacity to marry, one must not lack capacity to consent to sexual relations.[3] In *A Local Authority v JB* ,[4] the Court of Appeal suggested that the following factors may be relevant information for a person to be able to understand, retain, weigh and use in deciding whether to have sex:

(a) The sexual nature and character of the act of sexual intercourse, including the mechanics of the act;

(b) The fact that the other person must have the capacity to consent to the sexual activity and must in fact consent before and throughout the sexual activity;

(c) The fact that P can say yes or no to having sexual relations and is able to decide whether to give or withhold consent;

(d) That a reasonably foreseeable consequence of sexual intercourse between a man and a woman is that the woman will become pregnant; and

3 *London Borough of Southwark v KA and Others* [2016] EWCOP at [37].
4 [2020] EWCA Civ 735.

(e) That there are health risks involved, particularly the acquisition of sexually transmitted infections and the risk of sexually transmitted infections can be reduced by the taking of precautions such as the use of a condom.

8.11 Marriage is a more complex decision than whether to consent to sex, in *Southwark LBC v KA*,[5] Parker J identified the following information relevant to the decision to marry:

(a) The broad nature of the marriage contract;

(b) The duties and responsibilities normally attached to a marriage;

(c) That there may be financial consequences of the marriage; and

(d) The essence of the marriage is for two people to live together and love one another.

BEFORE A MARRIAGE WHERE PARTIES LACK CAPACITY TAKES PLACE

8.12 A local authority may become aware of a risk an adult lacking capacity shall be married through a number of different avenues. There may be a history of forced marriage in the family or the person may start expressing a desire to be married

8.13 If statutory services identify that a person who potentially lacks capacity to decide to marry or consent to sex is at risk of marriage, then a mental capacity assessment ought to be carried out as a matter of urgency. In circumstances where there appears to be an imminent risk of a forced marriage taking place it may be appropriate to make an urgent application for a Forced Marriage Protection order to be made on an interim basis pending the filing of further capacity evidence.

8.14 Once a mental capacity assessment has been carried out, if it is shown that the person lacks capacity to decide to marry or consent to sex then, if a risk of marriage exists, a Forced Marriage Protection Order ought to be applied for. Careful consideration also ought to be given as to whether an application to the Court of Protection is necessary.[6]

8.15 In most cases, a course of educative work ought to be commissioned in the hope that the person's capacity in respect of marriage and sex can be developed.

5 [2016] EWCOP 20.
6 See **Chapter 24**.

AFTER A MARRIAGE WHERE PARTIES LACK CAPACITY HAS TAKEN PLACE

8.16 Where statutory services become aware that an adult potentially lacking capacity has been married, a number of immediate steps ought to be taken:

(a) a mental capacity assessment ought to be carried out;

(b) consideration ought to be given as to what protective orders might be required, in particular, an application for a Forced Marriage Protection Order ought to be contemplated;

(c) the full circumstances of the marriage ought to be obtained and documented;[7] and

(d) in particular, services ought to consider whether notwithstanding the issue of capacity, the marriage was a forced marriage;

8.17 Once the person concerned is suitably protected, the question then arises of how to deal with the marriage. This issue is explored in **Chapter 5**. For those representing the victim, particular consideration ought to be given as to whether to apply for a decree of nullity. All parties shall need to actively consider an application for a declaration of non-recognition under the High Court's inherent jurisdiction.

SCOPE OF THE INHERENT JURISDICTION

8.18 The inherent jurisdiction was described by Lord Donaldson in *Re F (Mental Patient: Sterilisation)*[8] as 'the great safety net'. In *A Local Authority v DL*[9] Theis J held that the inherent jurisdiction's 'primary purpose is to help create a situation where the person concerned can receive outside help free of coercion, to enable him or her to weigh things up and decide freely what he or she wishes to do'. Upholding Theis J's decision, the Court of Appeal observed that the inherent jurisdiction was targeted 'solely at those adults whose ability to make decisions from themselves has been compromised by matters other than those covered by the Mental Capacity Act 2005'. Their Lordships also agreed with Theis J that the jurisdiction should be exercised in a 'facilitative' rather than a 'dictatorial' manner.[10]

8.19 The inherent jurisdiction can be used to provide additional protection to those lacking capacity when the remedy required does not fall within the Mental

7 HM Government, Chapter 4, Multi-Agency Practice Guidelines on handling forced marriage, 2014.

8 [1990] 2 AC 1.

9 [2011] EWHC 1022 (Fam).

10 *DL v A Local Authority* [2012] EWCA Civ 253.

Capacity Act 2005.[11] In *City of Westminster v C*,[12] the Court of Appeal specifically held that the Mental Capacity Act 2005 did not oust the High Court's inherent jurisdiction in relation to mentally handicapped adults to meet circumstances unmet by the scope to the legislation.

8.20 More commonly, however, it shall be deployed to protect vulnerable individuals who have mental capacity and therefore do not fall under the Mental Capacity Act 2005.[13]

8.21 Often cases shall involve allegations of abuse by others. For example, in *Southend on Sea Borough Council v Meyers*,[14] Hayden J made use of the inherent jurisdiction to deprive a 98-year-old man of his liberty in order to prevent him being subject to further abuse at the hands of his son his son.

TEST FOR VULNERABILITY

8.22 For the court to invoke the inherent jurisdiction, it must be satisfied that the adult concerned is:[15]

(a) under constraint;

(b) subject to coercion or undue influence; or

(c) for some other reason deprived of the capacity to make the relevant decision, or disabled from making a free choice, or incapacitated or disabled from giving or expressing a real and genuine consent.

8.23 In *Re DL*,[16] the Court of Appeal endorsed Munby J's summary of the test for the invoking of the inherent jurisdiction of the High Court as set out in *Re SA*:[17]

> 'i) Constraint: It does not matter for this purpose whether the constraint amounts to actual incarceration. The jurisdiction is exercisable whenever a vulnerable adult is confined, controlled or under restraint, even if the restraint is only of the kind referred to by Eastham J in *Re C (Mental Patient: Contact)* [1993] 1 FLR 940. It is enough that there is some significant curtailment of the freedom to do those things which in this country free men and women are entitled to do.
>
> ii) Coercion or undue influence: What I have in mind here are the kind of vitiating circumstances referred to by the Court of Appeal in *In re*

11 See, for example, *NHS Trust v Dr A* [2013] EWHC 2442 COP.
12 [2008] EWCA Civ 198.
13 See for example *Re DL* [2012] EWCA Civ 253; *London Borough of Wandsworth v M & Ors* [2018] 1 FLR 919; *Re SA* [2005] 2942(Fam).
14 [2019] EWHC 399 (Fam).
15 *Re SA* [2005] EWHC 2942 (Fam).
16 [2012] EWCA Civ 253.
17 [2005] EWHC 2942 (Fam).

T (Adult: Refusal of Treatment) [1993] Fam 95, where a vulnerable adult's capacity or will to decide has been sapped and overborne by the improper influence of another. In this connection I would only add … that where the influence is that of a parent or other close and dominating relative, and where the arguments and persuasion are based upon personal affection or duty, religious beliefs, powerful social or cultural conventions, or asserted social, familial or domestic obligations, the influence may, as Butler-Sloss LJ put it, be subtle, insidious, pervasive and powerful. In such cases, moreover, very little pressure may suffice to bring about the desired result

iii) Other disabling circumstances: What I have in mind here are the many other circumstances that may so reduce a vulnerable adult's understanding and reasoning powers as to prevent him forming or expressing a real and genuine consent, for example, the effects of deception, misinformation, physical disability, illness, weakness (physical, mental or moral), tiredness, shock, fatigue, depression, pain or drugs. No doubt there are others.'

8.24 Thus, there are a wide array of circumstances in which the High Court may determine somebody to be vulnerable and as such invoke the inherent jurisdiction. It seems clear that cases of forced marriage shall likely engage one or all three of the categories of cases identified by Munby J capable of giving rise to the court invoking the inherent jurisdiction. As such, careful consideration ought to be given to the making of an application under the inherent jurisdiction in circumstances where the victim requires support or protection not provided for by statute.

PROTECTIONS AVAILABLE

8.25 Once the inherent jurisdiction is involved, the court has an extremely broad discretion as to what order ought to be made. Examples of orders made include:

(a) In *A NHS Trust v Dr A*,[18] Baker J ordered the forcible feeding of Dr A under the inherent jurisdiction;

(b) In *DL v A Local Authority & Ors*,[19] the court granted an interim injunction protecting an elderly couple with capacity from their son;

(c) In *Croydon LBC v KR and ST*,[20] Lieven J declined to make an injunction under the inherent jurisdiction preventing a married couple from living with one another;

18 [2013] EWCOP 2442.
19 [2012] EWCA Civ 253.
20 [2019] EWHC 2498.

(d) In *Mazhar v the Lord Chancellor*,[21] Mostyn J had made an order under the inherent jurisdiction of the High Court authorising the use of reasonable force to bring a patient to hospital for treatment;

8.26 Thus, once the inherent jurisdiction is invoked, the court has extremely broad powers to make any orders it considers necessary to safeguard the adult's best interests. The single proviso to this broad and otherwise unfettered discretion is that the court must not do anything prohibited or inconsistent with statutory law.

21 [2019] EWCA Civ 1558.

CHAPTER 9

Organised exploitation and marriage for immigration purposes

Contents at a Glance:

INTRODUCTION

9.1 Forced marriage is internationally recognised as a form of modern slavery that can also give rise to human trafficking.[1] Of the 40.3 million people estimated to be enslaved around the world, 15.4 million are in forced marriages. Given the inherently international and cross-jurisdictional nature of forced marriage, human trafficking is a necessary facilitator of many forced marriages.[2]

9.2 Human trafficking, for the purposes of forced marriage, involves both internal, domestic journeys and victims being moved both into and out of the jurisdiction. For example, the National Crime Agency also identified European women being trafficked to the United Kingdom to marry Asian men not otherwise entitled to live in the United Kingdom as a form of human trafficking for forced marriage purposes.[3] Conversely, the phenomenon of British women being taken to foreign jurisdictions to be forcibly married and then returned to the United

1 International Labour Organisation, Global Estimates of Modern Slavery, Geneva 2017; Articles 1 and 2 United Nations Convention on the Abolition of Slavery, the Slave Trade and Institutions and Practices Similar to Slavery.
2 United Nations Office on Drugs and Crime, Global Report on Trafficking in Persons, 2016.
3 The National Crime Agency, the Nature and Scale of Human Trafficking in 2014.

Kingdom is well documented. Moving victims to other cities or parts of the UK for the purposes of forced marriage shall also come under the definition of human trafficking.

9.3 The United Nations has formulated the following definition of human trafficking which is largely adopted by the United Kingdom Government and agencies:[4]

> Trafficking in persons shall mean the recruitment, transportation, transfer, harbouring or receipt of persons, by means of the threat or use of force or other forms of coercion, of abduction, of fraud, of deception, of abuse of power or of a position of vulnerability or of the giving or receiving of payments or benefits to achieve the consent of a person having control of another person, for the purpose of exploitation. Exploitation shall include, at a minimum, the exploitation of the prostitution of others or other forms of sexual exploitation, forced labour or services, slavery or practices similar to slavery, servitude or removal of organs.

9.4 Human trafficking and modern slavery in the context of forced marriage is considered more fully at **Chapter 17**.

HUMAN TRAFFICKING

9.5 In 2016, within a global report undertaken by the United Nations Office on Drugs and Crime ('UNODC) it was recorded that trafficking for the purposes of forced or sham marriages accounted for 1.4 per cent of the total victims of trafficking.[5]

9.6 The UNODC data also noted that trafficking for marriage takes on 'a number of different permutations from involved organised irregular immigration and benefit fraud schemes in Europe, to traditional practices a in Central Asia and the Middle East, to the trade of women for marriages in South-East Asia'.

9.7 In 2017, the European Institute for Crime Prevention and Control, affiliated with the United Nations (HEUNI) reported that in five country studies there was convincing evidence that methods of recruitment for exploitative sham marriages were often the same as other forms of human trafficking and include luring victims with false promises and fake job offers/ opportunities. There is also a focus on young or inexperienced persons in insecure positions with financial difficulties, social problems and a history of marginalisation, low level education,

4 UN Protocol to Prevent, Suppress and punish Trafficking in Persons Especially Women and Children supplementing the United Nations Convention against Transnational Organized Crime.

5 The United Nations Office on Drugs and Crime, Global Report on Trafficking in Persons, 2016 available at https://www.unodc.org/documents/data-and-analysis/glotip/2016_Global_Report_on_Trafficking_in_Persons.pdf.

mental disabilities, lack of language skills weak social networks, and/or single mothers.[6]

ORGANISED EXPLOITATION

9.8 As noted within the United Nations Office on Drugs and Crime 2016 report, conflict can 'create favourable conditions for the trafficking of persons' and thus increase the use of organised exploitation. For example, in 2015, the International Organisation for Migration and the International Centre for Migration Policy Development reported that the 'Syrian conflict led to heightened vulnerability of many groups ... [with] ... many families and individuals adopting risky behaviours... including forced early marriages as a protective coping mechanism.[7]

9.9 Exploitation is also prevalent in areas of conflict as a result of armed groups 'engaging in trafficking in the territories in which they operate[8] 'with women being trafficked for the purpose of forced marriage and sexual slavery.

9.10 However, human trafficking for forced marriage does not stem exclusively from developing or conflict-ridden countries, nor is it a phenomenon that avoids affluent or developed countries. One example of organised exploitation for the purpose of marriage referred to within the 2016 report was that of a Chinese man who engaged Vietnamese persons with local knowledge to recruit females who were later moved across the border into Chinese territory and sold for marriage. Reference was also made to a 'different mode of trafficking' which has surfaced which takes the form of 'a large transnational organised crime group who recruited Central European women for sham marriages in Western Europe'.[9]

9.11 Therefore, practitioners and investigators ought to be aware that individual cases of forced marriages which are discovered may be indicative of wider, large scale networks facilitating and profiting from forced marriage.

6 European Institute for Crime Prevention and Control, Affiliated with the United Nations, HEUNI, Exploitative Sham Marriages: Exploring the Links between Human Trafficking and Sham Marriages, 2017 available at https://www.heuni.fi/material/attachments/heuni/policypaper/nn9cKy7Yd/HEUNI_HESTIA_PolicyPaper_final.pdf.

7 International Organization for Migration and the International Centre for Migration Policy Development Addressing Human Trafficking and Exploitation in Times of Crisis, Evidence and Recommendations for Further Action to Protect Vulnerable and Mobile Populations, 2015 available at https://publications.iom.int/system/files/addressing_human_trafficking_dec2015.pdf.

8 The United Nations Office on Drugs and Crime, Global Report on Trafficking in Persons, 2016 available at https://www.unodc.org/documents/data-and-analysis/glotip/2016_Global_Report_on_Trafficking_in_Persons.pdf.

9 The United Nations Office on Drugs and Crime, Global Report on Trafficking in Persons, 2016.

CIVIL AND CRIMINAL POWERS AVAILABLE

9.12 The United Nations Trafficking in Persons Protocol contains provisions for measures of protection and assistance that are not available under other legal frameworks. Adherence to the Protocol also triggers certain provisions under the UN Convention against Transnational Organized Crime (which the Protocol supplements).

9.13 Domestically, there are a number of remedies available. Offences under the Modern Slavery Act 2015, s 1, 2 or 4 may have been committed, as considered in **Chapter 17**. In terms of civil remedies, there are a number of options available to disrupt criminal networks.

Slavery and Trafficking Prevention Order

9.14 The Modern Slavery Act 2015 introduces two injunctive orders intended to disrupt and prevent slavery and human trafficking offences. Both have extra-territorial effect and severe penalties for breach. The first type of order is a slavery and trafficking prevention order ('STPO') made under created ss 14–22. The court may make a STPO where a person has been:

(a) convicted for a slavery or human trafficking offence;

(b) found not guilty of slavery or human trafficking offence by way of insanity; or

(c) found to be under a disability and has done the act charged against the defendant in respect of a slavery or human trafficking offence.

9.15 In order for the court to make a STPO it must be satisfied:

(a) that there is a risk the defendant shall commit a slavery or human trafficking offence; and

(b) it is necessary to make the order to protect persons generally or particular persons from the physical or psychological harm which would be likely to occur if the defendant committed such an offence.

9.16 Slavery and Trafficking Offences for the purpose of STPOs are listed in the Modern Slavery Act 2015, Sch 1. Forced marriage and breach of a forced marriage protection order are not offences listed within Sch 1.

9.17 Slavery and Trafficking Prevention Orders are made either on conviction or following an application under the Modern Slavery Act 2015, s 15 to a magistrates' court by the police, National Crime Agency or an immigration officer.

9.18 On hearing an application, the court must be satisfied:

(a) that the defendant is a relevant offender and since he was convicted of the relevant offences, has acted in a way which means that there is a risk the defendant may commit a slavery and human trafficking offence; and

(b) that it is necessary to make the order for the purposes of protecting persons generally, or particular persons, from the physical or psychological harm which would be likely to occur if the defendant committed such an offence.

9.19 A relevant offender is a person convicted, cautioned for or found not guilty by reason of insanity of an offence of slavery or human trafficking as defined by the Modern Slavery Act 2015, Sch 1. Alternatively, the defendant must have been convicted, cautioned for or found to have committed an equivalent offence overseas.

9.20 The court has a broad discretion to make any order it considers necessary for the purpose of protecting persons generally, or particular persons from the physical or psychological harm which would be likely to occur if the defendant committed a slavery or human trafficking offence.

9.21 A STPO may have effect for a fixed period of at least five years or until further order of the court. Individual provisions can last for longer or shorter periods than the rest of the order. Prohibitions on foreign travel, which may consist of a requirement for the defendant to surrender their passports, may last for a fixed period of not more than five years.

Slavery and Trafficking Risk Order

9.22 The second type of order created by the Modern Slavery Act 2015 are Slavery and Trafficking Risk Orders made pursuant to s 23. Such orders are made following application by a chief police officer, immigration officer or the director general of the national crime agency. A conviction is not required for the making an order, but the court must be satisfied that:

(a) the defendant has acted in a way which means that there is a risk that the they shall commit a slavery or human trafficking offence listed in Sch 1 to the Act; and

(b) it is necessary to make the order for the purpose of protecting persons generally, or particular persons, from the physical or psychological harm which would be likely to occur if the defendant committed such an offence.

9.23 Slavery and Trafficking Risk Orders may prohibit a defendant from doing anything necessary to protect others from physical or psychological harm which is likely to occur. Orders may last for a fixed period of at least two years or until further order. Prohibitions on foreign travel may only last up to five years. The Modern Slavery Act 2015, s 28 allows Slavery and Trafficking Risk Orders to be made on an interim basis.

9.24 Breach of a STRO is punishable with up to five years' imprisonment following trial on indictment.

MARRIAGE FOR IMMIGRATION PURPOSES

9.25 Forced marriage for immigration purposes is a widely reported phenomenon. There are a number of different forms of such marriages. For example, in 2014 Europol and the National Crime Agency reported Eastern European women being trafficked to the United Kingdom and forcibly married to Asian males without leave to remain in the United Kingdom.[10]

9.26 Separately, there has been widespread concern surrounding British women taken to other jurisdictions and forcibly married for immigration purposes. In some cases, it has been reported that women who have been forcibly married are being kept abroad until they are pregnant and then returned to the United Kingdom so that their child shall be British.[11]

9.27 Questions have been raised about how effectively the British Government is tackling the issue of forced marriage for immigration purposes, in 2017, in 47 per cent of cases where UK Visas and Immigration were made aware of potential abuse, spousal visas were still issued.[12]

9.28 Consideration has previously been given to a scheme whereby victims of forced marriage or domestic abuse would be able to confidentially inform the Home Office of the abuse concerned without the information being passed to the abuser or others. Such a scheme would conflict with the general public law procedural fairness requirement that applicants ought to know the basis upon which their application has been decided. Accordingly, to date, no such scheme has been adopted.

Reluctant sponsors

9.29 Under Part 8 of the Immigration Rules, British citizens are entitled to sponsor an application by their spouse to settle in the United Kingdom. Often victims of forced marriage shall be reluctant to sponsor spousal visas.

9.30 Unfortunately, it is not possible to block a visa application without all parties being made aware.[13] Instead, the victim would be required to sign a disclosable, public statement. The risk of harm which the signing said statement can cause a victim of forced marriage is obvious. Victims may also seek help from the Forced Marriage Unit who shall be able to advise on available options.

10 NCA Strategic Assessment, The Nature and Scale of Human Trafficking, 2014, Europol, Early Warning Notification, Marriages of Convenience, a link between illegal immigration and THB, 2014.

11 Forced marriage: Family visas and reluctant sponsors, House of Commons Library, 2018.

12 Forced marriage: Family visas and reluctant sponsors, House of Commons Library, 2018.

13 HM Government, Multi-Agency Practice Guidelines on Handling Cases of Forced Marriage, 2014, Ch 8.5.

9.31 Third parties may also notify the Home Office of potential abuse or suspicions of a forced marriage. Police Officers and Social Workers ought to actively consider whether such a disclosure is permissible or necessary.

Sham marriages

9.32 Sham marriages are defined under the Immigration and Asylum Act 1999, ss 24 and 24A[14] as a marriage to which 'one or both of the parties is not a British citizen or European Economic Area or Swiss national, there is no genuine relationship between the parties; either or both of the parties enter into the marriage or civil partnership for the purpose of circumventing (avoiding) UK immigration controls, including under the Immigration Rules or the Immigration (EEA) Regulations 2016.

9.33 Sham marriages usually occur when a non-European Economic Area national marries someone as a means of attempting to gain long term residency and the right to work and claim benefits.[15]

9.34 An example of a forced sham marriage is found in *A Local Authority v SY*.[16] The court was concerned with a marriage contracted between a failed asylum seeker married a vulnerable woman who lacked capacity to consent to marriage for immigration purposes. Keehan J held (at [50]):

> 'In my judgment it is important for SY that a declaration of non-marriage is made in respect of the June 2012 ceremony. There are also, in my judgment, compelling reasons of public policy why sham 'marriages' are declared non-marriages. It is vital that the message is clearly sent out to those who seek to exploit young and vulnerable adults that the courts will not tolerate such exploitation.'

HOME OFFICE DUTIES

9.35 In a domestic context, the Immigration Act 2014, Part 4 extended the notice period required for a marriage to take place from 15 days to 28 days. All proposed marriages and civil partnerships in the UK involving a non-EEA national with limited or no immigration status in the UK are to be referred to the Home Office by the registration official.[17] Home Office policy requires the Department to check all referrals against intelligence, evidence-based risk

14 As amended by Immigration Act 2014, s 55

15 Home Office, Criminal Investigations: Sham Marriage Version 2, 2019 page 5 available at https://assets.publishing.service.gov.uk/government/uploads/system/uploads/attachment_data/file/846190/criminal-investigations-sham-marriage-v2.0-ext.pdf.

16 [2013] All ER (D) 1996 (Nov).

17 Home Office, Criminal Investigations: Sham Marriage Version 2, 2019 page 5 available at https://assets.publishing.service.gov.uk/government/uploads/system/uploads/attachment_data/file/846190/criminal-investigations-sham-marriage-v2.0-ext.pdf.

profiles and other available information in order to identify suspicious proposed marriages.

9.36 Where the Home Office identifies a case for investigation on the basis there are reasonable grounds to suspect it is a sham, the Department must before the expiry of the 28 days' notice period, notify both the relevant registration official and the couple. The effect of said notification is that the notice period is extended to 70 days, giving the Department more time to investigate.

LOCAL AUTHORITY DUTIES

9.37 Local authorities are able to apply for declarations of non-recognition in circumstances where a marriage has been contracted with a vulnerable person for immigration purposes. In circumstances where the victim may lack capacity to consent to sex, marriage or to make decisions about contact with others, declaratory and injunctive relief from the Court of Protection may be necessary.

9.38 For cases involving an international element, local authorities ought to contact the Forced Marriage Unit for further advice and guidance, in particular with issues relating to spousal visas.

POLICE DUTIES

9.39 There are a number of offences which arise specifically in the context of forced or sham marriages for the purpose of immigration, in particular:

(a) Making a false statement with reference to a civil partnership contrary to the Civil Partnership Act 2004, s 80;

(b) Offences related to the recording of civil partnerships under the Civil Partnerships Act 2004, s 33;

(c) Offences relating to Registrar General's licence under the Civil Partnership Act 2004, s 32;

(d) Facilitation contrary to the Immigration Act 1971, s 25; or

(e) Conspiracy to facilitate.

9.40 Officers also ought to actively engage with the Forced Marriage Unit and social care services where it is suspected that a victim is being forced to marry for immigration purposes.

REGISTRARS' DUTIES

9.41 The Immigration Act 2014, s 24 creates a duty on the part of marriage registration officials to report suspected sham marriages once notice of the wedding has been taken. Those officiating marriages also ought to actively consider whether offences may be being committed and contact the police, or if appropriate, social services if they consider that they may of officiating over a forced or sham marriage.

9.42 In particular, those who officiate over marriages should familiarise themselves with the Forced Marriage Factsheet and Guidance for Registrars produced by the Forced Marriage Unit ('the Guidance').[18] The Guidance identifies the following warning signs:

(a) Either party showing sign of emotional distress.

(b) Either party showing signs of physical harm or assault.

(c) The bride and groom being accompanied by family or community members when giving notice to marry.

(d) When giving notice to marry, one party doing all the talking or showing reluctance to let the other party be spoken to alone.

(e) The parties being unable to converse in the same language.

(f) One party being unable to provide facts about the other person that one would expect a spouse to know, such as date of birth, occupation and address.

(g) Allegations of a forced marriage having been made by third parties.

9.43 In circumstances where a registrar suspects a forced marriage, the Guidance recommends that they ought to reassure the potential victim of confidentiality, speak with them alone in a private place and identify and respect the individual's wishes. It is particularly important to treat the individual in culturally sensitive way. The following specific steps ought to be taken:

(a) the Forced Marriage Unit or police ought to be contacted;

(b) an authorised interpreter ought to be contacted; and

(c) details of the police and the Forced Marriage Unit ought to be provided to the potential victim.

9.44 The Guidance notes that registrars should not speak to the individual's family or members of their community or allow family or community members act as an interpreter. It is also not appropriate for registrars to attempt to mediate between the parties. Finally, the registrar should not allow the individual to leave with members of their community of family if they may be in danger.

18 Forced Marriage Factsheet and Guidance for Registrars produced by the Forced Marriage Unit available at https://assets.publishing.service.gov.uk/government/uploads/system/uploads/attachment_data/file/320097/FM_Registrars_factsheet.pdf.

Part 2

Law and procedure in the family jurisdiction

CHAPTER 10

Interim Forced Marriage Protection Orders

Content at a Glance:

INTRODUCTION

10.1 Often cases of forced marriage shall involve fast moving events where urgent measures are required to protect and safeguard the potential victim. In such cases, putting the respondents on notice that an application has been made to the court may cause them to remove the person to be protected from the jurisdiction, avoid service, or otherwise cause the victim harm. Similarly, it shall almost always not be appropriate to wait to the conclusion of proceedings to obtain injunctive orders for the protection the potential victim. As such, interim Forced Marriage Protection Orders form an important part of the statutory scheme created by the Family Law Act 1996, Part 4A.

CHECKLIST

10.2

Who are the parties?	
Applicant	Person to be protected;
	Relevant third party;
	Other persons who may satisfy the court that they have sufficient connection to the person to be protected, knowledge of the circumstances of the person to be protected.

Respondent	The person who is subject to the proceedings (i.e. the person to be protected);
	Those who it is alleged have forced, attempt to force, or may attempt to force a person into a marriage;
	Any other persons who may become involved, including those who may aid, abet, counsel, procure or assist, conspire to force or attempt to force a person to enter into a marriage.
	If the person to be protected is a child, the court must review whether they should be named as a respondent to proceedings at every stage.
	Any other party the court seeks to join, for example a local authority or other public body.
Is leave required?	
Person to be protected	Leave not required
Relevant third party (local authority)	Leave not required
All other persons (police, Forced Marriage Unit or other connected persons)	Leave required, form FL403 to be submitted along with substantive application detailing the grounds on which leave is sought.
To which court is the application made?	
	Specified Family Court to be listed before a District or Circuit Judge or to the High Court Family Division.
What documents are required?	
	In readiness for an initial hearing, the application must be made on Form FL401A and be supported by a statement and draft order.
	Where an ex-parte order is sought, the statement must cover why the application is being made without notice.
	The applicant may also wish to append or file any other supporting evidence it seeks to rely upon (for example, police disclosure, multi-agency documents, local authority documents or other relevant statements).
	If contact details/ address to be kept confidential, Form C8 to be included with any application.

WHAT MEETS THE THRESHOLD FOR A FORCED MARRIAGE?

10.3

Family Law Act 1996, s 63A Forced Marriage Protection Orders

'(1) The court may make an order for the purposes of protecting:

(a) A person from being forced into a marriage or from any attempt to be forced into a marriage; or

(b) A person who has been forced into a marriage.

(2) In deciding whether to exercise its powers under this section and, if so, in what manner, the court must have regard to all the circumstances including the need to secure the health, safety and well-being of the person to be protected.

(3) In ascertaining that person's well-being, the court must, in particular, have such regard to the person's wishes and feelings (so far as they are reasonably ascertainable) as the court considers appropriate in the light of the person's age and understanding.

(4) For the purposes of this Part a person ('A') is forced into a marriage if another person ('B') forces A to enter into a marriage (whether with B or another person) without A's free and full consent.

(5) For the purposes of subsection (4) it does not matter whether the conduct of B which forces A to enter into a marriage is directed against A, B or another person.

(6) In this Part –

'force' includes coerce by threats or other psychological means (and related expressions are to be read accordingly); and

Forced Marriage Protection Order' means an order under this section.'

10.4 Practitioners must be aware that arranged marriages do not amount to a forced marriage 'a clear distinction must be drawn between, on the one hand, forced marriage as a form of domestic violence and a serious abuse of human rights, and, on the other, the concept of the consensual arranged marriage which is rightly perceived as a cultural norm in certain societies and thus wholly acceptable'.[1]

10.5 Similarly, cases where there is a loose commitment to marry in the future, absent of a formal engagement may not amount to forced marriage. In *West Sussex County Council and another v F and others*[2] in which Williams J having applied the dicta in *Chief Constable (above)* found that on the facts, there was a form of 'loose commitment' which was far closer to an arranged marriage:

> 'not undertaken with N's consent but not with the intention subsequently of her being forced to marry B whether she wanted to or not. The nature of the arrangement was such that had it endured to an age when she might legally have married I am satisfied she would have had a say and had she not wished it, it would not have proceeded' (at [1018]).

1 *Chief Constable & Anor v YK & Ors* [2010] EWHC 2438 (Fam) per Sir Nicholas Wall at para 9.
2 [2019] 1 FLR 992.

10.6 Force is not limited to physical force, it also encompasses financial or sexual abuse, emotional and psychological pressure and may be directed to another not only the person to be protected (Family Law Act 1996, s 63A(5), (6)). The court must be satisfied that 'the threats, pressure, or whatever it is such as to destroy the reality of consent and overbears the will of the individual'.[3]

MAKING AN APPLICATION FOR A FORCED MARRIAGE PROTECTION ORDER – GENERAL PROCEDURE

10.7 There is no fee for the making of the application for a Forced Marriage Protection Order.[4] A respondent's challenge to the order is free initially. However, should there be any further challenge the fee for such application is £95.00.[5]

10.8 An application for a Forced Marriage Protection Order is made using form FL401A[6] and must include with it:

(a) A sworn statement; and

(b) Draft order.

10.9 The statement of truth may be signed by a party, litigation friend or the legal representative of the party or litigation friend.[7]

10.10 There may be circumstances where statements are sought from those who are vulnerable, have disabilities or are unable to read or sign a document which is to be verified by a statement of truth. In those cases, the statement must contain a certificate made by an authorised person, which is a person able to administer oaths and take affidavits but need not be independent of the parties or their representatives.[8]

10.11 The authorised person must certify that the document has been read to the person signing it, that the person appeared to understand it and approved its content as accurate, that the person appeared to understand the declaration and the consequences of making a false declaration; and that the person signed or made his mark in the presence of the authorised person.[9]

3 *Hirani v Hirani* (1983) 4 FLR 232 CA at 234, later applied in *Re P (Forced Marriage)* [2011] 1 FLR 2060 per Baron J at paragraph 7 of Annex I of the judgment.

4 HMCTS, Civil and Family Court fee guidance, EX50 available at <https://assets.publishing.service.gov.uk/government/uploads/system/uploads/attachment_data/file/904862/ex50-eng.pdf>.

5 HMCTS, Civil and Family Court fee guidance, EX50 available at <https://assets.publishing.service.gov.uk/government/uploads/system/uploads/attachment_data/file/904862/ex50-eng.pdf>.

6 FPR 2010, PD 5A para 3.

7 FPR 2010, PD 5A paras 3.1, 3.7-3.10.

8 FPR 2010, PD 17A, paras 4.1-4.2.

9 FPR 2010, PD 17A, para 4.3.

10.12 Forced Marriage Protection Orders often involve circumstances where people, by virtue of coming forward to seek protection for themselves or others may be said to be placed at risk of significant harm. For example, a young adult may have fled their home to a confidential and secure location/refuge. Unless the court directs otherwise, a party is not required to reveal: (i) their home address or other contact details; or (ii) the address or contact details of any child or the person with whom the child is living.[10]

10.13 In circumstances where a party seeks to ensure the confidentiality of their placement/contact details are maintained an application using Form C8 should be appended to the substantive application for a Forced Marriage Protection Order.

10.14 Practitioners should be aware that withholding a party's details may only be a partial step to provide protection. The Government's Multi-Agency Guidelines: Handling Cases of Forced Marriages details that even those who are able to flee the family home are still at risk, as often perpetrators will go to considerable lengths to find the person to be protected including: (i) soliciting the help of others; involving the police by reporting them missing, or on occasion falsely accusing the victim of a crime, eg theft; (ii) tracing individuals through medical, dental records, bounty hunters, private investigators, local taxi drivers, members of the community and shop keepers; or (iii) through National Insurance Numbers, benefits records, school and college records.[11] The roles of public bodies to ensure confidentiality and therefore afford greater protection is considered further at **Chapter 25**.

Allocation and transfer of proceedings

10.15 An application for a Forced Marriage Protection Order may be made to the High Court of Justice or to one of the specific Family Court Centres designated to process such applications:

(a) Birmingham Civil and Family Justice Centre;

(b) Bradford Combined Court;

(c) Brighton Family Court Hearing Centre;

(d) Bristol Civil and Family Justice Centre;

(e) Cardiff Civil and Family Justice Centre;

(f) Central Family Court;

(g) Derby Combined Court;

(h) East London Family Court;

(i) Leeds Combined Court;

10 FPR 2010, r 29.1.

11 HM Government, Multi-Agency Guidelines: Handling Cases of Forced Marriage 2014.

(j) Leicester County Court and Family Court;

(k) Liverpool Civil and Family Court Hearing Centre;

(l) Luton County Court and Family Court;

(m) Manchester County Court and Family Court;

(n) Newcastle upon Tyne Combined Court Centre;

(o) Norwich Combined Court and Family Hearing Centre;

(p) Oxford Combined Court and Family Court Hearing Centre;

(q) Plymouth Combined Court;

(r) Portsmouth Combined Court Centre;

(s) Preston Family Court;

(t) Reading County Court and Family Court Hearing Centre;

(u) Sheffield Combined Court Centre;

(v) Teesside Combined Court; and

(w) West London Family Court.[12]

10.16 Lay justices do not have jurisdiction to hear applications for Forced Marriage Protection Orders.[13]

Who can apply?

10.17 Pursuant to the Family Law Act 1996, s 63C(2) the following persons are entitled to apply without permission of the court:

(a) The person who is to be protected;

(b) A relevant third party.

10.18 There is no age limit provided by the Family Law Act 1996, s 63(2)(a) which allows for children to apply to seek protection.

10.19 In cases involving children, if an application is made within other family proceedings (defined within the Family Law Act 1996, s 63(1), (2)), a guardian may already be appointed or the court may direct that one be appointed.[14]

10.20 However, if a guardian is not appointed, then the child must be deemed competent or must be appointed a litigation friend.[15] Careful consideration will

12 FL701 available at <https://assets.publishing.service.gov.uk/government/uploads/system/uploads/attachment_data/file/881315/fl701-eng.pdf>.

13 *Family Court Practice (the Red Book) 2020* Part I, Procedural Guide A9 paragraph [1.24].

14 See further FPR 2010, PD 16A, para 7.

15 See further, FPR 2010, PD 15.

need to be given as to whether it is appropriate for a family member to act as litigation friend in forced marriage cases. It will clearly not be appropriate in circumstances where the family member is alleged to be associated with the forced marriage.

10.21 If there are concerns that the person to be protected or other respondent lacks capacity, then directions may need to be made for cognitive/capacity assessments and the Family Procedure Rules 2010, Part 25 will apply. In the event any party is deemed to lack capacity then it may also be necessary to invite the Official Solicitor to act on their behalf.

10.22 Save for filing an application form or applying for a litigation friend, no further steps should be taken unless or until the issue of capacity is resolved by the court and a litigation friend, if required is appointed.[16]

Nationality/jurisdiction

10.23 Any British national may make an application to appeal to the High Court for protection, based on nationality alone.[17]

10.24 In *Re SA (Vulnerable adult with capacity: marriage)*[18] Munby J (as he then was) gave the following guidance when considering whether the court should invoke the inherent jurisdiction for the protection of vulnerable adults:

> '[37] The court exercises a 'protective jurisdiction' in relation to vulnerable adults, just as it does in relation to wards of court.
>
> [77] ….the inherent jurisdiction can be exercised in relation to a vulnerable adult who, even if not incapacitated by mental disorder, is, or is reasonably believed to be, either: (i) under constraint; or (ii) subject to coercion or undue influence; or (iii) for some other reason deprived of the capacity to make the relevant decision, or disabled from making a free choice, or incapacitated or disabled from giving or expressing a real and genuine consent.
>
> [78] … Constraint: It does not matter for this purpose whether the constraint amounts to actual incarceration. The jurisdiction is exercisable whenever a vulnerable adult is confined, controlled or under restraint … It is enough that there is some significant curtailment of the freedom to do those things which in this country free men and women are entitled to do …'

16 FPR 2010, r 15.3.

17 See *Re A (Jurisdiction: return of child)* [2013] UKSC 60 and *Re B (A child) (Habitual residence: inherent jurisdiction)* [2016] UKSC 4 and *Al-Jeffery v Al-Jeffery* [2016] EWHC 2151 (Fam) at para 49 whereby Holman J held that the same approach should apply to vulnerable adults.

18 [2005] EWHC 2942 (Fam).

10.25 However, when considering whether to exercise that jurisdiction, the court 'must not act exorbitantly but rather only with great caution or circumspection'.[19]

10.26 In *Re B (A child) (Habitual residence: inherent jurisdiction)*[20] Lady Hale and Lord Toulson held that there are three main reasons for caution when deciding whether or not to exercise jurisdiction with each factor being weighed in the balance:

(i) Doing so may conflict with the jurisdictional scheme applicable between the countries in question;

(ii) It may result in conflicting decisions between the countries in question; and

(iii) It may result in unenforceable orders.

10.27 It is worth noting that recent jurisprudence provides that the court may also consider whether the person to be protected was resident within the jurisdiction of England and Wales or, had been living within the jurisdiction for a period of time shortly prior to any application being made. In *Re KBH & Others v (FMPO: Non-Resident British Citizen)*[21] Holman J declined to make Forced Marriage Protection Orders in respect of three girls, who were resident in Somalia. As far as the court was aware, whilst they were British citizens, none of the girls nor the mother had set foot in the United Kingdom in the last ten years.

10.28 A distinction was drawn between the facts of that case and those in *Al Jeffery (Vulnerable Adult: British Citizen)*[22] which concerned a person to be protected detained in Saudi Arabia who had however, been in Wales prior to travelling. Ordering her return to England, Holman J specifically noted that she had lived, until the age of 17, in the United Kingdom where she was educated. His Lordship went on to say that he 'would have tak[en] a very different view if she had lived her whole life in Saudi Arabia but happened to be British by descent'[23].

Relevant third party

10.29 A relevant third party defines those named by an order of the Lord Chancellor. An example being, The Family Law Act 1996 (Forced Marriage) (Relevant Third Party) Order 2009) which has specified that local authorities fall within sub-section (b) and therefore do not require leave of the court for an application to be made.

19 *Re B (A child) (Habitual residence: inherent jurisdiction)* [2016] UKSC 4, *Al-Jeffery v Al-Jeffery (Vulnerable adult; British Citizen)* [2016] EWHC 2151 (Fam).
20 [2016] UKSC 4.
21 [2018] EWHC 2611 (Fam).
22 [2016] EWHC 2151.
23 *Al-Jeffery v Al-Jeffery* [2016] EWHC 2151 (Fam) at [55].

10.30 For all other persons, the leave of the court is required. When considering whether to grant leave the court must have regard to all the circumstances including:

(a) The applicant's connection with the person to be protected;

(b) The applicant's knowledge of the circumstances of the person to be protected;

(c) The wishes and feelings of the person to be protected so far as they are reasonably ascertainable and so far as the court considers it appropriate, in light of the person's age and understanding, to have regard to them.[24]

10.31 It may seem surprising that the police have not yet been made a relevant third party under the same principles. However, the recent case of *Metropolitan Police Service v Bille*[25] shows the potential difficulties that may arise. Holman J's judgment suggests that the police should be cautious before seeking leave to apply for a Forced Marriage Protection Order in circumstances where their connection to the person to be protected is limited.

10.32 The matter involved a girl ('M') who had travelled to Somalia to give birth to her child. The reasons for doing so, she said, were to avoid scrutiny from social services who had raised concerns in respect of her mental ill-health. The Metropolitan Police issued an application in the High Court for leave to apply for a Forced Marriage Protection Order. The application was supported by a witness statement from a female detective constable, the basis of which was said to be various tiers of hearsay, including that:

> 'a report had been made to the police by the FMU in 2018. The gist of the information received by the police from the FMU was said to be that the FMU had, in turn, received information from a named worker in a Somali charity based in Cardiff… that M had been forced to marry a named person in Somalia'.[26]

10.33 On the basis of that information alone, leave was granted to the police to make their application and such order was granted, without notice on an interim basis. Paragraph [7] of the judgment records the recitals of the order of the Deputy High Court Judge referring to 'all the circumstances' and the 'knowledge of M's history and current circumstances, but that there was no reference to the 'applicant's connection with the person to be protected'. Holman J concluded that this was because, in reality there was no connection between the Metropolitan Police and M at the time leave was sought. Whilst hearsay is admissible, the evidence relied upon was 'highly unsatisfactory' especially against both oral and written evidence having been relied upon by the father to the contrary. Instead, if anybody had the knowledge about M and her circumstances, it would have been the Forced Marriage Unit, not the Metropolitan Police. In circumstances where

24 Family Law Act 1996, s 63C(4).
25 [2019] EWHC 1868 (Fam).
26 *Metropolitan Police Service v Bille* [2019] EWHC 1868 (Fam) at [5].

a British citizen abroad requires protection, the Foreign and Commonwealth Office, through the Forced Marriage Unit should itself apply for an order.[27]

10.34 This does not however preclude the police from making such applications where a person directly affected, or a third party such as a friend approaches them to give information. This is because in such a situation, the police will more easily satisfy the requirement that they have 'a direct, or fairly direct connection with a person who is claiming that he or she has been, or may be, or may become a victim of a crime.[28] What is clear is that the criteria in the Family Law Act 1996, s 63C(6) must be stringently applied.

10.35 In cases relating to persons to be protected who have not been resident within the United Kingdom, their connection to this jurisdiction being by citizenship alone, it is open to, and may be most appropriate for, Her Majesty's Government itself acting, through the Foreign and Commonwealth Office and more specifically, the Forced Marriage Protection Unit to apply for protection orders.[29]

Application for leave

10.36 An application for leave to apply is to be made using Part 18 procedure using Form FL403.[30]

10.37 The Family Procedure Rules 2010 r.11.3(1)(a)-(b) provide that

(a) 'The application notice must set out:
   - (i) The reasons for the application, for the making of which permission is sought;
   - (ii) The applicant's connection with the person to be protected;
   - (iii) The applicant's knowledge of the circumstances of the person to be protected;
   - (iv) In relation to an application for permission to apply for a Forced Marriage Protection Order, the applicant's knowledge of the wishes and feelings of the person to be protected; and

(b) A draft of the proposed application, together with sufficient copies for one to be served on each respondent (and if different) the person to be protected'.

Where leave is sought, it is good practice that the decisions for granting or refusing leave are clearly recorded on the face of the order. Where permission is granted to apply for a forced marriage protection order, the application must proceed in accordance with the Family Procedure Rules 2010, r 11.2.[31]

27 *Metropolitan Police Service v Bille* [2019] EWHC 1868 (Fam) at [29]–[32].
28 *Metropolitan Police Service v Bille* [2019] EWHC 1868 (Fam) at [30].
29 *Re KBH & Others v (FMPO: Non-Resident British Citizen)* [2018] EWHC 2611 (Fam) at [7].
30 FPR 2010, PD 5A.
31 FPR 2010, r 11.3(4).

Order of the court's own motion

10.38 Pursuant to the Family Law Act 1996, s 63C(1)(b) the court may make a Forced Marriage Protection Order of its own motion within 'other family proceedings' in circumstances where it is considered necessary to protect a person; and the person who would be the respondent is a party to the current proceedings in which the order is being made, the person to be protected may or may not be party to current family proceedings.[32]

10.39 'Other family proceedings' are defined and listed within the Family Law Act 1996, ss 63(1), (2) and 63C(7) and include:

(a) Proceedings under the inherent jurisdiction of the High Court in relation to adults;

(b) Proceedings in which an emergency protection order has been made pursuant to the Children Act 1989, s 44 which includes an exclusion requirement as defined by s 44A (3) of that Act; and

(c) Proceedings in which the court has made an order under the Children Act 1989, s 50 (recovery of an abducted child, etc).

10.40 The court may therefore make orders in situations where the local authority, having not applied for protective orders, have become aware of a risk of forced marriage and seek to remove the child from their primary carer/ relative as a result under an Emergency Protection Order.

10.41 Where the court makes an order of its own motion, the procedure to be applied is set out in the Family Procedure Rules 2010, r 11.8(1) and must set out within the order –

(a) A summary of its reasons for making the order; and

(b) The names of the persons who are to be served with the order.

10.42 The court may order service of the order on –

(a) Any of the parties to the current proceedings;

(b) (if different) the person who is the subject of the proceedings; and

(c) Any other person whom the court considers should be served.[33]

10.43 The court must also give directions as to how the order is to be served.[34]

32 Family Law Act 1996, s 63C(6)(a)-(c).
33 FPR 2010, r 11.8(2).
34 FPR 2010, r 11.8(3).

Who can be named as a respondent?

10.44 Pursuant to the Family Law Act 1996, s 63B(2)(b) and (c) an application for a Forced Marriage Protection Order may name as a respondent any persons who are, or may be become involved in other respects as well as (or instead of) respondents who force or attempt to force, or may force or attempt to force, a person to enter into a marriage.

10.45 'Involvement in other respects' is defined by s 63B(3) of the Act:

(a) Aiding, abetting, counselling, procuring, encouraging or assisting another person to force, or attempt to force, a person to enter into a marriage; or

(b) Conspiring to force or attempt to force, a person to enter into a marriage.

10.46 Notice of the proceedings will need to be given to each respondent named, save in circumstance's where the application is expressly being made without notice.[35]

10.47 If an application is being made and those proceedings fall under Part 11 (which includes applications for Forced Marriage Protection Orders), the person who is the subject to those proceedings is to be a respondent to the application.[36]

Joinder and removal of parties

10.48 The court may, at any time, direct that a person be joined or removed as party to the proceedings.[37]

10.49 Importantly, where the person who is the subject of proceedings is not the applicant, and is a child, the court must consider at every stage in the proceedings, whether to make that child a party to the proceedings.[38]

10.50 In the event a child is joined to proceedings, consideration will need to be given as to the appointment of a guardian and/or litigation friend.[39]

10.51 Where a person is to be joined as a party to proceedings or cease to be a party, a person may file an application notice, using the Part 18 procedure.[40] The court may grant the application on the papers (in the event the application is for joinder), or list a hearing, or request that written representations be filed.[41]

35 FPR 2010, r 11.4(1)(a).
36 FPR 2010, r 18.3(1)(a)(ii).
37 FPR 2010, r 11.6(4).
38 FPR 2010, r 11.6(A1).
39 See FPR 2010, PD 16A, para 7 for further provisions in respect of when a child should be made party to proceedings generally.
40 FPR 2010, r 11.6(1)
41 FPR 2010, r 11.6(2)(a)-(c).

10.52 If a court directs the addition or removal of a party, it may also give directions about the service on a new party of a copy of the application for the protection order and other relevant documents; and any other directions for the management of the proceedings.[42]

TERMS OF AN ORDER

10.53 The Family Law Act 1996, s 63B(1) provides the court with a wide discretion for what terms may be included:

> 'A Forced Marriage Protection Order may contain such prohibitions, restrictions or requirements; and such other terms as the court considers appropriate for the purpose of the order'.

10.54 Importantly, the terms of the order may relate to, conduct both within and outside England and Wales.[43] The terms of the order sought will be fact specific and will need to be considered on a case by case basis. For example, where there is a risk that the person to be protected will be removed from the jurisdiction, terms will need to be sought to prevent such removal such as the surrender of passports.

10.55 Pursuant to the Family Law Act 1996, s 63F, Forced Marriage Protection Orders may be made for a specified period or until varied or discharged.

GENERAL RULES ON SERVICE

Service upon children and vulnerable persons

10.56 There may often be cases where an application for Forced Marriage Protection Orders are being made on behalf of a vulnerable person. The Family Procedure Rules 2010, r 11.2A requires that where a person who is the subject of proceedings is to be served with any documents or informed of any action taken by the court and that person is not the applicant and is:

(a) A child;

(b) A person, not being a party, who lacks or may lack capacity within the meaning of the 2005 Act; or

(c) A protected party

The court must give directions about the persons who are to be served or informed.[44]

42 FPR 2010, r 11.6(5).
43 Family Law Act 1996, s 63B(1), (2)(a).
44 See also FPR 2010, PD 6A, para 9.1.

10.57 There may be key workers, advocates, intermediaries or social workers who would be in a better position to inform the vulnerable person of any action taken by the court. In cases involving children, there is often a collaborative approach taken by both the allocated social worker and the guardian (if appointed) to notify the child of the outcome of proceedings in a focused and measured way using a narrative that can be understood. In proceedings relating to those who lack capacity, in addition to the above, advice may be taken (if applicable) from speech and language therapists working with the person to be protected as to how to effectively communicate information.

10.58 If there is any suggestion that a subject to proceedings falls within one of the above categories, this must be drawn to the attention of the court at the outset so that all appropriate steps can be taken, including consideration given as to how they may be represented and/or present their case.[45]

Service of orders on the police

10.59 Where the court makes a protection order, a copy of the order must be emailed to the centralised email address created and monitored by the Vulnerability Coordination Centre: fgm-fm-po@norfolk.pnn.police.uk.[46]

10.60 A copy of the order emailed must be accompanied by a statement showing that the respondent(s) and any other person whose breach of the order would be an offence have been served with the order or informed or its terms (whether by being present when the order was made or by telephone or otherwise).[47]

10.61 However, at the time of writing, this email address no longer works, and the central hub no longer appears to operate. Applicants therefore ought to serve orders accompanied by the necessary statement on the local police force responsible for the area in which the person to be protected lives.

10.62 The Family Procedure Rules 2010, r 11.12(3)[48] requires that both the order and the accompanying letter must be emailed by:

(a) The applicant, within two days of the order being served in accordance with r 11.7(3);[49] and

(b) The court officer, within one day of receipt of the certificate of service, where the order was served by the court following a request under r 11.7(4).[50]

10.63 Where an order is made varying, extending or discharging a protection order in accordance with the Family Procedure Rules 2010, r 11.10, the court

45 See also FPR 2010, PD 15, PD 16A.
46 FPR 2010, r 11.12(1) as amended by PD 36H 'pilot scheme'.
47 FPR 2010, r 11.12(2) as amended by PD 36H 'pilot scheme'.
48 As amended by FPR 2010, PD 36H 'pilot scheme'.
49 FPR 2010.
50 FPR 2010.

officer must immediately email a copy of that order along with a statement as referred to above and a copy of the original protection order to the centralised email address.[51] Again, at the time of writing, given the current status of the centralised system, this should be sent to the local police force.

Alternative service

10.64 There will regularly be an international element to Forced Marriage Protection Orders which can have an impact upon the ability to personally service named persons to the application. Similarly, in cases of 'organised' forced marriage, where persons move regularly to avoid detection, it may be difficult to establish a known address of the respondent(s).[52]

10.65 An application may therefore need to be made under the Family Procedure Rules 2010, r 6.19 for an alternative method of service of any document in proceedings.[53]

10.66 Such application may be made without notice[54] and if made prior to a document being served must be supported by the following evidence:

(a) The reason the order is sought;

(b) What alternative method or place is proposed;

(c) Why the applicant believes that the document is likely to reach the person to be served by the method or at the place proposed.[55]

10.67 If an application for an order is made after the applicant has taken steps to bring the document to the attention of the person to be served by an alternative method, or at an alternative place, then the application must be supported by the following evidence:

(a) The reason why the order is sought;

(b) What alternative method or alternative place was used;

(c) When the alternative method or place was used;

10.68 Why the applicant believes that the document is likely to have reached the person to be served by the alternative method or at the alternative place.[56]

10.69 The most common examples of alternative service are text, voicemail, email. As modern technology becomes more advanced, it is possible to use an electronic method which allows tracking of delivery and read receipts to ensure

51 FPR 2010, r 11.12(4) as amended by PD 36H 'pilot scheme'.
52 See further **Chapters 9** and **17**.
53 FPR 2010, r 6.35.
54 PDFPR 2010, PD 6A, para 6.1.
55 FPR 2010, PD 6A, para 6.2(a)-(c).
56 FPR 2010, PD 6A, para 6.3 (a)-(c).

the court can be satisfied that service has indeed been effective and the relevant persons have been made aware of the terms within the order.

WITHOUT NOTICE (EX-PARTE) APPLICATIONS

Procedure

10.70 The application procedure outlined above is to be followed for both applications for Forced Marriage Protection Orders on notice or ex-parte.

10.71 The court may, in any case where it considers that it is just and convenient to do so, make a Forced Marriage Protection Order even though the respondent has not been given notice of the proceedings as would otherwise be required by the court.[57]

10.72 Where such application is made it must be supported by a witness statement explaining why the application is being made without notice. Any application made by an organisation must state the name, address and position held within the organisation of the author.[58]

10.73 The statement must clearly set out before the court the underlying facts, based on admissible evidence.[59] Hearsay evidence is admissible and is likely to form the basis of any initial application, especially in cases where the applicant is a local authority or other public body which relies on record keeping and third-party communication/information or multi-agency liaison. However, even at the initial stage practitioners must begin to give thought to the primary evidence that may be required to be filed and subsequent directions sought at the case management/return hearing. Those who require leave to bring an application for a Forced Marriage Protection Order must also be cautious when relying upon hearsay as it may be that such evidence does not provide a basis for the court to be satisfied of the applicant's connection with the person to be protected.[60]

10.74 Whilst 'the making of any order ex-parte is a very serious step, with potentially very significant consequences'[61] there need not be a 'complex factual matrix'[62] at the initial stage.

10.75 Consideration will need to be given as to whether an interim order is truly necessary to ensure immediate protection or, whether further enquiries need to be made for example, with the person to be protected or with relevant agencies

57 Family Law Act 1996, s 63D(1).

58 FPR 2010, r 11.2.

59 *Re K (Passport Order)* [2020] EWCA Civ 190.

60 See above, *Metropolitan Police Service v Bille* [2019] EWHC 1868 (Fam).

61 *West Sussex County Council and another v F and others* [2018] EWHC 1702 (Fam) per Williams J at [20].

62 *Re A (Forced Marriage: Special Advocates)* [2010] EWHC 2438 (Fam) per Sir Nicholas Wall at [90].

(police, local authorities, Forced Marriage Protection Unit). Any ex-parte order requires full and frank disclosure from the applicant and caution must be taken not to overemphasise the case that comes before the court.

10.76 Practitioners representing applicants at any hearing without notice must ensure they take a careful note of what is being said and any judgment given, be that ex-tempore or otherwise.[63]

10.77 Pursuant to the Family Law Act 1996, s 63D(2), in deciding whether to exercise its powers under subsection (1) the court must have regard to all the circumstances including –

10.78 Any risk of significant harm to the person to be protected or another person if the order is not made immediately;

10.79 Whether it is likely that an applicant will be deterred or prevented from pursing an application if an order is not made immediately;

10.80 Whether there is reason to believe that:

(a) The respondent is aware of the proceedings but is deliberately evading service; and

(b) The delay involved in effecting substituted service will cause serious prejudice to the person to be protected or (if a different person) an applicant.

Circumstances in which ex-parte orders are likely to be sought

10.81 In cases of forced marriage, it may be necessary to act with speed and diligence to prevent further steps being taken which would place the person to be protected at risk of harm, whether that be to prevent the person to be protected from being subjected to a forced marriage, or, if the marriage has already taken place to prevent them suffering further harm.

10.82 Whilst each case will need to be considered on an individual basis, assessing the risk and urgency, the following situations are likely to give rise to an ex-parte order being sought.

10.83 There will often be situations where protection has been sought in confidence from a third party, friend or agency by the person to be protected whilst they remain within an environment which is unsafe. For example, a secretive phone call being made to report steps which are planned by family members in the coming hours, days or weeks which would result in the person being protected being forcibly married. The person to be protected or other family members may be placed at risk of harm if those who live with them are alerted to any order being sought.

63 FPR 2010, r 11.7(3)(b), as amended by PD 36H 'pilot scheme'.

10.84 There may be concerns that plans are in train for the person to be protected to be removed from the jurisdiction, where it is considered that alerting those involved may expedite the removal of person to be protected which would in turn, make enforcing protective orders, or ensuring the safety of the person to be protected far more difficult, placing them at risk of significant harm.

10.85 In some circumstances, those seeking protection may be afraid of the consequences of seeking an order, be that due to the strain it may place on their inter-familial relations or as a result of threats having already been made. Their willingness or ability to cooperate with agencies and/or seek an order may be diminished if they are not afforded protection or if notice were to be given. This aligns with the Governments Multi-Agency Guidance of the 'one chance rule', that professionals may only have 'one chance' to save a life.[64]

Mandatory vs prohibitory orders

10.86 A prohibitory order prevents a person from carrying out an act, or behaviour, a mandatory order actively requires a party to do something to comply. For example, an order requiring that the person to be protected be returned from another country in a mandatory order.

10.87 In *West Sussex County Council and another v F and others*[65] Williams J considered the previous guidance as set out in *Chief Constable and Another v YK and others*[66] quoting specifically paragraph [17] and [20] of Sir Nicholas Wall's judgment which reads as follows:

> '[17] The only criterion for protecting a respondent to such an order appears in section 63D(3), where the order is made ex parte and the court is required to give any respondent 'an opportunity to make representations' (see section 63D(3)). That opportunity must be 'as soon as just and convenient' (section 63D4(a)) and at an 'on notice' hearing (section 63D4(b)). The order otherwise lasts until varied or discharged (section 63F)'
>
> '[20] Thus the highest the case is put for any respondents are the requirements where there is an ex parte order; (1) for service and; (2) for the respondent to be given the opportunity to make representations.'

10.88 Williams J went on to clarify:

> '[20] The difference between the sorts of orders the President was discussing in that case and this is that he was referring purely to protective prohibitory orders which prevented a forced marriage and which could not be seriously objected to…

64 The Right to Choose: Multi-Agency Statutory Guidance for dealing with forced marriage, HM Government.
65 [2018] EWHC 1702 (Fam).
66 [2010] EWHC 2438 (Fam).

> When mandatory orders are concerned which require a person to do an act…it clearly involves a positive interference with the family life of the respondents and therefore has Article 6 ECHR implications which rights the President concluded were not engaged when the court was simply making prohibitory orders.
>
> Where mandatory orders are sought, whilst the section 63A criteria still apply…it seems to me that the court must be satisfied on appropriate evidence that the making of such an order is a necessary and proportionate response. Where the order is to bite almost immediately and in circumstances where the respondents will be placed under an obligation carrying potentially penal consequences before they will in practical terms be able to seek legal advice or return the matter to court, the approach of those applying for the injunction and the court considering it will necessarily need to be that much more robust'.

10.89 A distinction has therefore been made as to what an applicant must show when seeking to apply for mandatory order rather than a merely prohibitory order. Where a mandatory order is sought ex-parte the applicant must also show that the direction sought is necessary and proportionate.[67]

10.90 However, it is important to remember that at the initial or ex-parte hearing, no facts are yet established or found which may later be challenged and discounted. The court's primary role is protective and can be exercised without a detailed analysis of the underlying facts.[68] The court must be satisfied on the evidence it has before it that the person to be protected requires protection, applying the civil standard of proof.[69]

Service, ex-parte orders

10.91 The applicant must within two days of the order being made, unless otherwise directed by the court, serve personally:

(a) A copy of the order;

(b) A copy of the record of the hearing; and

(c) A copy of the application together with any statement supporting it.

On the respondent, the person who is the subject of the proceedings (if neither the applicant nor a respondent), and any other person named in the order.[70]

10.92 Where the applicant is an individual, the documents listed above must not be served personally by the applicant himself or herself.[71]

67 See further the interplay of this from a Human Rights perspective at **Chapter 6**.

68 *Re A (a child) (inherent jurisdiction)* [2020] EWHC 451 (Fam) at [49].

69 See *Re K (Forced Marriage: Passport Order)* [2020] EWCA Civ 190 at [47]–[49].

70 FPR 2010, r 11.7(3) as amended by PD 36H 'pilot scheme'.

71 FPR 2010, r 11.7(3A).

Steps to take if an ex-parte order is disputed

10.93 In general terms, where an order is made ex-parte, the respondent should seek to have the matter listed on notice to contest the order made rather than to appeal the ex-parte order itself.[72]

10.94 Where an order has been made ex-parte or on notice, it will remain in force for a specified period or until varied or discharged.[73]

10.95 However, where the order is made ex-parte, the court is required to give any respondent an opportunity to make representations.[74] Such opportunity must be as soon as is just and convenient to do so; and at a hearing which notice has been given to all parties.[75] In practice this is usually within 7–14 days.

10.96 Ex-parte orders may require that a respondent file a statement in response prior to any return hearing, signed by a statement of truth. Where, however, the continuation of a Forced Marriage Protection Order is contested, it will be necessary for the court to undertake an ordinary fact-finding evaluation of any potentially relevant factual issues.[76]

10.97 It will therefore be important for any respondent to carefully detail any factual matters which are disputed and those which are accepted. If a schedule of allegations has been provided, time will need to be given for a response to be filed and served from the respondent upon sight of all the relevant evidence relied upon by the applicant.

10.98 If, having heard from the respondent there is a factual dispute, unless the court is satisfied that the criteria as set out in the Family Law Act 1996, s 63A are no longer met, the order is likely to stand until the factual matrix is established.

72 See *Re P (a minor)* [1993] Fam Law 462, CA and *Re H (a minor)* [1994] 2 FLR 981.
73 Family Law Act 1996, s 63F.
74 Family Law Act 1996, s 63D(3).
75 Family Law Act 1996, s 63D(4).
76 *Re K (Forced Marriage: Passport Order)* [2020] EWCA Civ 190.

CHAPTER 11

With notice Forced Marriage Protection Orders

Contents at a Glance:

INTRODUCTION

11.1 It is not always necessary or appropriate to bring applications for Forced Marriage Protection Orders on a without notice basis. Further, all orders made on an ex-parte basis shall be followed by an *inter-partes* hearing. This chapter considers the differences in procedure when applying for final Forced Marriage Protection Orders on notice.

11.2 We also examine certain orders which may be applied for alongside Forced Marriage Protection Orders.

11.3 It also considers other protections which may be sought in the context of family law and what steps local authorities can take to ensure the safety and wellbeing of any relevant child.

APPLICATIONS MADE ON NOTICE

11.4 In the event that the test for making the application without notice is not met, then an application may be made on notice.

11.5 As already noted in **Chapter 10**, there is no difference in the procedure to be applied when making an application on notice save for the requirements for service, and that the statement need not address the grounds upon which the order is sought ex-parte.

11.6 At the initial hearing, the respondent will have been served with the application and the statement/s and grounds relied upon in support of the order,[1] unless any application has been made to withhold disclosure.[2]

11.7 In some circumstances a direction will have been made on issue, of the courts own motion, that the respondent file a statement in response to the application filed. If this has not already been directed, then the initial hearing will likely focus not only on whether an interim order should be made, but also, the position of the respondent. It is important to ascertain whether the application is itself challenged and specifically, whether there is any factual challenge. In circumstances where the order is opposed, the court will direct the respondent to file and serve a statement in response setting out such opposition. Where there is no challenge to the application, a final order may be made if the court is satisfied that the criteria as set out in the Family Law Act 1996, s 63A are met.

11.8 Where the application is opposed, the court may wish to consider case management directions at the initial hearing. Given the protective nature of Forced Marriage Protection Orders, it is unlikely that all evidence sought to be relied upon will be filed with the initial application, and indeed this is not required. Therefore, thought should be given what further evidence each party seeks permission to obtain, file and serve in support of, or in defence of the substantive application for a Forced Marriage Protection Order.

11.9 The evidence required will be dependent on whether the marriage has already taken place or whether the order is sought on the grounds that the person to be protected is at risk of being subjected to a forced marriage. As set out in *Metropolitan Police Service v Bille*:[3]

> 'clearly, in the situation where a marriage has not yet taken place, a court has to consider and evaluate the degree of risk or likelihood that a forced marriage is threatened, or may take place if not prevented. Such an evaluation no doubt requires a judgment as to future risk and likelihood, weighing all the known facts and circumstances of the case in point'.

11.10 In support of an application for a Forced Marriage Protection Order, practitioners may wish to consider obtaining the following evidence:

(a) Police disclosure;

(b) Supporting statements;

(c) Multi-agency reports;

(d) Local authority disclosure in cases involving children and young adults;

1 FPR 2010, r 11.4(1)(a).
2 See **Chapter 14**.
3 [2019] EWHC 1868 (Fam) at [19].

(e) Disclosure from schools or relevant educational facilities;

(f) Disclosure of information from the Forced Marriage Protection Unit (if applicable);

(g) Phone disclosure;

(h) MARAC reports;[4] and

(i) Expert evidence, capacity assessments.

11.11 In addition to the above, where it is alleged that a forced marriage has taken place the following evidence may be required:

(a) Photos/ videos of the celebration of marriage;

(b) Statements of third parties' who can attest to the marriage and circumstances which surrounded the same;

(c) Certificate of marriage (if obtainable);

(d) Details of travel/flights (in cases involving a foreign element).

11.12 Disclosure is considered in detail at **Chapter 12**; however, the general principle for third-party disclosure is as follows. The Family Procedure Rules 2010, r 21.2 provides general powers to the court to order disclosure from those who are not party to proceedings. Any application may be made without notice, and must be supported by evidence.[5] The court will need to be satisfied that the disclosure is necessary in order to dispose of the proceedings fairly or to save costs.[6]

11.13 Any order must specify clearly which documents are to be disclosed, and require the respondent to the order, when making disclosure, to specify any of those documents which: (i) are no longer in their control; or (ii) in respect of which the respondent claims a right or duty to withhold inspection.[7]

11.14 Where the respondent has not been present or on notice at the hearing where the disclosure order is made, it is good practice for there to be provision for an application to be made to vary or discharge the order upon notice. A person may not be requested to produce any document which that person could not be compelled to produce at the final hearing.[8]

Service of applications on notice

11.15 Where an application is made on notice, the applicant must serve a copy of the application, together with the notice of proceedings personally, not less

4 See further **Chapter 14**.
5 FPR 2010, r 21.2(2)(a)-(b).
6 FPR 2010, r 21.2(3).
7 FPR 2010, r 21.4(a)-(b).
8 FPR 2010, r 21.3(6).

than two days (unless time is abridged by the court)[9] before the date on which the application will be heard on:

- The respondent;
- A person who is the subject of the proceedings (if that person is neither the applicant nor respondent, for example if the application is made by a local authority or Police); and
- Any other person directed by the court.[10]

11.16 Where the application is served on the person who is the subject of the proceedings, it must be accompanied by a notice informing that person:

- How to apply to become a party to the proceedings; and
- Of that person's right to make representations orally or in writing at any hearing.[11]

11.17 If the applicant is an individual, then the application must not be served personally by the applicant himself/herself.[12] In the event an applicant is not represented or has limited funds, then a process server or other means of service is unlikely to be readily available. If the applicant, acting in person, requests then service of the application must be affected by the court.[13]

11.18 The applicant (or court bailiff) must within seven days of service of the application file a certificate of service stating the date and time of service.[14] It is good practice for any certificate of service to be retained in the event a party does not attend future hearings so that the court may be satisfied they were made aware of the terms of the order made.

11.19 The court may, and an application can be made, for the notice period to be abridged.[15] This may be appropriate in cases of urgency which fall outside the scope of orders sought ex-parte or where there may be difficulties with serving the application.

VARYING OR DISCHARGING AN ORDER

11.20 Pursuant to the Family Law Act 1996, s 63G(1), an application to discharge a Forced Marriage Protection Order may be made by: (i) any party to

9 FPR 2010, r 11.4(2).
10 FPR 2010, r 11.4(1).
11 FPR 2010, r 11.4(4).
12 FPR 2010, r 11.4(1A).
13 FPR 2010, r 11.4(3).
14 FPR 2010, r 11.4(6) as amended by PD 36H 'pilot scheme'.
15 FPR 2010, r 11.4(2).

the proceedings; (ii) the person to be protected by the order whether they are a party or not; or (iii) any person affected by the order.[16]

11.21 The court may vary or discharge a Forced Marriage Protection Order made of the courts own motion by virtue of the Family Law Act 1996, s 63C(1)(b) without a formal application being made to the court.[17]

11.22 However, where the court has directed that there is a need for the factual matrix to be established by way of a fact-finding it is unlikely that an order which is protective in nature would be varied or discharged unless the court is satisfied that the criteria as set out in the Family Law Act 1996, s 63A are no longer met.

11.23 An application to vary or discharge an order must set out the facts relied upon, be verified by a statement of truth and be made using Form FL403A.[18] Such application is made under the Family Procedure Rules 2010, Part 18.

11.24 Section 63D Family Law Act 1996 applies to the variation of a Forced Marriage Protection Order as it applies to the making of such order[19] and therefore any application to vary a Forced Marriage Protection Order may be made ex-parte.

11.25 The court may also when considering whether to vary or discharge an order consider undertakings.[20] Undertakings are an alternative to an interim order, or indeed any final order. The court may accept undertakings in the terms of any order made or proposed to be made at every stage including when considering an application to vary or discharge an order already made.

11.26 Undertakings are a solemn, binding promise to the court and effective as an order.[21]

11.27 Those giving an undertaking must be fully aware of the agreement they are entering into and the consequences of any breach and must make a signed statement to that effect as follows 'I understand the undertaking that I have given, and that if I break my promise to the court to pay any sum of money, I may be sent to prison'.[22]

11.28 The statement need not be given before the court in person. It may be endorsed on the court copy of the undertaking or may be filed in a separate document such as a letter.[23]

16 Under FPR 2010, r 11.10, rr s 11.7-11.9 apply to applications to extend or discharge a protection order.
17 Family Law Act 1996, s 63G(2).
18 FPR 2010, PD 5A.
19 Family Law Act 1996, s 63G(3).
20 Family Law Act 1996, s 63E.
21 *Hussain v Hussain* [1986] 2 FLR 271.
22 FPR 2010, PD 33A, para 2.3.
23 FPR 2010, PD 33A, para 2.4.

11.29 Practitioners must ensure their clients understand and are aware of the different levels of protection afforded by undertakings and an order. If breached, undertakings are enforced by way of an application for committal whereas breach of a Forced Marriage Protection Order is an arrestable offence with up to five years' imprisonment.

11.30 Further, the court may not accept undertakings if:

- It appears that the respondent has used or threatened violence against the person to be protected; and
- It is necessary to make a Forced Marriage Protection Order so that may breach may be punishable as an offence under the Family Law Act 1996, s 63CA.[24]

THE '*RE K*' ROUTE MAP TO 'FINAL' FORCED MARRIAGE PROTECTION ORDERS

11.31 A clear framework has been provided in the recent case of *Re K (Forced Marriage: Passport Order)*.[25] Having carried out a comprehensive review of the relevant authorities, the President of the Family Division set out a four-stage test to be applied which is summarised as follows.

Stage One

11.32 The following key points can be taken from paragraphs 46-49 of the judgment:

- At the first hearing where the application is made ex-parte, the courts role is protective.
- The court will need to establish the underlying facts, based on admissible evidence on the balance of probabilities. The burden of proof lies with the applicant.
- If the order is contested the court will need to undertake an ordinary fact-finding evaluation of any relevant factual issues.

Stage Two

11.33 The law operates in a binary system, something either happened or it did not.[26]

24 Family Law Act 1996, s 63E(2)(a).
25 [2020] EWCA Civ 190.
26 *Re B (Children)* [2008] UKHL 35 at [2].

11.34 Therefore, as reflected at paragraph 50 of the judgment, it is the fact-finding exercise that will enable the court to determine, on the facts found: (i) what the risks are; and (ii) determine 'whether or not there is a need to protect a person from any attempt to be forced into a marriage, or that person has been forced into a marriage'.

Stage Three

11.35 Based upon the facts that have been found, the court must then assess both the risks and the protective factors. In *Re K* it was suggested that a balance sheet of the positives and negatives may assist.

11.36 At paragraph 52, the court held that:

> 'At the conclusion of Stage Three, the court must explicitly consider whether or not the facts as found are sufficient to establish a real and immediate risk of the subject of the application suffering inhumane or degrading treatment sufficient to cross the ECHR, Article 3 threshold'.

11.37 **Chapter 6** considers in detail the interplay between Human Rights and Forced Marriage Protection Orders. It is worth however noting that:

- Ill-treatment must attain a minimum level of severity to fall within Article 3, the assessment of this minimum dependents on all the circumstances of the case, such as the duration of the treatment, its physical or mental effects and in some cases, the age, sex and state of health of the victim.[27]
- Failure to protect from domestic abuse may fall within the definition of inhumane and degrading treatment.[28]

Stage Four

11.38 At paragraph 53 of the judgment the court set out that at fourth stage:

> 'if there a risk that the person to be protected will suffer conduct sufficient to satisfy Article 3, the court must achieve an accommodation between the need to protect the subject of the application of that risk, and the need to respect their family life and private life under Article 8, including their respect for autonomy'.

11.39 It should be remembered that a court is a public body within the meaning of the Human Rights Act 1998, s 6(3)(a) and thus, must act in a manner which is compatible with the Convention rights of the person to be protected. This

27 *Ireland v United Kingdom* (1978) (Application No 5310/71).
28 *Volodina v Russia* (2019) (Application No 41261/17).

duty includes a requirement to discharge the courts positive obligations under Article 3 of the Convention as an absolute right.

11.40 Once a court is put on notice that a person to be protected may be placed at risk of suffering or has suffered cruel or degrading treatment within the meaning of Article 3, they must take all reasonable steps to provide effective protection.[29] Should a public authority breach someone's Convention rights in a forced marriage context by failing to put in effective protective measures when put on notice of a forced marriage, the Human Rights Act 1998, s 7 allows the victim to bring proceedings against the public authority.

11.41 The above is reflected within *Re K* at paragraph 53 in which the court held that when considering the accommodation between Article 3 and 8, it must not be 'a strict balancing exercise as there is a necessity for the court to establish the minimum measures necessary to meet the risk that has been established under Article 3'.

Duration and terms of the order

11.42 The following key points can be taken from paragraphs 54-55 of the judgment:

- The court should have in mind the high degree of flexibility which is afforded to the court by the open wording of the FLA 1996, s 64A.
- A bespoke order should be drawn up in each case which pitches the intrusion on private and family life at the point which is necessary in order to meet the duty under Article 3, but no more.
- The length, terms and breadth of the order should vary to reflect the particular factual context. The length should be considered with the notion that circumstances might change.
- A date should be fixed on which the order, or a specific provision within it, is reviewed by the court. Only in the most serious and clear cases is the court likely to be able to see far enough into the future to make an open-ended order. In other cases, the court should look at far as it can in assessing risk but no further.

INTERNATIONAL CASES AND WARDSHIP

11.43 There will be, in many forced marriage cases, an international element, be that because: (i) the person to be protected/other relevant persons are abroad; (ii) that there is a risk that the person to be protected may be taken abroad; or (iii)

29 *Osman v UK* (Application No 23452/94) (2000) 29 EHRR 245.

that the person to be protected has already been taken abroad for the purpose of a marriage.

11.44 As the court noted in *Re K*, the wording of the Family Law Act 1996, s 63B(1), is 'open and flexible;[30] and therefore permits the court to make an order containing such prohibitions, restrictions for the purposes of protecting a person from being forced into a marriage, or from any attempt to do so, or protecting a person who has been forced into a marriage.

Passport orders

11.45 At an early stage, being proactive to prevent the risk of the person being protected coming to harm is crucial. This was emphasised by Munby J (as he then was) in *X City Council v MB*[31] 'that in this kind of case one needs to bear in mind that prevention is better than a cure'.

11.46 It may therefore be necessary within the initial application to request that a term of the order made be to prevent travel and require that the person to be protected passport be surrendered to the court or named solicitors acting for them or another.

11.47 Similarly, at the conclusion of proceedings when making a final order the court may assess the risk to be that the safety of the person to be protected requires a passport order to be made for a specified period of time.

11.48 Guidance in respect of passport orders has been provided in *Re K (Forced Marriage: Passport Order)*[32] which can be summarised as follows:

- The wishes and feelings of the individual are to be assessed as part of the court's overall analysis of that person's 'wellbeing' and to the extent that the court considers appropriate to have regard to that person's wishes and feelings, whether they have capacity to make decisions about marriage and travel or not.
- Where an adult lacks capacity and expresses wishes and feelings to pursue a course of action, the court will have jurisdiction to make orders protecting that person from doing that which s/he wishes to do in circumstances where the court considers that the facts established and the assessment of the Article 3 risk so justify. The court can make an order protecting a person from themselves.
- In appropriate cases, this may extend to make an express injunction against the person to be protected from leaving the jurisdiction. However, such a step should only be taken after a careful analysis of the risks and the degree to which such protection is necessary.

30 *Re K (Forced Marriage: Passport Order)* [2020] EWCA Civ 190 at 56.
31 [2006] EWHC 168 (Fam) at [27].
32 [2020] EWCA Civ 190 at [62]–[67].

- Open-ended passport orders or travel bans should only be imposed in the most exceptional of cases and where the court can look sufficiently far into the future to be satisfied that highly restrictive orders of that nature will be required indefinitely. In all other cases, the court should impose a time limit when making such orders.
- Unless the court can see with clarity that there will be no need for any continuing order after a particular date, for example when it is clear that the circumstances will change so that the risk is removed, the appropriate course will be for the court to list the matter for further review a short time before the passport and/or travel ban will otherwise expire.

11.49 Further in *Re B (A Child) (Removal from Jurisdiction: Removal of Family's Passports as Coercive Measure)*[33] it was held that 'the removal or retention of an individual's passport cannot be a 'coercive measure' so as to ensure compliance or future compliance of orders.

Port alert

11.50 In cases where the court directs that there be a restriction upon travel outside the jurisdiction and circumstances arise in which there is a likelihood that a child will be removed from the jurisdiction in breach of that order, an application may be made for a port alert, also known as an 'all ports warning'.

11.51 The police will, if considered appropriate, institute the 'port alert' if the danger of the removal is real (not just by way of insurance) and imminent (within 24–48 hours).[34]

11.52 Where the risk pertains to a child (under 16) a port alert can be implemented by the police without the need for a court order, a request being made directly. However, if an order has been obtained it should be produced to the police. In respect of children 16 and above, an order restricting or restraining removal from the jurisdiction must be obtained before seeking police assistance.[35]

11.53 If the relevant child has been made a ward of court, the courts permission is required to remove that child from the jurisdiction. If no permission has been obtained and the police assistance is sought to prevent removal of the ward, the applicant must produce evidence that the child is a ward such as:

- An order confirming wardship;
- An injunction; or
- Where the matter is urgent and no order has been made, a certified copy of the wardship application.[36]

33 [2015] 1 All ER 230.
34 FPR 2010, PD 12F para 4.6(a)-(b).
35 FPR 2010, PD 12F para 4.3.
36 FPR 2010, PD 12F, para 4.4.

11.54 The application for police assistance must be made by the applicant or his/her legal representative to the applicant's local police station. Applications may be made to any police station in urgent cases, where the wardship application has just been issued; or where the court has just made the order relied upon.[37]

11.55 Any request for police assistance must be accompanied by as much of the following information as possible:

- The child*:* the name, sex, date of birth, physical description, nationality and passport number; if the child has more than one nationality or passport, provide details;
- The person likely to remove*:* the name, age, physical description, nationality, passport number, relationship to the child, and whether the child is likely to assist him or her; if the person has more than one nationality or passport, provide details;
- Person applying for a port alert*:* the name, relationship to the child, nationality, telephone number and (if appropriate) solicitor's or other legal representative's name and contact details; if the person has more than one nationality, provide details;
- Likely destination;
- Likely time of travel and port of embarkation and, if known, details of travel arrangements;
- Grounds for port alert (as appropriate):
  - suspected offence under the Child Abduction Act 1984, s 1 or 2;
  - the child is subject to a court order.
- Details of person to whom the child should be returned if intercepted.[38]

11.56 Once a port alert is issued all other police forces and immigration offices will be made aware of the child's details under the 'stop list' for a period of 4 weeks, unless a further application is made.[39]

Wardship and return orders

11.57 Prior to the enactment of the FLA 1996, s 63, the High Court had used wardship as a method to ensure the protection from forced marriages and seek return of British nationals to the jurisdiction.[40] Such approach is also recommended by the Multi-Agency Guidelines on Handling cases of Forced Marriage.[41]

37 FPR 2010, PD 12F, para 4.5.
38 FPR 2010, PD 12F para 4.7(a)-(g).
39 FPR 2010, PD 12F para 4.8.
40 See *Re KR (Abduction: Forcible Removal by Parents)* [1999] 2 FLR 542.
41 HM Government, Multi-Agency Guidelines on Handling Cases of Forced Marriage, June 2014.

11.58 Once a child has been made a ward 'no important step can be taken in the child's life without the permission of the court'.[42] Further, pursuant to the Marriage Act 1949, s 3(6), a ward of court may not marry without leave of the court.

11.59 Therefore, the protections offered by wardship the closest thing to those afforded by enactment of s.63 Family Law Act 1996. However, despite there now being a statutory power for protection, wardship remains used regularly in cases of forced marriage as noted in *Y (A Minor: Wardship)*[43] per Hayden J:

> '[12] I have noted that when reference is made to "wardship" the public have little understanding of it. Why should they? For the most part it belonged to the past. It is rooted in feudal history and ultimately it is derived from the delegated performances of the duties of the Crown to protect its subjects. That does not sound obviously applicable to modern child protection but it has proved to be particularly useful in extreme circumstances, for example, when urgent medical treatment is required or when forced marriage is anticipated or, more commonly, where there has been threatened child abduction.'

11.60 In cases involving persons under 18 who are no longer within the jurisdiction of England and Wales, an application may be made under the inherent jurisdiction to make them a ward of court to help facilitate their return alongside making a Forced Marriage Protection Order or, if they are still within the jurisdiction, to protect them from being removed.[44]

11.61 In *Re M (Wardship)*[45] Munby P (as he then was) summarised the relevant case law as follows:

> '[31] Thus, as is well recognised in the authorities, the court may make a child who is a British subject a ward of court even if the child, at the time the order is made, is outside the jurisdiction: see *A v A and another (Children: Habitual Residence) (Reunite International Child Abduction Centre and others intervening)* [2013] UKSC 60, [2014] AC 1 , paras 60-65, 70, referring to various authorities including *Re B, RB v FB and MA (Forced Marriage: Wardship: Jurisdiction)* [2008] EWHC 1436 (Fam), [2008] 2 FLR 1624 and *Re N (Abduction: Appeal)* [2012] EWCA Civ 1086, [2013] 1 FLR 457 . Other examples, seemingly not cited to the Supreme Court, of the warding of a child who is a British subject, at a time when the child is outside the jurisdiction, can be found in In *re Liddell's Settlement Trusts* [1936] Ch 365 (see the facts as summarised by Slesser LJ at 369) and, more recently, in *Re KR (Abduction: Forcible Removal by Parents)* [1999] 2 FLR 542 (see the facts at 544 and the form of order at 546). For

42 *S, Re (Infants)* [1967] 1 All ER 202 per Cross J at [209].
43 [2015] EWHC 2098 (Fam).
44 See *Re M (Wardship)* [2015] EWHC 1433 (Fam) at per Munby P (as he then was) at [32].
45 [2015] EWHC 1433 (Fam).

the corresponding exercise of jurisdiction by the old Probate, Divorce and Admiralty Division see *Harben v Harben* [1957] 1 WLR 261'

11.62 An application for wardship may also be considered in cases where the local authority is statute barred[46] from making an application for care or supervision order as a result of the age of the person to be protected i.e. once they turn 17 years of age. However, the court cannot make an adult (persons over 18) a ward of court.[47]

11.63 The courts wardship jurisdiction is part of and not separate from the court's inherent jurisdiction.[48] Proceedings should not be commenced unless it is clear that the issues concerning the child cannot be resolved under the Children Act 1989.[49]

11.64 Any person with a genuine interest may apply to make a child a ward of court, which permits applications by a child.[50] For example, whilst not in the context of forced marriage in *E v X LBC*[51] a child applied ex-parte to be made a ward and such application was granted by Munby J (as he then was).

11.65 Such applications must be made using Form C66[52] and must be started in the High Court.[53] However, consideration should be given to transferring the case in whole or in part to the Family Court where a direction has been given confirming the wardship and directing that the child remains a ward of court during his minority or until further order.[54] There may therefore be cases in which a final hearing or fact-finding hearing to determine whether Forced Marriage Protection Orders should be made is heard by the Family Court despite the child being a ward.

11.66 A local authority seeking to invoke the inherent jurisdiction, including making any application that a young person be made a ward requires leave of the court.[55]

11.67 The Family Law Act 1986, s 38 provides that a ward may not leave the jurisdiction of England and Wales without leave of the court unless: (i) proceedings for divorce, nullity or judicial separation in respect of the marriage of his/her parents are continuing in a court in another part of the UK; (ii) proceedings for dissolution or annulment or legal separation in respect of the

46 Children Act 1989, s 5(3) provides that no care or supervision order may be made with respect to a child who has reached the age of 17 (or 16 in the case of a child who is married).
47 *Re SA (Vulnerable Adult with Capacity: Marriage)* [2005] EWHC 2942 (Fam), [2006] 1 FLR 867, at [84].
48 FPR 2010, PD 12D, para 1.3.
49 FPR 2010, PD 12D, para 1.1.
50 FPR 2010, r 12.3.
51 [2005] EWHC 2811 (Fam) at [6].
52 FPR 2010, PD 5A para 3.1.
53 FPR 2010, r 12.36(1).
54 FPR 2010, PD 12D, para 2.1 .
55 Children Act 1989, s 100(3).

civil partnership of his/her parents are continuing in a court in another part of the UK; or (iii) he/she is habitually resident in another part of the UK. In those circumstances, the child may be removed without the consent of any court, to the other part of the UK as applicable.

11.68 There is some debate around whether a married child can be made wards. Although, in *Re Elwes (No 2)*,[56] E had entered into a 'runaway marriage' whilst being a ward. The court held that despite her marriage, she would remain a ward, such actions making it more important than ever that she be subject to the supervision of the court.

11.69 Further, in cases of forced marriage it would seem wholly contrary to public policy for the court to decline to exercise its protective powers over a child who had been already forced into the marriage.

OTHER ORDERS TO BE SOUGHT IN CONJUNCTION WITH A FORCED MARRIAGE PROTECTION ORDER

11.70 The Family Law Act 1996, s 63R(1) provides that the relevant provisions relating to forced marriage do not affect any other protection or assistance available to a person who:

- is being or may be, forced into a marriage or subject to an attempt to be forced into a marriage; or
- has been forced into a marriage.

11.71 The Family Law Act 1996, s 63R(2) makes clear that in particular it does not affect –

- The inherent jurisdiction of the High Court;
- Any criminal liability;
- Any civil remedies under the Protection from Harassment Act 1997;
- Any right to an occupation order or a non-molestation order under the FLA 1996, Part 4;
- Any protection or assistance under the Children Act 1989;
- Any claim in tort; or
- The law of marriage.

11.72 There are a number alternative and/or secondary orders which may be sought in addition to a Forced Marriage Protection Order which are also considered in **Chapter 3**. In a family law context, the alternative orders which may

56 (1958) Times July 30.

be sought are examined below. **Chapter 24** may also assist practitioners when considering diplomatic assistance in respect of repatriation to the jurisdiction.

Secondary orders under the inherent jurisdiction

11.73 In cases where the whereabouts of a person to be protected is unknown or has been unlawfully removed from placement and/or the jurisdiction (be that a child or a vulnerable adult that lacks capacity) there are a number of orders which may be sought against third-parties under the inherent jurisdiction to ascertain their whereabouts.

11.74 Such orders may be directed against third parties where there is reason to believe they might be able to provide information which may lead to the location of the missing person, even if those third parties were innocent of involvement in the abduction,[57] and to order searches for such information; legal professional privilege is no defence to such orders.[58] Such orders may be made ex parte and in secret[59] and must be made to the High Court using Form C66.[60]

11.75 The following orders which may be made were referenced in *PH v KM and Another*:[61]

- Orders against public authorities (for example, HM Revenue and Customs, the Benefits Agency, the DVLA, local authorities, local education authorities) requiring them to search their records with a view to informing the court whether they have any record of the child or the child's parent or other carer.
- Orders directed against telephone and other IT service providers.
- Orders directed against banks and other financial institutions.
- Orders directed against airline and other travel services providers with a view to finding out whether the missing person has in fact left the jurisdiction and if so, how for what destination.
- Freezing Orders to restrain the assets of those who have control over the person to be protected. In the event such person was in contempt of court, a sequestration order. Sequestered funds could then be used to fund litigation abroad to secure the return of the person to be protected to the jurisdiction.
- Tipstaff Orders directing Tipstaff[62] to locate and collect the person to be protected, to enter a private residential property, if need be using force to open doors, with a view to searching for, removing and taking into custody anything (for example a computer or a mobile phone or other similar device)

57 *PM v KH and Another* [2010] EWHC 870 (Fam).
58 *PM v KH and Another* [2010] EWHC 870 (Fam) at [38] applying *Burton v Earl of Darnley* (1869) LR 8 Eq 576n and *Ramsbotham v Senior* (1869) LR 8 Eq 57.
59 See *PH v KM and Another* [2010] EWHC 870 at [37].
60 FPR 2010, PD 5A, para 3.1.
61 [2010] EWHC 870 at [36].
62 The role of Tipstaff is set out at FPR 2010, PD 12D paras 7.1–7.4.

which there is reason to believe may contain information throwing light as to whereabouts.[63] Practitioners should make sure that Tipstaff are notified directly of any applications. The court may request that Tipstaff attend court and give their views on the most appropriate orders to be made in the circumstances.

- The court can also require the attendance at court to give oral evidence anyone who there is reason to believe may be able to provide relevant information. Compliance with such orders can, where appropriate be enforced by endorsing the order with a penal notice and then, in the event of non-compliance, issuing a bench warrant for the arrest and compulsory production in court of the defaulter. Such orders are usually confined to relatives, friends or associates.

Non-molestation order

11.76 An application for a non-molestation order is made using Form FL401 and supported by a witness statement.[64] They can be made ex-parte where the court considers it is just and convenient to do so[65] having consideration to the all the circumstances including:

- Any risk of significant harm to the applicant, or relevant child, attributable to the conduct of the respondent, if the order is not made immediately;
- Whether it is likely that the applicant will be deterred or prevented from pursuing the application is an order is not made immediately;
- Whether there is reason to believe that the respondent is aware of the proceedings but is deliberately evading service and that the applicant or relevant child will be seriously prejudiced by the delay involved in effecting service.[66]

11.77 Where an application is made without notice, the statement in support must cover the reasons why the applicant avers notice should not be given.[67]

11.78 The standard terms/protections offered by a non-molestation order are that the named respondent(s) must not:

- Use or threaten violence toward the applicant or any relevant child;
- Intimidate, harass or pester the applicant or any relevant child;
- Contact the applicant or any relevant child directly, or indirectly including by way of social media and messaging platforms;

63 Reference made to *Re S (Ex Parte Orders)* [2001] 1 WLR 211, [2001] 1 FLR 308 at 320.
64 FPR 2010, r 10.2(1).
65 Family Law Act 1996, s 45(1).
66 Family Law Act 1996, s 45(2)(a)-(c).
67 FPR 2010, r 10.2(4).

- Attend a specified area in which the applicant lives, works or the respondent knows the applicant to be. This is commonly known as a zonal order;
- Damage, attempt to damage or threaten to damage the family home or property belonging to the applicant; and
- Instruct any other person to take the actions prohibited by the respondent.

11.79 A non-molestation order can only be applied for by a person who is associated with the respondent. As a result, they may not always be available as a source of protection in forced marriage cases where the person to be protected is not the applicant themselves as they cannot be applied for on their behalf. Although, the court may make a non-molestation order of its own motion in proceedings to which the respondent is a party if it considers that the order should be made for the benefit of any other party to the proceedings or any relevant child.[68]

11.80 Pursuant to the Family Law Act 1996, s 62(3) and (4) a person is associated with the other if they fall into one of the following categories:

- They are, were or intend to be married to each other;
- They are, were or intend to be civil partners to each other;
- They are or were cohabitants;
- They live or have lived in the same household in a familial relationship;
- They are relatives, this includes: (i) parent, stepparent, child, stepchild, grandparent, grandchild of that person or of that person's spouse, former spouse, civil partner or former civil partner; or (ii) the brother, sister, uncle, aunt, niece, nephew or first cousin (whether of the full blood or the half blood or by marriage or civil partnership) of that person or of that person's spouse, former spouse, civil partner or former civil partner. It also includes those in relation to a person who, is cohabiting or has cohabited with another person, any person who would fall within the above definitions if, the parties were married or civil partners;[69]
- They have had an intimate personal relationship for a significant duration with each other;
- In relation to a child they are:
  - A parent of the child; or
  - Have or have had parental responsibility for the child.

11.81 Persons under 16 years of age may only apply for a non-molestation order with the leave of the court[70] and permission may only be granted where the child has sufficient understanding to make the proposed application.[71]

68 Family Law Act 1996, s 42(2)(b).
69 Family Law Act 1996, s 63(1).
70 Family Law Act 1996, s 43(1).
71 Family Law Act 1996, s 43(2).

11.82 In deciding whether to grant a non-molestation order and on what terms, the court shall have regard to all the circumstances, including the need to secure the health, safety and well-being of the applicant and of any relevant child.[72]

11.83 In addition, the following principles should also be considered in deciding whether to grant a non-molestation order:

- There must be evidence of molestation.[73]
- Molesting is intentionally not defined but has been considered to be synonymous with 'to pester'[74]
- It is conduct which can properly be regarded as constituting such a degree of harassment as to call for the intervention of the court.[75]
- The court must be satisfied on the balance of probabilities that judicial intervention is required to control the respondent's behaviour that is the subject of the complaint; and the applicant or relevant child must require protection.
- In cases requiring protection of a relevant child, there need not be direct interaction between the respondent and the relevant child if the conduct is by proxy, significantly harmful to them if it were to continue.[76]

Occupation order

11.84 An occupation order (previously known as ouster orders) regulates who may occupy the family home and specified areas around the home. The terms may include 'zonal orders' preventing the respondent from coming within a set distance. An application is made using the same procedure as a non-molestation order (above) using Form FL401.[77]

11.85 The severity of an occupation order has long been recognised, in *Chalmers v John*[78] Thorpe LJ observed that:

> 'the gravity of an order requiring a respondent to vacate a family home, an order overriding proprietary rights, was recognised in cases under the Domestic Violence and Matrimonial Proceedings Act 1976 and a string of authorities in this court emphasise the Draconian nature of such an order, and that it should be restricted to exceptional cases. I do not myself think that the wider statutory provisions contained in the Family Law Act 1996 obliterate that authority. The order remains Draconian, particularly in the perception of the respondent. It remains an order that overrides proprietary

72 Family Law Act 1996, s 42(5).
73 *C v C (Non-molestation order: jurisdiction)* [1998] 1 FLR 554.
74 *Vaughan v Vaughan* [1973] 1 WLR 1159.
75 *Horner v Horner* (1983) 4 FLR 50.
76 *Re T (non-molestation order)* [2018] 2 WLR 1570.
77 FPR 2010, PD 5A, para 3.1.
78 [1999] 1 FLR 392.

rights and it seems to me that it is an order that is only justified in exceptional circumstances.'

11.86 In all cases in which the court is considering making an occupation order it should also consider whether to make a non-molestation order.[79]

11.87 As with non-molestation orders, occupation orders can only be applied for by a person who is associated with the respondent and the same definition of associated persons applies.

11.88 It is crucial to know what the applicant's property rights are within the family home/dwelling house as it will alter which provision of the Family Law Act 1996 applies to the application for an occupation order. There is a distinction to be made between those who are 'entitled' to occupy the family home and those who are not.

11.89 Pursuant to the Family Law Act 1996, s 33(1)(a), an applicant is entitled if: (i) he or she is entitled to occupy the dwelling house by virtue of, a beneficial estate or interest or contract or by virtue of any enactment giving him/her the right to remain in occupation; or (ii) has home rights in relation to a dwelling-house; and pursuant to s 33(1)(b) the dwelling-house: (i) is or at any time has been the home of the person entitled and of another person with whom he is associated, or (ii) was at any time intended by the person entitled and any such other person to be their home.

11.90 Where an applicant is not 'entitled', a declaratory order will need to be sought prior to any orders seeking to regulate the occupation of the family home which will provide the applicant with the same occupancy rights as the respondent.

11.91 Home rights apply to those as civil partners and spouses. They were previously known as matrimonial home rights, however were renamed following the extension to civil partners.[80] Home rights are defined under the Family Law Act 1996, s 30(2) as:

- If in occupation, right not to be evicted or excluded from the dwelling-house or any part of except with the leave of the court given by an order under the Family Law Act 1996, s 33;
- If not in occupation, a right with leave of the court so given to enter into and occupy the dwelling-house.

Entitled applicants

11.92 Where an applicant is 'entitled' orders may be sought in the terms as specified by the Family Law Act 1996, s 33(3).

79 Family Law Act 1996, s 42(4A).
80 Family Law Act 1996, s 30(1) (as amended by Civil Partnership Act 2004, Sch 9).

11.93 When applying under the Family Law Act 1996, s 33, pursuant to sub-s (7):

> 'If it appears to the court that the applicant or any relevant child is likely to suffer significant harm attributable to conduct of the respondent if an order under this section containing one or more of the provisions mentioned in subsection (3) is not made, the court shall make the order unless it appears to it that—
>
> (a) the respondent or any relevant child is likely to suffer significant harm if the order is made; and
>
> (b) the harm likely to be suffered by the respondent or child in that event is as great as, or greater than, the harm attributable to conduct of the respondent which is likely to be suffered by the applicant or child if the order is not made'.

11.94 The wording is therefore mandatory, where the court is satisfied that the balance of harm falls in favour of the applicant.

11.95 If the balance of harm test (above) is not met, *Chalmers v John*[81] confirms the court can make an occupation order via the 'core criteria' test and other factors listed in the Family Law Act 1996, s 33(6). In accordance with this section, the court has a discretionary power to grant an injunction and should have regard to all circumstances including, but not limited to:

- The housing needs and resources of each of the parties and of any relevant child
- The financial resources of each of the parties
- The likely effect of any order, or of any decision by the court not to exercise its powers…on the health, safety or well-being of the parties and of any relevant child
- The conduct of the parties in relation to each other and otherwise.

Entitled respondents

11.96 Where an application is brought under the Family Law Act 1996, s 35, the court may make an order in the terms set out in sub-ss (3), (4) and (5).

11.97 In addition to the Family Law Act 1996, s 33(6) 'core criteria' (above), the court must consider the following factors:

- the length of time that has elapsed since the parties ceased to live together;
- the length of time that has elapsed since the marriage [or civil partnership] was dissolved or annulled; and

81 [1999] 1 FLR 392.

- the existence of any pending proceedings between the parties—
  - for an order under the Matrimonial Causes Act 1973, s 34A or 24 (property adjustment orders in connection with divorce proceedings etc.);
  - for a property adjustment order under the Civil Partnership Act 2004, Sch 5, Pt 2;
  - for an order under the Children Act 1989, Sch 1, para 1(2)(d) Or (e) (orders for financial relief against parents); or
  - relating to the legal or beneficial ownership of the dwelling-house.

11.98 The court must, by virtue of the Family Law Act 1996, s 35(8), where it decides to make an order under s 35, and it appears to it that if the order does not include terms as set out at s 35(5), that the applicant or any relevant child is likely to suffer significant harm attributable to conduct of the respondent, then the court shall include the terms as set out in s 35(5) unless it appears to the court that:

- The respondent or any relevant child is likely to suffer significant harm if the provision is included in the order; and
- The harm likely to be suffered by the respondent or child in that event is as great as or greater than the harm attributable to conduct of the respondent which is likely to be suffered by the applicant or child if the provision is not included.

Cohabitants

11.99 Where an application is brought under the Family Law Act 1996, s 36 the court shall in addition to the 'core criteria' have regard to –

- The length of time during which they have cohabited;
- Whether there are or have been any children who are children of both parties or for whom both parties have or have had parental responsibility;
- The length of time that has elapsed since the parties ceased to live together; and
- The existence of any pending proceedings between the parties—
  (i) for an order under the Children Act 1989, Sch 1, para 1(2)(d) or (e) (orders for financial relief against parents); or
  (ii) relating to the legal or beneficial ownership of the dwelling-house.

11.100 The Family Law Act 1996, s 36(7) provides that where the court is deciding whether to exercise its powers to include one or more of the provisions as set out in s 36(5) and in what manner, the court shall have regard to all the circumstances, in addition to those outlined above,[82] the questions mentioned in s 36(8) which are:

82 Family Law Act 1996, s 36(6).

- Whether the applicant or any relevant child is likely to suffer significant harm attributable to conduct of the respondent if the s 36(5) provision is not included in the order; and
- Whether the harm likely to be suffered by the respondent or child if the provision is included is as great as or greater than the harm attributable to conduct of the respondent which is likely to be suffered by the applicant or child if the provision is not included.

11.101 Where an application is brought under the Family Law Act 1996, s 38 the court shall have regard to the core criteria, and also, by virtue of s 38(4)(e) and (5) when considering whether to make an order under s 38(3) have regard to –

- Whether the applicant or any relevant child is likely to suffer significant harm attributable to conduct of the respondent if the s 38(3) provision is not included in the order; and
- Whether the harm likely to be suffered by the respondent or child if the provision is included is as great as or greater than the harm attributable to conduct of the respondent which is likely to be suffered by the applicant or child if the provision is not included.

Unentitled parties

11.102 Where an application is brought under the Family Law Act 1996, s 37, the court can only make orders as specified under s 37(5).

11.103 The Family Law Act 1996, s 37(4) requires that s 33(6) and (7), are applied to the exercise by the court of its powers under s 37. Therefore, the court must apply the balance of harm test, and the 'core criteria' test as set out at **13.89–13.92**.

Orders pursuant to the Children Act 1989, s 8

11.104 There may be circumstances in which one parent has concerns that their child is at risk of being removed from the jurisdiction or their primary care for the purposes of a forced marriage by the other parent/relative. There may also be concerns raised by one parent that the child would be at risk from the other as a result of a risk of forced marriage when considering contact and residence orders.

11.105 Given the broad scope of the Family Law Act 1996, s 63B(1) a Forced Marriage Protection Order is likely to incorporate the terms which could be sought by virtue of prohibited steps, specific issue orders and potentially, child arrangements orders. However, the latter may still be sought to prevent contact between the child and the parent and define the child's living arrangements in circumstances where it is felt that the child may be at risk should such orders not be made or to regulate arrangements made following a forced marriage.

11.106 For example, *B v B* [83]in which the child, who was 11 years' old sought a residence order for her to live with her paternal uncle and aunt. She had previously lived in Bangladesh and had been married to H, who was 20 years' old. She had returned to the UK to live with her paternal aunt and uncle and the marriage was declared void ab initio.

11.107 The child's welfare is the court's paramount consideration when deciding whether or not to make any Children Act 1989, s 8 order and when considering the terms of the same. The court shall have particular regard to the welfare checklist, pursuant to the Children Act 1989, s 1(3).

11.108 The court may make a s 8 order 'in any family proceedings in which a question arises with respect to the welfare of the child' where an application has been made either by a person entitled to apply, or by a person who has obtained leave of the court.[84] The court may also, of its own motion, make a s 8 order whenever it considered that the order should be made.[85]

11.109 An application may be made without leave for any s 8 order by (i) a parent, guardian or special guardian of the child; (ii) any person with parental responsibility pursuant to the Children Act 1989, s 4A; and (iii) any person in whose favour a lives with is in force.[86] Such applications must be made using Form C100.[87]

11.110 The following persons are entitled to apply to the court for an order determining a child's living and contact arrangements may be applied for (in addition to those named above) by:

- Any party to a marriage in relation to whom the child is of the family (whether or not subsisting);
- Any civil partner in relation to whom the child is of the family (whether or not subsisting);
- Any person with whom the child has lived for a period of at least three years;
- A person who is not the parent or guardian of the child but is named in a child arrangement order as a person with whom the child is to spend time or otherwise have contact with and the child arrangements order has provided that they have parental responsibility for the child concerned under the Children Act 1989, s 12(2A);
- Any person who –
  - in any case where a residence order is in force with respect to the child, has the consent of each of the persons in whose favour the order was made;

83 [2008] EWHC 938 (Fam).
84 Children Act 1989, s 10(1)(a), (2)(a), (b).
85 Children Act 1989, s 10(1)(b).
86 Children Act 1989, 10(4).
87 FPR 2010, PD 5A.

- in any case where the child is in the care of a local authority, has the consent of that authority; or
- in any other case, has the consent of each of those (if any) who have parental responsibility for the child.[88]

11.111 Local authority foster parents and relatives of a child are entitled to apply for a lives with order in respect to a child if the child has lived with them for a period of at least one year immediately preceding the application.[89]

11.112 A relative of a child is entitled to apply for a child arrangements order, if the arrangements regulated by the order relate only to either or both: (a) with whom the child is to live; (b) and when the child is to live with any person, if the child has lived with that relative for a period of at least one year immediately prior to the application.[90]

11.113 'Relative of the child' is defined as grandparent, brother, sister, uncle or aunt (whether of the full or half-blood) by marriage or civil partnership, or stepparent.[91]

11.114 A court is not permitted to make a s 8 order in respect of a child who is under local authority care, either by virtue of an interim or full care order and no application can be made by a local authority for a child-arrangements order and orders cannot be made in favour of a local authority.[92]

LOCAL AUTHORITY INTERVENTION

Duties to protect children

11.115 Pursuant to the Children Act 1989, s 17(1) every local authority has a general duty to:

- Safeguard and promote the welfare of children within their area who are in need; and
- So far as is consistent with that duty, to promote the upbringing of such children by their families;

by providing a range and level of services appropriate to those children's needs.

11.116 The Children Act 1989, s 47(1) provides that where a local authority are: (a) informed that a child who lives, or is found, in their area (i) is the subject of an emergency protection order, or (ii) is in police protection; or (b) have reasonable cause to suspect that a child who lives, or is found, in their area is suffering, or

88 Children Act 1989, s 10(5).
89 Children Act 1989, s 10(5A), (5B).
90 Children Act 1989, s 10(5B), (5C).
91 Children Act 1989, 105(1).
92 Children Act 1989, s 9(1), (2).

is likely to suffer, significant harm the authority must make, or cause to be made, such enquires as they consider necessary to enable them to decide whether they should take any action to safeguard or promote the child's welfare.

11.117 As a result, where a local authority is informed that a relevant child within their area has been, or may be, at risk of being subjected to a forced marriage there is a statutory duty to ensure all necessary enquiries are made.

Emergency protection

11.118 The Multi-Agency Guidance makes specific reference to emergency protection orders in circumstances where 'immediate emergency action is necessary to protect a child or young person from being forced to marry or being abducted'.[93]

11.119 The Children Act 1989, s 44 allows the court to make an emergency protection order, granting the applicant temporary parental responsibility, authorises the applicant to: (i) remove the child to accommodation provided by or on behalf of the applicant; (ii) prevents removal of the child from hospital or other place where he/she was accommodated prior to the order being granted; and (iii) compels any person who is in a position to do so to comply with a request to produce the child to the local authority.[94]

11.120 An application would need to be made using Form C110A[95] and accompanied by a statement in support. Pursuant to the Family Procedure Rules, r 12.3, the respondents shall be:

- Every person whom the applicant believes to have parental responsibility for the child;
- Where the child is subject of a care order, every person whom the applicant believes to have had parental responsibility immediately prior to the making of the care order;
- In the case of an application to extend, vary or discharge an order, the parties to the proceedings leading to the order which it is sought to have extended, varied or discharged; and
- The child.

11.121 The duration of such order will initially be limited to eight days, although there can be further extension for a period of seven days.[96]

93 HM Government, Multi-Agency practice guidelines: Handling cases of Forced Marriage, June 2014.

94 Children Act 1989, s 44(4).

95 FPR 2010, PD 5A, para 3.1.

96 Children Act 1989, s 45.

11.122 If the whereabouts of the child in need of protection is unknown, an application may be required for the court to authorise that the applicant enter a specified premises to search for the child.[97]

11.123 Similarly, where the court is satisfied that there is reasonable cause to believe that there may be another child on those premises with respect to whom an emergency protection order ought to be made, it may make an order authorising the applicant to search for that other child on those premises.[98] If such an order has been made and a child is found on the premises and the applicant is satisfied that the grounds for the making of the emergency protection order exist with respect to that child, the order shall have affected as if it were an emergency protection order.[99]

11.124 Under the Children Act 1989, s 48(9) where, on an application made by any person for a warrant under this section, it appears to the court: (a) that that a person attempting to exercise powers under an emergency protection order has been prevented from doing so by being refused entry to the premises concerned or access to the child concerned; or (b)that any such person is likely to be so prevented from exercising any such powers, it may issue a warrant authorising any constable to assist the person mentioned in (a) or (b) in the exercise of those powers using reasonable force if necessary.

11.125 Pursuant to the Children Act 1989, s 44(1)(a)–(c) the court may only make an emergency protection order in favour of a local authority where the court is satisfied that:

- There is reasonable cause to believe that the child is likely to suffer significant harm if:
  - S/he is not removed to accommodation provided by or on behalf of the applicant;
  - He does not remain in the place in which he is then being accommodated.
- In cases of an application made by a local authority:
  - Enquires are being made with respect to the child under the Children Act 1989, s 47(1)(b);
  - Those enquires are being frustrated by access to the child being unreasonably refused to a person authorised to seek access and that application has reasonable cause to believe that access to the child is required as a matter of urgency.
- In cases of an application made by an 'authorised person':
  - The applicant has reasonable cause to suspect the child is suffering, or is likely to suffer significant harm;
  - The applicant is making enquiries with respect to the child's welfare; and

97 Children Act 1989, s 48(3).
98 Children Act 1989, s 48(4).
99 Children Act 1989, s 48(5)

- Those enquires are being frustrated by access to the child being unreasonably refused to a person authorised to seek access and that application has reasonable cause to believe that access to the child is required as a matter of urgency.

11.126 Harm is defined as any 'ill-treatment, or impairment of health or development, including, impairment suffered from seeing or hearing the ill-treatment of another'.[100]

11.127 In cases where the court is satisfied that an emergency protection order should be made and makes such order, it may include an 'exclusion requirement' if:

- There is reasonable cause to believe that, if a person is excluded from a dwelling-house in which the child lives then:
  - In cases where an order is made under the Children Act 1989, s 44(1)(a) the child will not be likely to suffer significant harm, even though the child is not removed, or does not remain; or
  - In cases where an order is made under the Children Act 1989, s 44(1)(b) or (c) that the enquiries referred to will cease to be frustrated; and
- That another person living in the dwelling-house (whether a parent of the child or other person):
  - Is able and willing to give to the child the care which it would be reasonable to expect a parent to give him; and
  - Consents to the inclusion of the exclusion requirement.[101]

11.128 An exclusion requirement is a provision:

- Requiring the relevant person to leave the dwelling-house in which he is living with the child;
- Prohibiting the relevant person from entering a dwelling-house where the child lives; and
- Excluding the relevant person from a defined area in which a dwelling-house in which the child lives is situated.[102]

11.129 A power of arrest may be attached to an exclusion requirement.[103]

11.130 Pursuant to the Children Act 1989, s 31(9) an authorised person means: (a) the NSPCC and any of its officers; and (b) any person authorised by order of the Secretary of State to bring proceedings and officer of a body which is so authorised.

100 Children Act 1989, s 31(9).
101 Children Act 1989, s 44A(2).
102 Children Act 1989, s 44A(3).
103 Children Act 1989, s 44A(5).

11.131 The no order principle applies, and the court should not make an order unless making such order is better than no order being made[104].

11.132 Emergency protection orders are to be made when there is an emergency and unless action is taken the child will be at risk of significant harm during the period of the order.[105] Such an order should not be made unless the court is satisfied that it is both necessary and proportionate and that no other less radical form of order will achieve the essential end of promoting the welfare of the child. Separation is only to be contemplated if immediate separation is essential to secure the child's safety: 'imminent danger' must be 'actually established'.[106]

11.133 Emergency protection orders can be made without notice[107] but only in wholly exceptional circumstances where there is a genuine emergency or compelling reason to believe the child's welfare might otherwise be compromised if notice is given.[108]

11.134 There is no route of appeal against a decision to make, or not to make an emergency protection order, the extension or refusal to extend the order, the period during which such order is to have effect, to discharge or not to discharge the order, or the giving of or refusal to give any direction in connection with such an order.[109]

Interim care orders

11.135 Following receipt of information that a child is at risk of forced marriage or has been subjected to a forced marriage, the local authority will likely initiate a joint investigation or hold a legal planning meeting to ascertain whether an application shall be made for an interim care/ supervision orders and/or care order/ supervision orders.

11.136 Such application is made using Form C110A[110] and must be supported by a statement, signed with a statement of truth.

11.137 The court must be satisfied pursuant to the Children Act 1989, s 38(2), that there are reasonable grounds to believe that criteria as set out in s 31(2) are met, namely, that:

> 'The child has suffered or is at risk of suffering significant harm, and that the harm, or likelihood of harm is attributable to (i) the care given to the child, or likely to be given to him if the order were not made, not being

104 Children Act 1989, s 1(5).
105 *Re C and B (Care Order: Future Harm)* [2001] 1 FLR 611.
106 *Re X (Emergency protection Orders)* [2006] 2 FLR 701.
107 FPR 2010, PD 12E, para 12.16.
108 *Re X (Emergency protection Orders)* [2006] 2 FLR 701.
109 CA 1989, s 45(1); *Essex County Council v F* [1993] 1 FLR 847.
110 FPR 2010, PD 5A, para 3.1.

what it would be reasonable to expect a parent to give him; or (ii) the child's being beyond parental control'.

11.138 Harm is defined as any 'ill-treatment, or impairment of health or development, including, impairment suffered from seeing or hearing the ill-treatment of another'.[111]

11.139 In cases where the court is satisfied that the criteria for the making of an interim care order are met and such order is made, it may include an 'exclusion requirement' if:

- There is reasonable cause to believe that, if a person is excluded from the dwelling-house in which the child lives, the child will cease to suffer, or cease to be likely to suffer significant harm; and
- That another person living in the dwelling-house (whether a parent of the child or some other person) –
  - Is able and willing to give the child the care which it would be reasonable to expect the parent to give him; and
  - Consents to the inclusion of the exclusion requirement.[112]

11.140 An exclusion requirement is a provision:

- Requiring the relevant person to leave the dwelling-house in which he is living with the child;
- Prohibiting the relevant person from entering a dwelling-house where the child lives; and
- Excluding the relevant person from a defined area in which a dwelling-house in which the child lives is situated.[113]

11.141 A power of arrest may be attached to an exclusion requirement.[114]

11.142 An interim care order will allow the local authority to share parental responsibility for the subject child/ren and take steps to promote and ensure their welfare.

11.143 Whether there is a need for interim care orders where these are sought in circumstances where Forced Marriage Protection Orders are in place was considered in *London Borough of Camden v RZ and Others*.[115] MacDonald J held that the Forced Marriage Protection Orders already in place adequately addressed the risk of forced marriage in respect of one of the children and the removal from the jurisdiction of another. As a result, His Lordship held that 'there was no proper basis for continuing the interim care orders in respect of the children,

111 Children Act 1989, s 31(9).
112 Children Act 1989, s 38A(2).
113 Children Act 1989, s 38A(3).
114 Children Act 1989, s 38A(5).
115 [2017] 1 FLR 873.

those interim care orders should be discharged and that the children should return to the care of their father pending the final determination of the local authority's substantive applications' [at 81].

11.144 In the alternative, parent/s may authorise their children to be accommodated by the local authority pursuant to the Children Act 1989, s 20 whilst there is further investigation into the risks posed as a result of any alleged forced marriage or risk of forced marriage. The Children Act 1989, s 20, does not allow the local authority or share parental responsibility and where the child is under sixteen, the consent of the parents is required. It may therefore not be suitable in cases of forced marriage which involve concerns in respect of the family.

11.145 The Children Act 1989, s 20(3) imposes a duty that every local authority shall provide accommodation for any child in need within their area who has reached the age of 16 and whose welfare the local authority consider is likely to be seriously prejudiced if they do not provide them with accommodation. The Multi-Agency Guidelines provides that 'a young person who has been the subject of a forced marriage and is at risk of harm from their family is likely to fall within this definition'.[116]

11.146 Following the making of Forced Marriage Protection Orders, the court may also direct that a local authority undertakes a Children Act 1989, s 37 report to which requires the local authority to undertake an investigation of the child's circumstances and consider whether they should: (i) apply for a care order or supervision order in respect of the child; (ii) provide services or assistance for the child and the family; or (iii) take any other action with respect of the child.[117]

11.147 Where public law proceedings are initiated, alternative family members may be approached when considering interim placement of a child, the family support network and when making further enquiries to ensure the child's safety and wellbeing.

11.148 However, the Multi-agency Guidance provides that 'ideally, family group conferenced should not be used in cases where a child or young person is at risk of forced marriage because of the physical danger and potential emotional manipulation they may experience during this type of session with their parents and other members of their community'.[118]

116 HM Government, Multi-Agency practice guidelines: Handling cases of Forced Marriage, June 2014.

117 *A v SM and HB (Forced Marriage Protection Orders)* [2012] EWHC 435 (Fam).

118 HM Government, Multi-Agency practice guidelines: Handling cases of Forced Marriage, June 2014.

CHAPTER 12

Disclosure into related proceedings and evidential difficulties in cases of forced marriage

Contents at a Glance:

INTRODUCTION

12.1 This Chapter considers the nature of confidentiality of private family proceedings and deals with the use of material from family proceedings in other related proceedings. It also provides guidance for seeking disclosure orders when evidence gathering in cases of forced marriage, either as the applicant or when defending an application for a Forced Marriage Protection Order. Forced marriage cases often involve vulnerable persons and children may also apply in their own right for protection, the Chapter therefore also covers some of the evidential difficulties that may arise with such persons giving evidence and what directions may be sought to assist.

CHECKLIST

Key Principles		
Private Proceedings:	**Disclosure:**	**Vulnerable persons and children**
Proceedings in respect of a Forced Marriage Protection Order are proceedings in private.	Where disclosure is sought from previous or concurrent family proceedings an application is required to be made to the Family Court.	Where it is suggested that a child should be called to give evidence, the court must apply the relevant case law and guidance from the Family Justice Council Guidance in relation to children giving evidence in family proceedings.
In cases of forced marriage it is important to remember that it will be contempt of court to publish information from proceedings, where those proceedings relate to: (i) the exercise of the inherent jurisdiction of the High Court; or (ii) wholly or mainly to the maintenance or upbringing of a minor; or are (iii) proceedings brought under the Mental Capacity Act 2005; or in circumstance's where (iv) the court expressly prohibits the publication of all information relating to the proceedings or of information of the description which is published.	Applications for disclosure should, if possible, be made to the judge who heard the proceedings and on notice to all relevant persons within those proceedings so that objections may be made as to the disclosure.	The court must consider whether the quality of the evidence given by a party or witness a party's participation in the proceedings (other than by way of giving evidence) is likely to be diminished by reason of vulnerability and, if so, whether it is necessary to make one or more participation directions. This does not apply to a party who is a child.
There is a prohibition on any publication of material which is intended to, or likely to identify a child as being involved in proceedings before the family court.	For disclosure of material from the police, the relevant Protocols and Good Practice Guidance should be followed and third-party disclosure orders should be made early within proceedings and if possible at the first the Case Management Hearing.	

Key Principles		
Private Proceedings:	**Disclosure:**	**Vulnerable persons and children**
In proceedings which relate to children, the Family Procedure Rules 2010 provide exceptions as to when information from such proceedings may be shared and with whom.	The general position is that each party is entitled to have disclosure of all materials which may be taken into account by the court when reaching a decision adverse to them. However, an application may be made to withhold disclosure in certain circumstances.	
Where disclosure of information is not covered by those Rules, an application is required to be made to the Family Court for an order granting or permitting disclosure.		

PRIVATE PROCEEDINGS

12.2 Proceedings in respect of an application for a Forced Marriage Protection Order are proceedings to which the Family Procedure Rules 2010 apply. As such, the proceedings are to be held in 'private' and the public have no right to be present unless the court directs otherwise.[1]

12.3 Further, the Family Procedure Rules 2010, r 11.7 specifies that 'any hearing relating to an application for a protection order must be in private unless the court directs otherwise'. This incorporates any application for a Forced Marriage Protection Order.

12.4 It should be noted that applications for matrimonial and civil partnership proceedings (most importantly in the context of forced marriage, petitions for a decree of nullity) are as a general rule, hearings in public[2] although there are exceptions to this and the court may order that the hearing or part of it be heard in private.[3]

12.5 Pursuant to the Children Act 1989, s 97(2)[4] there is a prohibition on any publication of material which is intended to or likely to identify a child as being involved in proceedings before the Family Court. This must be borne in mind where the Forced Marriage Protection Order application involves matters

1 FPR 2010, r 27.10(1), (2).
2 FPR 2010, r 7.16(1).
3 FPR 2010, r 7.16(3).
4 As amended by Children Act 2004, s 62.

relating to children, be that that because a child is the subject of the proceedings and the person to be protected or involved in other safeguarding respects.

12.6 The Administration of Justice Act 1960, s 12 sets out the proceedings in which publication of material would be contempt of court. For the purposes of forced marriage, the relevant provisions of s 12 are: sub-s 12(1)(a)(i) proceedings relating to the inherent jurisdiction of the High Court; there will be cases in which there are concurrent wardship proceedings for example, to facilitate or necessitate the return or security of a child who may be subjected to forced marriage or the risk of forced marriage; sub-s 12(1)(a)(iii) proceedings which relate wholly or mainly to the maintenance or upbringing of a minor; applications for Forced Marriage Protection Orders may run alongside or within public law care proceedings or applications for contact and residence, it may also be said that the application for a Forced Marriage Protection Order falls within this provision; sub-s 12(1)(b) proceedings brought under the Mental Capacity Act 2005 or under any provision of the Mental Health Act 1983 authorising an application or reference to be made to the First-tier Tribunal, the Mental Health Review Tribunal for Wales or the county court; applications for Forced Marriage Protection Orders in respect of adults lacking capacity are often brought within or alongside proceedings within the Court of Protection; sub-s 12(1)(e) where the court expressly prohibits the publication of all information relating to the proceedings or of information of the description which is published.

12.7 The Administration of Justice Act 1960, s 12(2) provides that 'a summary of the whole or part of an order made by a court sitting in private is not itself contempt of court save for when the court expressly prohibits publication'. Indeed, as has been noted in **Chapter 10**, the Family Procedure Rules 2010, r 11.12(3) requires that a Forced Marriage Protection Order be served upon the police, such order in practice will usually recite the findings of the court and the basis upon which the order is being made.

12.8 In *Re B (A Child: Disclosure)*,[5] Munby J (as he then was) provided a summary of the relevant principles in respect of the Administration of Justice Act 1960, s 12, following concerns that there was 'a widespread misunderstanding as to its ambit'.[6] The following are key points to be taken from the judgment and must be applied cautiously by practitioners:

- Contempt of court requires knowledge that the proceedings in question are the type referred to in the Administration of Justice Act 1960, s 12(1)(a).
- Publication means dissemination, oral or written, unless communication of information by someone to a professional, each acting in furtherance of the protection of children. Publication includes to a journalist, Member of Parliament, a Minister of the Crown, a Law Officer, the Director of Public Prosecutions, the police (except when exercising child protection functions), the General Medical Council, or any other public body or public official.

5 [2004] All ER (D) 500.
6 *Re B (A Child: Disclosure)* [2004] All ER (D) 500 at [81].

- The following information is not prohibited by the Administration of Justice Act 1960, s 12:
  - (a) the fact, if it be the case, that a child is a ward of court and is subject to wardship proceedings, or that a child is the subject of residence or other proceedings under the Children Act 1989 or of proceedings relating wholly or mainly to his maintenance or upbringing;
  - (b) the name, address or photograph of such a child;
  - (c) the name, address or photograph of the parties (or, if the child is a party, the other parties) to such proceedings;
  - (d) the date, time or place of a past or future hearing of such proceedings;
  - (e) the nature of the dispute in such proceedings;
  - (f) anything which has been seen or heard by a person conducting himself lawfully in the public corridor or other public precincts outside the court in which the hearing in private is taking place;
  - (g) the name, address or photograph of the witnesses who have given evidence in such proceedings;
  - (h) the party on whose behalf such a witness has given evidence; and
  - (i) the text or summary of the whole or part of any order made in such proceedings.
- The following are prohibited by the Administration of Justice Act 1960, s 12:
  - (a) accounts of what has gone on in front of the judge sitting in private;
  - (b) documents such as affidavits, witness statements, reports, position statements, skeleton arguments or other documents filed in the proceedings, transcripts or notes of the evidence or submissions, and transcripts or notes of the judgment (this list is not necessarily exhaustive);
  - (c) extracts or quotations from such documents; and
  - (d) summaries of such documents.

  These prohibitions apply whether or not the information or the document being published has been anonymised.
- However, irrespective of ambit of the Administration of Justice Act 1960, s 12, in cases involving children, the Children Act 1989, s 97(2) applies and there is a prohibition on any publication of material which may identify a child as being involved in proceedings before the family court.[7]

Proceedings which relate to children

12.9 The Family Procedure Rules 2010, r 12.73 permits the communication of information in proceedings held in private (whether or not contained in a document filed with the court) to:

7 See also *A v A Ward* [2010] 1 FLR 1497 in which the court disapplied s 12 in a case where care proceedings had been initiated but dismissed by the trial judge and the parents wished to disclose information to the BBC.

- A party;
- The legal representative of a party;
- A professional legal adviser;
- An officer of the service or a Welsh family proceedings officer;
- The welfare officer;
- The Director of Legal Aid Casework (within the meaning of the Legal Aid, Sentencing and Punishment of Offenders Act 2012, s 4);
- An expert whose instruction by a party has been authorised by the court for the purposes of the proceedings;[8]
- A professional acting[9] in furtherance of the protection of children;[10]
- An independent reviewing officer appointed in respect of a child who is, or has been, subject to proceedings to which this rule applies.

12.10 The Rules also permit communication of information in circumstances where the courts give permission, and subject to any direction of the court, in accordance with The Family Procedure Rules 2010, r 12.75 and PD 12G. Nothing contained within r 12.73 (above) permits the communication to the public at large, or any section of the public, of any information relating to the proceedings.

12.11 The Family Procedure Rules 2010, r 12.75 also allows communication of information for the purposes connected with proceedings as follows:

> '(1) A party or the legal representative of a party, on behalf of and upon the instructions of that party, may communicate information relating to the proceedings to any person where necessary to enable that party –
>
> (a) by confidential discussion, to obtain support, advice or assistance in the conduct of the proceedings;

8 For example, any expert instructed to carry out a capacity assessment of a party.

9 Pursuant to FPR 2010, r 2.3, a professional acting in furtherance of the protection of children' includes: (a) an officer of a local authority exercising child protection functions; (b) a police officer who is– (i) exercising powers under CA 1989, s 46; or (ii) serving in a child protection unit or a paedophile unit of a police force; (c) any professional person attending a child protection conference or review in relation to a child who is the subject of the proceedings to which the information regarding the proceedings held in private relates; (d) an officer of the National Society for the Prevention of Cruelty to Children; or (e) a member or employee of the Disclosure and Barring Service, being the body established under Protection of Freedoms Act 2012, s 87(1).

10 Baker J held in *S v SP and Cafcass* [2016] EWHC 3673 (Fam) that when considering the scope of a professional acting in furtherance of the protection of children 'it must be given a broad interpretation. Too narrow an interpretation of the rules would jeopardise the welfare of children. It is axiomatic that the administration of justice and the protection of children requires disclosure of information between professionals to ensure that children are protected' at [36]. His Lordship encouraged that 'in cases of doubt, professionals should always, as a precautionary step, apply to the court for permission to disclose information' at [38].

(b) to attend a mediation information and assessment meeting, or to engage in mediation or other forms of non-court dispute resolution;

(c) to make and pursue a complaint against a person or body concerned in the proceedings; or

(d) to make and pursue a complaint regarding the law, policy or procedure relating to a category of proceedings to which this Part applies.

(2) Where information is communicated to any person in accordance with paragraph (1)(a) of this rule, no further communication by that person is permitted.

(3) When information relating to the proceedings is communicated to any person in accordance with paragraphs (1)(b),(c) or (d) of this rule –

(a) the recipient may communicate that information to a further recipient, provided that –

(i) the party who initially communicated the information consents to that further communication; and

(ii) the further communication is made only for the purpose or purposes for which the party made the initial communication; and

(b) the information may be successively communicated to and by further recipients on as many occasions as may be necessary to fulfil the purpose for which the information was initially communicated, provided that on each such occasion the conditions in sub-paragraph (a) are met.'

12.12 The Family Procedure Rules 2010, PD 12G, para 2.1 provides a table which gives further provision for information that may be shared by for other purposes. Notably, it allows for a party in family proceedings or any person lawfully in receipt of information to give the 'text or summary of the whole or part of a judgement given in the proceedings' to a police officer for the purposes of a criminal investigation or to a member of the Crown Prosecution Service 'to enable the department to discharge its functions under any enactment'.

APPLICATIONS FOR DISCLOSURE OF DOCUMENTS FROM CONCURRENT OR PREVIOUS FAMILY PROCEEDINGS

12.13 Forced marriages cases often involve young adults or children, in some circumstance's disclosure may be required from either concurrent or previous private law or public law children proceedings. Documents from such proceedings may contain important information pertaining to the risk that a respondent may pose to the person to be protected or other relevant information that a party may seek to rely upon.

12.14 It may be that one party to the application for Forced Marriage Protection Orders will be aware of, or have access (in principle, for example a local authority who were previously party to public law proceedings) to papers or information from such previous proceedings. Where there is some suggestion that there may have been prior local authority involvement or proceedings a direction may be sought for a statement from the relevant local authority to inform what involvement, if any, there has been so as to assist the court when evaluating risk. As noted in *Re D (Minors) (Adoption Reports: Confidentiality)*[11] 'It is a fundamental principle of fairness that a party is entitled to the disclosure of all materials which may be taken into account by the court when reaching a decision adverse to that party'.

12.15 It is also important that practitioners must keep at the forefront of their mind that:

> 'it is the duty owed to the court both by the parties and the parties and their legal representatives to give full and frank disclosure… in all matters in respect of children…. The parties and their advisers must also use their best endeavours: (a) to confine the issues and the evidence called to what is reasonably considered to be essential for the proper presentation of their case; (b) to reduce or eliminate issues for expert evidence; and (c) in advance of the hearing to agree which are the issues or the main issues'.[12]

12.16 A party's mere possession of documents from previous family proceedings does not then permit their automatic disclosure/ dissemination into proceedings, permission of the court is required.[13] This applies to both: (i) situations where documents are sought to be disclosed from proceedings relating to an application for a Forced Marriage Protection Order; and (ii) where documentation from other family proceedings is sought to be disclosed into proceedings relating to the application for a Forced Marriage Protection Order. An application must be made to the court pursuant to the Family Procedure Rules 2010, r 12.73(b) (above) for an order granting permission to obtain and/or disclose papers from the relevant proceedings.

12.17 There is no specified application form suggested within the Family Procedure Rules 2010 however, such applications are usually made using Form C2. So far as is possible all persons to whom the documents seeking to be disclosed would relate to should be put on notice and given an opportunity to make representations as to whether they oppose disclosure. A direction should be sought for permission to serve a redacted copy of the order on those who may wish to oppose disclosure. The application for disclosure should be made to the judge who has conduct of the proceedings, in so far as is possible although this is not a necessary requirement.

11 [1996] AC 593.

12 *Practice Direction: Case Management* [1995] 1 FLR 456.

13 FPR 2010, r 12.73(b).

12.18 In cases where there are concurrent family proceedings and/or other family proceedings which have been consolidated with the application for Forced Marriage Protection Orders, the court will usually direct that there be cross disclosure of the relevant papers. The same principles will apply with directions made for interested persons to be given an opportunity to make representations as to whether disclosure should be permitted. In line with the overriding objective[14] parties will likely be directed by the court to agree a list of core documents that will form part of the proceedings rather than blanket disclosure of all material.

DISCLOSURE INTO RELATED PROCEEDINGS

12.19 In some cases, an application may be made for information/documentation relating to ongoing proceedings to be disclosed into other forms of litigation including the Court of Protection. An application made pursuant to the Family Procedure Rules 2010, r 12.73(b) is required on notice to all relevant person. For example, disclosure has been made by the family court to the General Medical Council in *A County Council v W (Disclosure)*[15] and *A Health Authority v X (Discovery: Medical Conduct)*.[16]

12.20 When considering such applications, the following dicta of Munby P (as he then was) is relevant:

> 'Family courts should not stand in the way of, and should, on the contrary, take all appropriate steps to facilitate the proper administration of justice elsewhere. This principle is well recognised in authorities both in relation to the criminal justice system and in relation to tribunals as varied as those dealing with medical discipline and criminal injuries compensation. It is of course, equally applicable in relation to the civil justice system'.[17]

DISCLOSURE OF FAMILY PROCEEDINGS MATERIAL TO THE POLICE

12.21 Proceedings within the family courts are often concluded prior to any criminal investigation or criminal proceedings, especially where the matter relates to the welfare and future upbringing of children.

12.22 In cases in respect of children, whilst the Family Procedure Rules 2010, PD 12G, para 12.1 allows for a party in family proceedings or any person lawfully in receipt of information to give the 'text or summary of the whole or part of a judgement given in the proceedings' to: (i) a police officer for the purposes of a criminal investigation; or (ii) to a member of the Crown Prosecution Service 'to

14 FPR 2010, r 1.1.
15 [1997] 1 FLR 574.
16 [2001] 2 FLR 673.
17 *Re W* [2017] EWFC 61, [2017] 3 FCR 709.

enable the department to discharge its functions under any enactment' it does not allow for the disclosure of other documentation such as statements, reports, assessments, medical or other expert evidence.

12.23 Forced Marriage Protection Orders may be sought alongside public law proceedings under the Children Act 1989, Part IV or V. There are a number of authorities which provide guidance as to when the court may order onward disclosure of documentation from those proceedings which are covered by the Children Act 1989, s 98 which provides that:

> 'in any proceedings in which a court is hearing an application for an order under Part IV or V, no person shall be excused from:
>
> (a) Giving evidence on any matter; or
>
> (b) Answering any question put to him in the course of giving evidence.
>
> On the ground that doing so might incriminate him or his spouse or civil partner of an offence.
>
> (2) A statement or admission made in such proceedings shall not be admissible in evidence against the person making it or his spouse or civil partner in proceedings for an offence other than perjury.'

12.24 No such provision exists under the Family Law Act 1996 however, there does not appear anything contained within the jurisprudence that would prevent the same principles being applied where a court is faced with an application for onward disclosure of documents, from proceedings relating to a Forced Marriage Protection Orders made in respect of children over and above that set out in PD 12G, with the obvious caveat that the Children Act 1989, s 98 does not apply.

12.25 In *Re C (A Minor) (Care Proceedings: Disclosure)*[18] Swinton Thomas LJ, gave guidance in respect of such applications. Such guidance sets out as separate factors to consider those cases to which the Children Act 1989, s 98(2) applies:

> 'In the light of the authorities, the following are among the matters which a judge will consider when deciding whether to order disclosure. It is impossible to place them in any order of importance, because the importance of each of the various factors will inevitably vary very much from case to case:
>
> a. The welfare and interests of the child or children concerned in the care proceedings. If the child is likely to be adversely affected by the order in any serious way, this will be a very important factor.
>
> b. The welfare and interests of other children generally.
>
> c. The maintenance of confidentiality in children cases.

18 [1997] 2 WLR 322 sub nom *Re EC (Disclosure of Material)* [1996] 2 FLR 725, at 733.

d. The importance of encouraging frankness in children's cases. All parties to this appeal agree that this is a very important factor and is likely to be of particular importance in a case to which s 98(2) applies. The underlying purpose of s 98 is to encourage people to tell the truth in cases concerning children, and the incentive is that any admission will not be admissible in evidence in a criminal trial. Consequently, it is important in this case. However, the added incentive of guaranteed confidentiality is not given by the words of the section and cannot be given.

e. The public interest in the administration of justice. Barriers should not be erected between one branch of the judicature and another because this may be inimical to the overall interests of justice.

f. The public interest in the prosecution of serious crime and the punishment of offenders, including the public interest in convicting those who have been guilty of violent or sexual offences against children. There is a strong public interest in making available material to the police which is relevant to a criminal trial. In many cases, this is likely to be a very important factor.

g. The gravity of the alleged offence and the relevance of the evidence to it. If the evidence has little or no bearing on the investigation or the trial, this will militate against a disclosure order.

h. The desirability of co-operation between various agencies concerned with the welfare of children, including the social services departments, the police service, medical practitioners, health visitors, schools, etc. This is particularly important in cases concerning children.

i. In a case to which s 98(2) applies, the terms of the section itself, namely, that the witness was not excused from answering incriminating questions, and that any statement of admission would not be admissible against him in criminal proceedings. Fairness to the person who has incriminated himself and any others affected by the incriminating statement and any danger of oppression would also be relevant considerations.

j. Any other material disclosure which has already taken place.'

12.26 In *Re M (Children)*[19] Sir Andrew McFarlane P considered whether the 'Re C' checklist remained fit for purpose and held that:

> 'despite the passage of over twenty years all counsel in the present appeal accepted that Swinton Thomas LJ's distillation of the relevant law in *Re C* has continued to be the leading authority to which all levels of the Family Court regularly turn when determining applications for disclosure of material to the police'.

19 [2019] EWCA Civ 1364 at [30].

DISCLOSURE FROM THE POLICE

12.27 Forcing a person into a marriage is a criminal offence pursuant the Anti-social Behaviour, Crime and Policing Act 2014, s 121.

12.28 In normal circumstances a breach of an order would be punishable by application for committal. Further, pursuant to the Family Law Act 1996, s 63CA[20] it is also a criminal offence to breach a Forced Marriage Protection Order which is punishable with a maximum penalty for up to five years' imprisonment. If there is a breach as a result of the Family Law Act 1996, s 63CA and a person has been convicted, they cannot then be punished by contempt as a result of the same conduct and vice versa.[21]

12.29 Where there have been proceedings in the criminal courts the evidence adduced will be a matter of public record. It is therefore good practice to seek disclosure from those proceedings and/or send a representative to take a 'noting brief' of matters unfolding within the proceedings.

12.30 The Family Procedure Rules 2010, Part 21 governs the disclosure and inspection of documents. Rule 21.2 enables an order for disclosure to be made against persons who are not parties to the proceedings:

> '(3) The court may make an order under this rule only where disclosure is necessary in order to dispose fairly of the proceedings or to save costs.
>
> (4) An order under this rule must:
>
> a. Specify the documents or the classes of documents which the respondent must disclose; and
>
> b. Require the respondent, when making disclosure to specify any of those documents –
>
> (i) which are no longer in the respondent's control; or
>
> (ii) in respect of which the respondent claims a right or duty to withhold inspection.
>
> (5) Such an order may –
>
> a. Require the respondent to indicate what has happened to any documents which are no longer in the respondent's control; and
>
> b. Specify a time and place for disclosure and inspection.
>
> (6) An order under this rule must not compel a person to produce any document which that person could not be compelled to produce at the final hearing.
>
> (7) This rule does not limit any other power the court may have to order disclosure against a person who is not party to proceedings.'

20 As inserted by Anti-social Behaviour, Crime and Policing Act 2014, s 120.
21 Explanatory notes to Anti-social Behaviour, Crime and Policing Act 2014, s 120, at para [317].

12.31 Police disclosure orders will regularly be made at the initial hearing, or, at the case management hearing. Where the police have not been present, the disclosure order should record that the relevant police force are able to vary or discharge the terms of the order on notice.

12.32 The police may make an application pursuant to the Family Procedure Rules 2010, r 21.3 to withhold any requested disclosure advancing that it would injurious to the public interest to do so (see **12.52–12.55** *et seq)*

12.33 Where a criminal prosecution has been brought by the Crown Prosecution Service or there is an ongoing police investigation it is likely that disclosure/ sharing of information will be required. In such circumstances, parties should in the first instance invoke the Police Protocol and/or make the relevant request to obtain information from the police.

12.34 Forced marriage is defined by the Forced Marriage Unit as a form of child abuse, allegations of such nature may also form the basis of public law proceedings.

12.35 Since 2014, in cases involving criminal investigations into child abuse (child victims who were ages 17 and under at the time of the alleged offending) and/or Family Court proceedings concerning a child (aged 17 and under), the procedure relating to disclosure from and to the police/ criminal justice system is governed by the 'Protocol and Good Practice Model, Disclosure of information in cases of alleged child abuse and linked criminal and care directions hearings, 2013' (hereinafter "the 2013 Protocol").

12.36 Where a request for disclosure is to be made by the local authority, Part A, paragraph (4) the 2013 Protocol should be applied. In the event the request is refused, an order may be sought against the relevant police force from the family court for the necessary disclosure and Part A, paragraph 7, of the 2013 Protocol should be applied.

12.37 It should also be noted that each police force may also have their own local protocols which are followed.[22] However, most police forced have adopted the standard Disclosure Protocol between the Family Court and the police.[23]

EVIDENTIAL DIFFICULTIES AND DISCLOSURE

Multi Agency Risk Assessment Conference (MARAC) reports

12.38 MARAC reports are confidential documents. A respondent to an application may wish to make an application for disclosure of documents relied upon under the Family Procedure Rules 2010, r 21.2.

22 See for example see *A Local Government v A and others* [2018] EWHC 1819 (Fam).
23 See Law Society, Related Family and Criminal Proceedings Guide, Appendix 2.

12.39 When dealing with, or making such an application practitioners should be aware of and familiarise themselves with the Family Justice Council Guidance MARACs and Disclosure into Court Proceedings.[24] The key provisions of which are outlined below:

- The essential purpose of a MARAC is to share information about risk, devise a co-ordinated safety plan for the adult victim, to liaise with appropriate agencies to address safety of children and include as needed safety actions in the plan, to address the behaviour of the alleged perpetrator and to address the safety of staff working with the family;
- A MARAC is not a legal entity and therefore the owner of information shared at a MARAC is the original supplying agency;
- MARACs should only be required to disclose information by an order of the court;
- Any request for information must be an informed request setting out the nature of the information sought, ie there must be no 'fishing expedition';
- The question of disclosure should always be considered well in advance of a contested hearing and dealt with by an order for directions.
- Notice should ordinarily be given to the Chair of the MARAC, if this is not practicable, the order should allow a MARAC representative to appear and object before compliance is required.
- Any order should be addressed to the Chair of the MARAC.
- When served with the order the Chair of the MARAC, the Chair is under a duty to raise formal objection if any disclosure will interfere significantly with a safety plan or may cause harm to any relevant child. If, however, a decision is made not to make a formal objection –
  - The MARAC Chair should identify the documents currently held (which in practice will usually only be the minuets);
  - If the minuets refer to information supplied and held by another organisation the court should be invited to make an order directed to that organisation unless the Chair of that organisations has consented to disclosure;
  - If any document ordered to be disclosed is believed by the Chair to be unreliable, the court should be so informed;
  - If a MARAC is in doubt whether to disclose they may set out to the court their concerns and reservations but in so doing accept that the court may nevertheless order the disclosure;
  - MARAC workers should not ordinarily be called a witness in court proceedings.

24 Working Party of the Family Justice Council, MARACs and disclosure into court proceedings, 2011 available at <https://www.judiciary.uk/wp-content/uploads/2014/10/fjc_marac_guidance_dec2011.pdf>.

Withholding disclosure

12.40 Documents disclosed within forced marriage proceedings may contain highly sensitive information which has the ability to place both the person to be protected, and the sharer of information at significant risk should the respondent be made aware of its contents. Practitioners must therefore be familiar with the relevant disclosure principles. As set out within *Chief Constable and Another v YK, RB, ZS, SI, AK and MH*:[25]

> 'Although the court is required to take into account "all the circumstances" when deciding whether or not to make an order there is nothing in the Act which requires the court to apply any given criteria beyond the matters identified in s 63A (2). There is, moreover, nothing in the Act to stop the court acting on hearsay evidence, or information provided to it by the police which has not been disclosed to the respondents.'

12.41 However, within family proceedings, there is a presumption that as a starting point any party is entitled to have disclosure of all materials which may be taken into account by the court when reaching a decision adverse to them.[26] The leading authority remains *Re B (Disclosure to other Parties)*[27] (approved by the Court of Appeal in *A Local Authority v A*[28] in which Munby J (as was) at [67]). The key principles are summarised below.

12.42 Parties are entitled to a fair trial under Article 6 of ECHR, these cannot be qualified by anyone else's right under Article 8 of ECHR, they are entitled to be involved in the decision-making process, seen as a whole, to a degree sufficient to provide them with the requisite protection of their interests.

12.43 Parties must be able to participate in such a way as will enable them to influence the outcome and assess their prospects of making an appeal, they must have a reasonable opportunity to present their case, including their evidence under conditions that do not place them at a substantial disadvantage to their opponents;

12.44 Parties must have knowledge of and comment on observations filed or evidence adduced by other parties.

12.45 There may be a limited qualification of a party's right to see a document if it is reasonably directed toward a clear and proper objective such as another's rights under Article 8 of ECHR. There may be circumstances in which having balanced one party's Article 6 right to see all relevant documents and the Article 8 rights of others, the balance is struck in such a way as to permit withholding of material from a party, or at least some of the documents.

25 [2010] EWHC 2438 (Fam), [2012] Fam 102, [2011] 2 WLR 1027, [2011] 1 FLR 1493 at [18].
26 *Re D (Minors) (Adoption Reports: Confidentiality)* [1996] AC 593, [1995] 2 FLR 687.
27 [2001] 2 FLR 1017.
28 [2009] EWCA Civ 1057.

12.46 Non-disclosure can only be justified when the case for doing so is 'compelling' or 'strictly necessary', the court must be 'rigorous' in its examination of the risk and gravity of the feared harm of those whose Article 8 rights are said to be engaged.[29] Any difficulties caused to a party by limitation of their right to see the documentation must be sufficiently counterbalanced by procedures designed to ensure they receive a fair trial.

12.47 Following the court receiving notice that there is a dispute as to disclosure of documents within proceedings they may either: (i) seek for written submissions to be filed so that the matter may be determined on paper; or (ii) list a contested hearing so that oral submissions may be made. In *A County Council v SB, MA and AA*,[30] the then President, Sir Nicholas Wall held at [35] 'that clearly in some forced marriage or 'honour' based violence cases[31] disclosure of information might put a witness, or the source of the information at risk'. In such circumstances, the approach adopted by McFarlane J at paragraph 112(i) of his judgment in *Re T (Wardship: Review of Police Protection Decision) (No 2)*[32] should be adopted. Namely, that full disclosure should be made to the court of the relevant material, and that the court should then decide whether the Article 6 rights of the parties require disclosure. His Lordship endorsed the approach taken in *Re B (Disclosure to Other Parties)*.[33]

12.48 The Family Procedure Rules 2010, r 11.7(2) allows for the court to direct that withholding of submissions made, or any evidence adduced, for or at any hearing in proceedings:

- To protect the person who is the subject of the proceedings or any other person;
- For any other good reason.

12.49 Where an order is made under the Family Procedure Rules 2010, r 11.7, the court may direct that a hearing be held in order to consider any representations made by any of the persons named in, or directed to be served with, the order.[34]

12.50 Pursuant to the Family Procedure Rules 2010, r 21.3:

> '(3) A person who wishes to claim a right or a duty to withhold inspection of a document, or part of a document, must state in writing –
>
> (a) the right or duty claimed; and
>
> (b) the grounds on which that right or duty is claimed.
>
> (4) The statement referred to in paragraph (3) must be made to the person wishing to inspect the document.

29 *Campbell and Fell v United Kingdom* (1984] 7 EHRR 165.
30 [2010] EWHC 2528 (Fam).
31 See further **Chapter 7**.
32 [2008] EWHC 196 (Fam), [2010] 1 FLR 1026.
33 [2001] 2 FLR 1017.
34 FPR 2010, r 11.9.

(5) A party may apply to the court to decide whether a claim made under paragraph (3) should be upheld.

(6) Where the court is deciding an application under paragraph (1) or (5) it may –

(a) require the person seeking to withhold disclosure or inspection of a document to produce that document to the court; and

(b) invite any person, whether or not a party, to make representations.

(7) An application under paragraph … (5) must be supported by evidence.'

12.51 It is good practice for any application to withhold evidence to be contained within the lead application so that relevant directions may be made and further delay is not caused.

Public interest immunity

12.52 An application may be made to withhold evidence on the basis that its disclosure would be injurious to the public interest advancing the argument of public interest immunity.

12.53 There are essentially three steps required when considering a claim for the withholding of documents on the grounds of public interest immunity:

- First, whether the material is relevant and passes the threshold test for disclosure in the applicable proceedings;
- Secondly, if the threshold test is passed, whether the material identified as relevant and subject to disclosure attracts public interest immunity. The test is whether there is a real risk that disclosure would cause 'real damage' or 'serious harm' to the public interest;
- Thirdly, if applying the 'real damage' test, the material attracts public interest immunity, the question arises as to whether the public interest in non-disclosure is outweighed by the public interest in disclosure for the purpose of doing justice in the proceedings.[35]

12.54 Each document should generally be assessed individually for materiality.[36] The court will require disclosure of all material relevant to the allegation and its investigation at the earliest possible stage and establish a process to evaluate the public interest immunity claim. The usual course of which will involve the court hearing directly from the representative of the party seeking to assert public interest immunity in private and in the absence of other parties.

35 See *Re C (a child) (No 2) (Application for Public Interest Immunity)* [2017] EWHC 692 (Fam) at [29].

36 See *Durham County Council v* Dunn [2012] EWCA Civ 1654 at [50].

12.55 The court may wish to consider whether it is necessary for a different judge to hear the substantive application for relief in the event the public interest immunity claim succeeds. The court must also, at an early stage, consider whether it is necessary request that the Attorney General appoint a special advocate.[37]

Special advocates

12.56 The use of special advocates will always be exceptional, never automatic and a course of last resort.[38] Their use in forced marriage cases was considered in *Chief Constable and another v YK and Others*[39] and the following key points can be taken from the judgment:

- The use of special advocates will rarely, if ever, be appropriate in forced marriage cases (at [89] [109]);
- This is because the nature of the relief given by the Act is protective, quasi-injunctive and did not depend on a complex factual matrix. If there was a proper basis for the court's exercise of its jurisdiction under the Act an order under the Act may be made ex-parte (at [90]);
- If an order is made, then that order would stand in its protective capacity, and in that capacity might allow for information not to be disclosed, be that under a claim for public interest immunity or under the ECHR, such determination can, usually, be properly undertaken by the judge without the intervention of special advocates (at [91], [92], [100]);
- In a different case, whether of forced marriage or 'honour' based violence, the problems which faced McFarlane J in *Re T (Wardship: Impact of Police Intelligence)* [2010] 1 FLR 1048 may arise.
- The right to a fair trial manifestly does not entitle a party either to see all the documents in the case or to have all the information in the possession of the court[40]).

Children giving evidence

12.57 There may be cases in which the account of a child is the evidence upon which a Forced Marriage Protection Order is sought, for example where the child is themselves the applicant.

12.58 In most circumstances any allegations made by a child, and relied upon to satisfy the test for a Forced Marriage Protection Order, will have been relayed to another, be that a professional, a family member or otherwise. In such circumstances, a statement should be sought directly from the person to whom

37 See *Re T (Wardship: Impact of Police Intelligence)* [2010] 1 FLR 1048.
38 *R v H, R v C* [2004] HL 3 at [98].
39 [2010] EWHC 2438 (Fam).
40 *Re B (Disclosure to other Parties)* [2001] 2 FLR 1017 at [101].

such allegations were made in conjunction with all other supporting evidence including all contemporaneous notes taken.

12.59 In reaching its conclusion as to whether a child should give evidence, the court must apply the guidance from relevant case law and guidance of the Family Justice Council in relation to children giving evidence in family proceedings.[41]

12.60 It had previously been that within family proceedings, there was a presumption that a child would not be called to give evidence. In *Re W*[42]Baroness Hale confirmed that this 'could not be reconciled with the approach of the European Court of Human Rights, which always aims to strike a fair balance between competing Convention rights.'

12.61 Her Ladyship continued:

> 'when the court is considering whether a particular child should be called as a witness, the court will have to weigh two considerations: the advantages that that will bring to the determination of the truth and the damage it may do to the welfare of this or any other child. A fair trial is a trial which is fair in the light of the issues which have to be decided' (at [24].

In stand-alone applications for Forced Marriage Protection Orders, the court will likely have in mind that 'the nature of the relief given by the Family Law Act is protective, quasi-injunctive and [does] not depend on a complex factual matrix'.[43]

12.62 The following factors as set out in *Re W* (above) and within the subsequent guidelines issued by the Family Justice Council, Working Party on Children Giving Evidence[44] are to be weighed in the balance by the court when considering whether a child is to be permitted to be called to give evidence:

(a) The child's wishes and feelings; in particular their willingness to give evidence; as an unwilling child should rarely if ever be obliged to give evidence;

(b) The child's particular needs and abilities;

(c) The issues that need to be determined;

(d) The nature and gravity of the allegations;

(e) The source of the allegation;

(f) Whether the case depends on the child's allegations alone;

(g) Corroborative evidence;

(h) The quality and reliability of the existing evidence;

41 FPR 2010, PD 3AA, para 5.1.

42 [2010] UKSC 12 at [22].

43 *Chief Constable and another v YK and Others* [2010] EWHC 2438 (Fam) at [90].

44 [2012] Family Law 79.

(i) The quality and reliability of any ABE interview;

(j) Whether the child has retracted allegations;

(k) The nature of any challenge a party which to make;

(l) The age of the child; generally, the older the child the better;

(m) The maturity, vulnerability and understanding, capacity and competence of the child; this may be apparent from ABE or from professionals' discussions with the child;

(n) The length of time since the events in question;

(o) The support or lack of support the child has;

(p) The quality and importance of the child's evidence;

(q) The right to challenge evidence;

(r) Whether justice can be done without further questioning;

(s) The risk of further delay;

(t) The views of the guardian who is expected to have discussed the issue with the child concerned if appropriate and those with parental responsibility;

(u) Specific risks arising from the possibility of the child giving evidence twice in criminal or other and family proceedings taking into account that normally the family proceedings will be heard before the criminal;

(v) The serious consequences of the allegations ie whether the findings impact upon care and contact decisions.

12.63 The court must also consider alternatives to a child giving evidence, which shall include further questions being put to the child on an occasion distinct from the substantive hearing so as to avoid oral examination.[45] The following further key points in respect of procedure of any child giving evidence can be taken from *Re E*:[46]

- Any question of a child giving evidence must be raised and decided at the earliest stage and prior to any trial process (at [58]);
- The court undertaking a Re W determination will need to engage in a relatively full and sophisticated evaluation of the relevant factors; simply paying lip-service to Re W is not acceptable (at [60]);
- It is plainly good practice for the court to be furnished with a written report from the children's guardian and submissions on behalf of the child before deciding whether that child should be called as a witness (at [61]).

45 Family Justice Council, Working Party on Children Giving Evidence [2012] Family Law 79 at [12].

46 [2016] EWCA Civ 473.

12.64 In both *Re E* and *Re W* (above), the court was concerned with public law care proceedings, where the burden of proof lies with a local authority and public law orders are being sought. That may be the case in cases where applications for Forced Marriage Protection Orders coincide with public law proceedings, but in circumstances where the application for a Forced Marriage Protection Order is made by another lay third party, or by a parent within proceedings relating to contact and residence, the following dicta of *Re W*[47] should be kept in mind:

> '[29] ... there are specific risks to which the court must be alive. Allegations of abuse are not being made by a neutral and expert local authority which has nothing to gain by making them, but by a parent who is seeking to gain an advantage in the battle against the other parent. This does not mean that they are false but it does increase the risk of misinterpretation, exaggeration or downright fabrication. On the other hand, the child will not routinely have the protection and support of a Cafcass guardian. There are also many more litigants in person in private proceedings. So, if the court does reach the conclusion that justice cannot be done unless the child gives evidence, it will have to take very careful precautions to ensure that the child is not harmed by this'.

12.65 The guidance provided in *Re W*[48] was endorsed and applied within private law proceedings in *Re B (a child) (private law proceedings: child evidence)*.[49] Whilst applications for Forced Marriage Protection Orders may be free standing without issues of contact and residence being determined, Black LJ's comments in respect of when a parent may call a child to give evidence are pertinent to cases of forced marriage where parents seek to dispute allegations made that the child is at risk of, or has been subjected to a forced marriage:

> '[28] .... A parent's decision to call or not to call their child to give evidence is not a clinical or forensic decision such as a lawyer would make but involves (or should involve) the exercise of parental concern for the child. As Baroness Hale said (above), "[a] wise parent with his child's interests truly at heart will understand" the harm that calling the child will do to him or her. It is not likely therefore to be routine that parents have recourse to the evidence of their child. Indeed, one would expect that they would need to be persuaded by a very good reason before they would even contemplate it'.

12.66 The guidelines set out in *Re W* have also been held to apply in cases involving non-party children giving evidence in proceedings.[50]

47 [2010] UKSC 12.
48 [2010] UKSC 12.
49 [2014] EWCA Civ 1015.
50 See *Re B (a child) (removal from jurisdiction: removal of family's passports as coercive measure)* [2014] EWCA Civ 843.

Vulnerable parties/witnesses

12.67 Cases of forced marriage will likely involve vulnerable parties and witnesses. The court must consider whether a party's participation in the proceedings (other than by way of giving evidence) is likely to be diminished by reason of vulnerability and, if so, whether it is necessary to make one or more participation directions.[51] The court must also consider whether the quality of the evidence given by a party or witness is likely to be diminished by reason of vulnerability and, if so, whether it is necessary to make one or more participation directions.[52] The court must consider any views expressed by the party about participating in the proceedings before making any participation directions.[53]

12.68 'Participation direction' means –

(a) General case management direction made for the purpose of assisting a witness or party to give evidence or participate in proceedings; or

(b) A direction that a witness or party should have the assistance of one or more of the measures in the Family Procedure Rules 2010, r 3A.8; and

(c) References to the 'quality of evidence' are to its quality in terms of completeness, coherence ad accuracy; and for this purpose, "coherence" refers to a witlessness's or a party's ability in giving evidence to give answers which address the questions put to the witness or the party and which can be understood both individually and collectively.[54]

12.69 The Family Procedure Rules 2010, r 3A.3[55] provides that when considering the vulnerability of a party or witness, the court must have regard to the matters set out in the Family Procedure Rules 2010, r 3A.7(2)(a), (j) and (m), which read as follows:

> 'When deciding whether to make one or more participation directions the court must have regard in particular to—
>
> (a) The impact of any actual or perceived intimidation, including any behaviour towards the party or witness on the part of—
>
> (b) Any other party or other witness to the proceedings or members of the family or associates of that other party or other witness; or
>
> Any members of the family of the party or witness;
>
> (c) Whether the party or witness—

51 FPR 2010, r 3A.4(1). However, this does not apply to a party who is a child by virtue of FPR 2010, r 3A.2.

52 FPR 2010, r 3A.5(1). However, this does not apply to a party who is a protected party by virtue of FPR 2010, r 3A.2.

53 FPR 2010, rr 3A.4(2) and 3A.5(2).

54 FPR 2010, r 3A.1.

55 This does not apply to a party who is a protected party by virtue of FPR 2010, r 3A.2.

i. Suffers from mental disorder or otherwise has a significant impairment of intelligence or social functioning;

ii. Has a physical disability or suffers from a physical disorder; or

iii. Is undergoing medical treatment;

(d) The nature and extent of the information before the court;

(e) The issues arising in the proceedings including (but not limited to) any concerns arising in relation to abuse;

(f) Whether a matter is contentious;

(g) The age, maturity and understanding of the party or witness;

(h) The social and cultural background and ethnic origins of the party or witness;

(i) The domestic circumstances and religious beliefs of the party or witness;

(j) Any questions which the court is putting or causing to be put to a witness in accordance with section 31G(6) of the 1984 Act( );

(k) Any characteristic of the party or witness which is relevant to the participation direction which may be made;

(l) Whether any measure is available to the court;

(m) The costs of any available measure; and

(n) Any other matter set out in Practice Direction 3AA.'

12.70 'Abuse' includes any concerns arising in relation to any of the following:

- domestic abuse, within the meaning given in FPR 2010, PD 12J;
- sexual abuse;
- physical and emotional abuse;
- racial and/or cultural abuse or discrimination;
- forced marriage or so called 'honour-based violence';
- female genital or other physical mutilation;
- abuse or discrimination based on gender or sexual orientation; and
- human trafficking.[56]

12.71 The Family Procedure Rules 2010, PD 3AA, para 3.1 requires that when considering whether any of the above factors may mean that the participation of any party or witness is likely to be diminished by reason of vulnerability. When

56 FPR 2010, PD 3AA, para 2.1.

addressing this question, the court should consider the ability of the party or witness to:

- understand the proceedings, and their role in them, when in court;
- put their views to the court;
- instruct their representative/s before, during and after the hearing; and
- attend the hearing without significant distress.

12.72 Measures referred to, which may be put in place are:

- to prevent a party or witness from seeing another party or witness;
- to allow a party or witness to participate in hearings and give evidence by live link;
- to provide for a party or witness to use a device to help communicate;
- to provide for a party or witness to participate in proceedings with the assistance of an intermediary;
- to provide for a party or witness to be questioned in court with the assistance of an intermediary; or
- to do anything else which is set out in PD 3AA.[57]

12.73 In addition to the above, the court may use its general case management powers as it considers appropriate to facilitate the party's participation. For example, the court may decide to make directions in relation to matters such as the structure and the timing of the hearing, the formality of language to be used in the court and whether (if facilities allow for it) the parties should be enabled to enter the court building through different routes and use different waiting areas.[58]

12.74 The Family Court, or the High Court may make a direction for a measure which is not available where the court is sitting and may direct that the court will sit at the nearest or most convenient location where the family court sits and the measure is available.[59] However, the court does not have the power to direct that public funding is available to provide such measure.[60] If such measure is considered necessary but is not available then the reasons for why the measure is not available must be recorded in the order.[61]

12.75 An application for participation directions or special measures may be made on the application form initiating proceedings or during the proceedings any person filing an application notice. The application form or application notice must contain the matters as set out in the Family Procedure Rules 2010, PD 3AA

57 FPR 2010, r 3A.8(1).
58 FPR 2010, PD 3AA para 4.2.
59 FPR 2010, r 3A.8(2)-(3).
60 FPR 2010, r 3A.8(4).
61 FPR 2010, r 3A.8(5).

and subject to this, the Part 18 procedure applies to an application for directions made during the proceedings.[62]

12.76 The application should contain the following information, as applicable:

- why the party or witness would benefit from assistance;
- the measure or measures that would be likely to maximise as far as practicable the quality of that evidence;
- why the measure or measures sought would be likely to improve the person's ability to participate in the proceedings; and
- why the measure or measures sought would be likely to improve the quality of the person's evidence.[63]

12.77 The court may also make any participation direction of its own motion.[64] Where the court proposes to make an order of its own initiative it may give any person likely to be affected by the order an opportunity to make representations; and where it does so it must specify the time by and the manner in which the representations must be made.[65] The court may make an order of its own initiative without hearing the parties or giving them an opportunity to make representations.[66] However, where the court proposes to hold a hearing to decide whether to make the order, it must give each party likely to be affected by the order at least five days' notice of the hearing.[67]

12.78 Where the court has made an order of its own motion without hearing from any party, a party affected by the order may apply to have it set aside, varied or stayed; and the order must contain a statement of the right to make such application.[68]

12.79 If an application is being made to set aside, vary or stay the order it must be made within such period as specified by the court; or if the court does not specify a period, within seven days beginning with the date on which the order was served on the party making the application.[69]

12.80 Albeit prior to 27 November 2017 when the Family Procedure Rules 2010, Part 3, PD 3AA came into force and involving a case in respect of a decree of nullity (a hearing in public), the case of *NS v MI*,[70] reflects such practices being implemented in cases of forced marriage in which Munby J (as he then was) noted:

62 FPR 2010, r 3A.10(1)-(3).
63 FPR 2010, PD 3AA, para 6.1.
64 FPR 2010, r 3A.11.
65 FPR 2010, r 4.3(2).
66 FPR 2010, r 4.3(4).
67 FPR 2010, r 4.3(3).
68 FPR 2010, r 4.3(5).
69 FPR 2010, r 4.3(6).
70 [2007] 1 FLR 444.

> '[38] ...there may be cases of this kind where a petitioner will be reluctant to give evidence if, for example, members of her family are present... like vulnerable witnesses in other forensic settings, should be able to give evidence from behind a screen or by video link...in an appropriate case, the court would do whatever it could to afford the petitioner proper protection whilst at the same time safeguarding both the interests of the respondent and, indeed, the wider public interest in the proper administration of justice.... If special arrangements are to be sought in any particular case, the court must be alerted to the issue in good time, and before the day of hearing, so that it can have a proper opportunity to consider whether the request should be granted and, if it is, adequate time in which to make the necessary practical arrangements.'

12.81 In *Re C (Female Genital Mutilation and Forced Marriage Fact Finding)*,[71] (heard following the enactment of Part 3 and PD3AA), at paragraphs 15-17, Ms Justice Knowles reflected upon the rules and protections afforded to vulnerable witnesses. It was noted that whilst the rules contained within Part 3 and PD3AA were intended to maximise the ability of those deemed vulnerable to give their best evidence and participate fully, they did not address the substance of the evidence given by a vulnerable person. Her Ladyship concluded that the standard of proof which applies is not to be modified, irrespective of the characteristics of a witness, including a vulnerable witness. It remains the courts duty to take an entirely dispassionate approach to the process of determining whether, on the available, relevant and admissible evidence, the facts alleged by the vulnerable witness are established on the balance of probabilities.

71 [2019] EWHC 3449 (Fam).

CHAPTER 13

Appeals

Contents at a Glance:

CHECKLIST

Relevant forms	
FP161	Appellant's notice (Family Division of the High Court)
FP162	Respondent's notice (Family Division of the High Court)
N161	Appellant's notice (Family Court)
N162	Respondent's notice (Family Court)

Key principles	
Test for appeal	The decision was wrong; or
	Unjust because of a serious procedural or other irregularity in the proceedings in the lower court.
Timescales for appeal notices	Appeal notice must be filed within such period directed by the lower court, or if there is no such direction within 21 days beginning with the date of the decision of the lower court. Unless the appeal is being made against a case management decision or an interim public law order whereby the appeal notice must be filed within 7 days of the decision of the lower court.
Timescales for respondent's notice	The respondent's notice shall be filed within the period directed by the lower court, or if there is no direction given by the lower court within 7 days in appeals against case management decisions and 14 days for all other decisions.
	In general terms, it is a matter for the respondent whether they seek to file a respondent's notice (the wording being 'may' file) unless:

	(i) the respondent seeks permission from the appeal court; or (ii) wishes the appeal court to uphold the order of the lower court for reasons other than those given by the lower court. If (i) or (ii) applies a respondent's notice must be filed.
Is permission to appeal required in cases of forced marriage?	Permission will always be required in cases of forced marriage. Lay justices do not have jurisdiction to hear applications for Forced Marriage Protection Orders nor are such proceedings given an automatic right of appeal. The appellant must show that the appeal has: (i) a real prospect of success; or (ii) that there is some other compelling reason why the appeal should be heard. In cases where the appeal is being made against a case management decision the court will also have regard to: (i) The issue is of sufficient significance to justify an appeal; (ii) The procedural consequences of an appeal (e.g. the impact upon the timetable) outweigh the significance of the case management decision; (iii) It would be more convenient to adjourn the determination of the issue.

GROUNDS OF APPEAL

13.1 Appeals within family proceedings are governed by the Family Procedure Rules 2010, Part 30, PD 30A. 'It is sometimes easy to think that an appeal is from a judgment. But it is not; it is from an order'.[1]

13.2 The appeal court will allow an appeal where the decision of the lower court was:

- wrong; or
- unjust because of a serious procedural or other irregularity in the proceedings in the lower court.[2]

13.3 Every appeal will be limited to a review of the decision of the lower court unless:

- An enactment or practice direction makes different provision for a particular category of appeal; or
- The court considers that in the circumstances of an individual appeal it would be in the interests of justice to hold a re-hearing.[3]

1 *Vaughan v Vaughan* [2007] EWCA Civ 1085 per Wilson LJ at [8].
2 FPR 2010, r 30.12(3)(a)-(b).
3 FPR 2010, r 30.12(1)(a)-(b).

13.4 Unless it orders otherwise the appeal court will not receive oral evidence or evidence which was not before the lower court.[4]

13.5 Unless the appeal court or the lower court orders otherwise, an appeal does not operate as a stay of any order or decision of the lower court.[5]

Human Rights Act 1998 appeals

13.6 Cases involving forced marriage may involve appeals on Human Rights grounds. This is discussed in detail within **Chapter 6**.

13.7 Where the appellant seeks to rely on any issue under the Human Rights Act 1998; or a remedy available under the Act for the first time in an appeal the appellant must include in the appeal notice.[6]

13.8 An appellant who seeks to rely on any provision of or right arising under the Human Rights Act 1998 or seeks a remedy available under that Act for the first time in an appeal, they must within the appeal notice, inform the court specifying:

- The Convention right which it is alleged has been infringed and details of the alleged infringement; and
- The relief sought and whether this includes a declaration of incompatibility.[7]

IS PERMISSION REQUIRED?

13.9 There is an automatic right of appeal where the appeal is against a committal or secure accommodation order, a refusal to grant habeas corpus for release in relation to a minor, or against an order or decision made by a lay justice or a bench of two or three lay justices.[8]

13.10 Given that applications for Forced Marriage Protection Orders shall not be heard by lay justices[9] it is likely that permission will be required.

13.11 An application for permission to appeal should be made orally at the hearing at which the decision to be appealed against is made.[10] Permission to appeal may be given only where:

4 FPR 2010, r 30.12(2).
5 FPR 2010, r 30.8.
6 FPR 2010, PD 30A, para 5.2, the information required by r 29.5(2) and PD 29A will apply as if referenced to the directions hearing were to the application for permission to appeal.
7 FPR 2010, r 29.5(2), PD 30A, para 5.2.
8 FPR 2010, r 30.3(1B)-(2), PD 30A, paras 2.1-2.2 and 4.1.
9 *Family Court Practice* (the Red Book) 2020 Part I, Procedural Guide A9 paragraph [1.24].
10 FPR 2010, PD 30A para 4.2.

- The court considers that the appeal would have a real prospect of success; or
- There is some other compelling reason why the appeal should be heard.[11]

13.12 "Real prospect of success' is to say that the prospect of success must be realistic rather than fanciful, no other floss should be placed on the words of the rules'.[12]

13.13 Where no application is made for permission to appeal at the hearing or the lower court refuses permission to appeal an application for permission to appeal may be made to the appeal court.[13]

TIMESCALES AND APPEAL NOTICES

13.14 The Family Procedure Rules 2010, r 30.4 sets out the relevant time limits for bringing of appeals.

13.15 Save for where the appeal is against a case management decision or interim public law order,[14] where a party seeks to appeal a decision, the appellant must file their appeal notice within 21 days beginning with the date of the decision of the lower court,[15] unless such timescales is extended or reduced.[16]

13.16 The respondent to an appeal may file and serve a respondent's notice.[17] Where the respondent seeks permission to appeal from the appeal court; or wishes to ask the appeal court to uphold the order of the lower court for reasons different from or additional to those given by the lower court, the wording is mandatory, stating that the respondent must file a respondent's notice.[18]

13.17 Where the respondent seeks permission from the appeal court, it must be requested within the respondent's notice.[19]

13.18 The respondent's notice shall be filed within the period directed by the lower court, or if there is no direction given by the lower court within seven days in appeals against case management decisions and 14 days for all other decisions.[20]

11 FPR 2010, r 30.3(7)(a)-(b).
12 *Tanfern Limited v. Cameron MacDonald & Anor* [2000] 1 WLR 1311, *CR v SW* [2013] EWHC 1155 (Fam), *H v G (Adoption Appeal)* [2013] EWHC 2136 (Fam), *R(A Child)* [2019] EWCA Civ 895.
13 FPR 2010, PD30A, para4.3(a)-(b).
14 Children Act 1989, s 38(1).
15 FPR 2010, r 30.4(2)(b).
16 FPR 2010, r 30.4(2)(a).
17 FPR 2010, r 30.5.
18 FPR 2010, r 30.5(2)(a)-(b).
19 FPR 2010, r.30.5(3).
20 FPR 2010, r 30.5(4), (4A).

13.19 When permission to appeal has been given by the lower court, or permission is not required then the date to file the respondent's notice runs from the date of service of the appellant's notice. If permission has been given by the appeal court, then the date on which the respondent is served with notification that such permission has been given. If the substantive appeal hearing is to be heard following the permission hearing, the date on which the respondent is served with the application for permission to appeal.[21]

13.20 Unless the appeal court orders otherwise, a respondent's notice must be served on the appellant, any other respondent and the persons referred to the Family Procedure Rules 2010, r 30.4(5)[22] as soon as practical; and in any event not later than seven days after it is filed.[23]

13.21 Any application to vary the time limit for filing an appeal notice must be made to the appeal court,[24] the parties may not agree to extend any date or time limit set by these rules, Practice Direction 30A, or an order of the appeal court or the lower court.[25]

13.22 An appeal notice may not be amended without the permission of the appeal court.[26]

APPEALS AGAINST CASE MANAGEMENT DECISIONS AND INTERIM ORDERS

13.23 A case management decision includes decisions made under the Family Procedure Rules 2010, r 4.1(3) and decisions about disclosure, filing of witness statements or experts' reports, direction about the timetable of the proceedings and adding a person to the proceedings.[27]

13.24 Any appeal against a case management decision or interim order requires the appellant to file the appellant's notice within seven days beginning with the date of the decision of the lower court.[28]

13.25 Where the application is for permission to appeal from a case management decision, the factors to which the court is to have particular regard include whether:

21 FPR 2010, r 30.5(5)(a)-(c).
22 (a) any children's guardian, welfare officer, or children and family reporter; (b) a local authority who has prepared a report under s 14A(8) or (9) of the 1989 Act; (c) an adoption agency or local authority which has prepared a report on the suitability of the applicant to adopt a child; (d) a local authority which has prepared a report on the placement of the child for adoption.
23 FPR 2010, r 30.5(6).
24 FPR 2010, r 30.7(1).
25 FPR 2010, r 30.7(2).
26 FPR 2010, r 30.9.
27 FPR 2010, PD 30A, para 4.5B.
28 FPR 2010, r 30.4.

- The issue is of sufficient significance to justify an appeal.
- The procedural consequences of an appeal (eg the impact upon the timetable) outweigh the significance of the case management decision.
- It would be more convenient to adjourn the determination of the issue.[29]

13.26 Clients should be carefully advised that the appeal court is encouraged to support robust but fair case-management decisions.[30]

13.27 Unless the court concludes that there is 'so blatant an error in the conclusion that it could only have been reached if the judge erred in method of decision'[31] or; that the lower court took into account irrelevant matters, failed to take into account relevant matters, or came to a decision so plainly wrong that it must be regarded as outside the generous ambit of the discretion entrusted to the judge,[32] then the appeal court is likely to be slow to interfere or allow the appeal.

13.28 Where permission is granted, the order granting permission may limit the issues to be heard; and be made subject to conditions.[33]

13.29 If the lower court refuses an application for permission to appeal, a further application may be made at the appeal court.[34] Where the appeal court, without a hearing, refuses permission to appeal, the person seeking permission may request the decision to be re-considered at a hearing.[35]

13.30 However, where a judge of the High Court, or, in the Family Court, a judge of the High Court or Designated Family Judge refuses permission to appeal without a hearing and considers that the application is totally without merit, the judge may make an order that the person seeking permission may not request the decision to be reconsidered at a hearing.[36]

13.31 Where a party requests that permission to appeal be reconsidered at a hearing, they must file such request within seven days beginning from the date on which the notice that permission has been refused was served.[37]

29 FPR 2010, PD 30A, para 4.5A.

30 *Deripaska v Cherney* [2012] EWCA Civ 1235, paras 17, 30, and *Stokors SA v IG Markets Ltd* [2012] EWCA Civ 1706, paras 25, 45, 46 applied in *Re TG (Care Proceedings: Case Management: Expert Evidence)* [2013] EWCA Civ 5 [2013] 1 FLR 125 at [35].

31 *Re W (Relocation: Removal Outside Jurisdiction)* [2011] 2 FLR 409 at [9] and [10] applying the dicta of Sir John Arnold in *G v G (Minors: Custody Appeal)* [1985] 1 WLR 647, [1985] FLR 894 (at 650D–G and 896 respectively).

32 *Re TG* [2013] EWCA Civ 5 at [35] applying *Royal & Sun Alliance Insurance plc v T & N Ltd* [2002] EWCA Civ 1964, paras 37-38, 47; *Walbrook Trustee (Jersey) Ltd v Fattal* [2008] EWCA Civ 427, para 33, and *Stokors SA v IG Markets Ltd* [2012] EWCA Civ 1706, para 46.

33 FPR 2010, r 30.4(8).

34 FPR 2010, r 30.3(4).

35 FPR 2010, r 30.3(5).

36 FPR 2010, r 30.3(5A).

37 FPR 2010, r 30.4(5), (6).

13.32 The respondent's notice must be filed within such a period as may be directed by the lower court; or where the court makes no such direction, seven days beginning with:

- The date on which the respondent is served with the appellant's notice where: (i) permission to appeal was given by the lower court; or (ii) permission to appeal is not required;
- The date on which the respondent is served with notification that the appeal court has given the appellant permission to appeal; or
- The date on which the respondent is served with notification that the application for permission to appeal and the appeal itself are to be heard together.[38]

APPEALING FINDINGS OF FACT

13.33 It is usual practice for fact-finding hearings to take place within proceedings for a Forced Marriage Protection Order where a party seeks to challenge the factual matrix upon which the order is sought.[39] Practitioners should advise their clients of the inherent difficulties of appealing findings made by the lower court.

13.34 The following key principles should be noted:

- An appeal court will rarely even contemplate reversing a trial judge's findings of primary fact'. Unless a finding is insupportable on any objective analysis it will be immune from review.[40]
- The judge at first instance has had the opportunity to make a comprehensive assessment of all the information – written, verbal, non-verbal and visual – when reaching a conclusion.[41]
- This court should therefore only interfere with findings of fact in limited circumstances, for example where there has been a material error of law, or the making of a critical finding of fact which has no basis in the evidence, or a demonstrable misunderstanding of relevant evidence, or a demonstrable failure to consider relevant evidence.[42]
- An error in the balancing exercise justifies intervention only if it gives rise to a conclusion that the judge's determination was outside the generous ambit

38 FPR 2010, r 30.5(4A)–(5).

39 *Re K (Forced Marriage: Passport Order)* [2020] EWCA Civ 190.

40 *Re A (No 2) (Children: Findings of Fact)* [2019] EWCA Civ 1947 at [92] applying *Re B (A Child)* [2013] UKSC 33 per Lord Neuburger at [52].

41 *Re A (No 2) (Children: Findings of Fact)* [2019] EWCA Civ 1947 at [92].

42 *Re A (No 2) (Children: Findings of Fact)* [2019] EWCA Civ 1947 applying *Henderson v Foxworth Investments Ltd* [2014] UKSC 41at [67].

of reasonable disagreement or wrong within the meaning of the various expressions to which he had referred.[43]

- However, this does not mean that an appeal on fact can never succeed, if the court is convinced that the judge was plainly wrong, it is his duty to interfere.[44]

WHO DO YOU APPEAL TO?

13.35 The Family Procedure Rules 2010, PD 30A provides the following helpful tables at paras 2.1 and 2.2 detailing the 'routes of appeal'.

13.36 In summary, forced marriage, cases will not be heard by lay justices,[45] any appeal from a District Judge will be to a Circuit Judge, judge of the High Court level sitting in the family court or a Judge of the High Court where it raises an important point of principle or practice. Where an appeal is from a decision of a Circuit Judge, the appeal will be to the High Court, Forced Marriage Protection Orders not falling within the specified category of proceedings under PD 30A para 2.1(5), unless it is a second appeal. Any appeal against a decision of a judge of the High Court will be to the Court of Appeal save where the appeal is against a decision of a judge sitting as a Deputy High Court Judge.

43 *Re B (A Child) (Care Proceedings: Threshold Criteria)* [2013] UKSC 33) per Lord Wilson at [40].

44 *Sherrington v Sherrington* [2005] EWCA Civ 326 at [33] applied in *A and R (Children)* [2018] EWHC 2771 (Fam).

45 *Family Court Practice* (the Red Book) 2020 Part I, Procedural Guide A9 paragraph [1.24].

CHAPTER 14

Decrees of nullity

Contents at a Glance:

CHECKLIST

Key provisions for relief:	
Was the marriage undertaken when one of the parties were a child?	YES: the marriage is void and a decree of nullity may be sought (Matrimonial Causes Act 1973, s 11(1)(a)(ii)).
Did one, or both parties, lack capacity to consent to the marriage when it was celebrated as a result of duress, mistake, unsoundness of mind or otherwise?	YES: the marriage is voidable and a decree of nullity may be sought (Matrimonial Causes Act 1973, s 12(1)(c)) UNLESS the proceedings were instituted three years after the date of the marriage. Where three years has past, the court may grant leave to bring an application for nullity if[1] (i) the petitioner has some time during that period suffered from mental disorder within the meaning of the Mental Health Act 1983; and (ii) the court considers in all the circumstance's it would be just to grant leave. In circumstances where no decree of nullity can be sought by virtue of a lapse of 3 years or otherwise, consideration should be given to applying for a declaration of non-recognition (see **Chapter 15**).

1 Matrimonial Causes Act 1973, s 13(4).

Procedure:	
Who can apply	Husband, wife or civil partner. If the petitioner lacks capacity, the Official Solicitor on their behalf. The petition should be made using Form D8N.
Who is the respondent	The spouse/ civil partner whom the petition is being bought against. The respondent must within 7 days beginning with the date on which the application for decree is served, file an acknowledgment of service, using form D10. If the respondent wishes to defend the case they must file and serve an 'answer' (using form D8B) within 21 days beginning with the date the acknowledgment of service was required to be filed. Any cross application to be made by a respondent must be made within 21 days beginning with the date by which the respondent's acknowledgment of service is required to be filed, unless the court gives permission for an application to be made after that time has passed.

THE EFFECT OF A DECREE OF NULLITY

14.1 Aside from an application for a Forced Marriage Protection Order, where a marriage has taken place, an application may be required for a decree of nullity. This has been examined as an overview within **Chapter 5**. This chapter aims to give a more comprehensive review and assist practitioners with the procedure.

14.2 Nullity is a reactive rather than proactive measure, however, as Munby J (as he then was) expressed in *NS v MI*:[2]

'[9] If the court cannot intervene in time to prevent what Singer J in *Re SK*,[3] at paragraph [5] aptly described as these 'gross transgressions of an individual's integrity', then the court must attempt, wherever possible, to remedy their consequences. The primary remedy is, of course, a suit for nullity. I emphasise, a suit for nullity, not a suit for divorce'.

14.3 Once a decree of nullity is granted, the marriage will be null and void. However, there is an important distinction to be made between marriages which

2 [2007] 1 FLR 444.
3 [2004] EWHC 3202 (Fam).

are 'void' and marriages which are 'voidable' and the effect the decree of nullity has in respect of the marriage in law.

14.4 In most forced marriages cases, save for those in respect of children (under the age of 16) the marriage will likely be challenged as voidable pursuant to the Matrimonial Causes Act 1973, s 11(1)(c).

VOID MARRIAGES

14.5 It is important to have a grasp of the key provisions which may render a marriage void.

14.6 A marriage is considered as void where it does not meet the requirements of a legal marriage under the Matrimonial Causes Act 1973, s 11. The effect of a void marriage is that it will be treated as though the marriage never took place.

14.7 The requirements pursuant to the Matrimonial Causes Act 1973, s 11(1) are as follows:

> '(a) That it is not a valid marriage under the provisions of the Marriage Acts 1949-1986 that is to say where –
>
> i. The parties are within prohibited degrees of relationship;
>
> ii. Either party is under the age of sixteen;
>
> iii. The parties have intermarried in disregard of certain requirements as to formation of marriage;
>
> (b) That at the time of the marriage either party was already lawfully married (or a civil partner).
>
> (c) …
>
> (d) In the case of polygamous marriage entered into outside England and Wales, that either party was at the time of the marriage domiciled in England and Wales.'

'Prohibited degrees of relationship'

14.8 The Marriage Act 1949, Sch 1, Part 1 defines which inter-familial relationships fall within such exclusion as:

> '(1)
>
> (a) Adoptive child;
>
> (b) Adoptive parent;
>
> (c) Child;

(d) Former adoptive child;

(e) Former adoptive parent;

(f) Grandparent

(g) Grandchild

(h) Parent

(i) Parent's sibling

(j) Sibling; and

(k) Siblings child.

(2) in the list, 'sibling' means a brother, sister, half-brother or half-sister.'

14.9 It is also a criminal offence for a person to have a sexual relationship with those falling within the prohibited degree of relationship to him/her.[4]

14.10 Pursuant to the Marriage Act 1949, s 1(2), a marriage solemnised between a person and any person mentioned in the list in Sch 1, Part 2 shall be also void, unless pursuant to s 1(3), if both the parties to the marriage have attained the age of 21 at the time of the marriage and the younger party has not at any time before attaining the age of 18 been a child of the family in relation to the other party. These include:

(a) Child of a former civil partner.

(b) Child of a former spouse.

(c) Former civil partner of grandparent.

(d) Former civil partner of parent.

(e) Former spouse of a grandparent.

(f) Former spouse of a parent.

(g) Grandchild of former civil partner.

(h) Grandchild of former spouse.

14.11 The Marriage Act 1949 was amended by the Marriage Act 1949 (Remedial) Order 2007,[5] following the case of *B v UK*[6] in which the European Court of Human Rights held that the previous regime was breached Article 12 insomuch as it was required that –

(a) in the case of a marriage between a man and the former wife of his son, after death of both his son and the mother of his son;

4 Sexual Offences Act 2003, s 64.
5 SI 2007/438.
6 [2005] 3 FCR 35.

(b) in the case of a marriage between a woman and the father of a former husband of hers, after the death of both the former husband and the mother of the former husband

14.12 The court considered the original protections of preventing a marriage and concluded that such circumstances did not fall into such aims and thus the Act was amended to remove such provisions:

> 'The bar on marriage was aimed at protecting the integrity of the family (preventing sexual rivalry between parents and children) and preventing harm to children who might be affected by the changing relationships of the adults around them. While those aims were legitimate, the bar on such marriages did not prevent the relationships occurring and was not subject to an absolute prohibition'.[7]

14.13 Cousins, both second and first may marry and there is no prohibition on the same in principle.

'In disregard to the formation of the marriage'

14.14 For marriages conducted within the jurisdiction of England and Wales, pursuant to the Marriage Act 1949, s 49, the marriage shall be void:

> 'if any persons knowingly and wilfully intermarry under the provisions of this Part of this Act –
>
> (a) Without having given due notice of marriage to the superintendent registrar;
>
> (b) Without a certificate for marriage having been duly issued, in respect of each of the persons to be married, by the superintendent registrar to whom notice of the marriage was given;
>
> (c) ....
>
> (d) On the authority of certificates which are void by virtue of subsection (2) s.33 of this Act;
>
> (e) In any place other than a church, chapel, registered building, office or other place specified in the notices of marriage and certificates of the superintendent registrar;
>
> (ee) In the case of marriage purporting to be in pursuance of s.26(1)(bb) of this Act, on any premises that at the time the marriage is solemnized are not approved premises

7 *B and L v UK* (2005) (App no 36536/02, p 353).

(f) In the case of marriage in a registered building (not being a marriage in the presence of an authorised person), the absence of a registrar district in which the registered building is situated;

(g) In the case of a marriage in the office of a superintendent registrar, in the absence of the superintendent registrar.

(gg) in the case of a marriage on approved premises, in the absence of the superintendent registrar of the registration district in which the premises are situated or in the absence of a registrar of that district; or

(h) in the case of a marriage to which section 45A of this Act applies, in the absence of any superintendent registrar or registrar whose presence at that marriage is required by that section';

14.15 In cases involving marriages according to the rites of the Church of England, the Marriage Act 1949, s 25 also stipulates that:

'(1) 'A marriage shall be void in any of the following cases.

(2) Case A is where any persons knowingly or wilfully intermarry according to the rites of the Church of England (otherwise than by special licence) –

a. Except in the case of a marriage in pursuance of s.26(1) (dd) of this Act, in any place other than a church or other building in which banns may be published.

b. without banns having been duly published, a common licence having been obtained, or certificates having been duly issued under Part III of this Act by a superintendent registrar to whom due notice of marriage has been given; or

c. on the authority of a publication of banns which is void by virtue of subsection (3) of section three or subsection (2) of section twelve of this Act, on the authority of a common licence which is void by virtue of subsection (3) of section sixteen of this Act, or on the authority of certificates of a superintendent registrar which are void by virtue of subsection (2) of section thirty-three of this Act;

d. in the case of a marriage on the authority of certificates of a superintendent registrar, in any place other than the church building or other place specified in the notices of marriage and certificates as the place where the marriage is to be solemnized.

(3) Case B is where any persons knowingly and wilfully consent to or acquiesce in the solemnization of a Church of England marriage between them by a person who is not in Holy Orders.

(4) Case C is where any persons of the same sex consent to or acquiesce in the solemnization of a Church of England marriage between them.

(5) In subsections (3) and (4) "Church of England marriage" means a marriage according to the rites of the Church of England.'

14.16 In cases in which the above requirements have not been complied a declaration of marriage may be sought pursuant to the Family Law Act1986, s 55(1).[8]

14.17 In *Akhter v Khan*,[9] at first instance Williams J had summarised the principles adopted by Moylan J in *A v A (Attorney General intervening)*[10] in respect of what would be considered as a marriage falling within the Matrimonial Causes Act 1973, s 11 as follows:

> '(a) "Unless a marriage purports to be of the kind contemplated by the [1949 Act] it will not be within section 11"; (b) "What brings a ceremony within the scope of the Act or at what stage the cumulative effect of the failures is to take the ceremony wholly outside the scope of the 1949 Act has to be approached on a case by case basis"; and (c) the court should take various factors into account.'

Foreign and international marriages

14.18 Many forced marriage cases will involve a marriage that has taken place overseas and therefore practitioners must be aware of the relevant legal principles relating to foreign and overseas marriages.

14.19 Pursuant to the Matrimonial Causes Act 1973, s 14:

> '(1) Subject to subsection (3) where, apart from this Act, any matter affecting the validity of a marriage would fail to be determined (in accordance with the rules of private international law) by reference to the law of a country outside England and Wales, nothing in s.11, 12 or 13(1) shall –
>
> a. Preclude the determination of the matter as aforesaid; or
>
> b. Require the application to the marriage of the grounds or bar there mentioned except so far as applicable in accordance with those rules.
>
> (2) In the case of a marriage which purports to have been celebrated under the Foreign Marriage Acts 1892 to 1947 or has taken place outside England and Wales and purports to be a marriage under common law, section 11 above is without prejudice to any ground on which the marriage may be void under those Acts or, as the case may be, by virtue of the rules governing the celebration of marriages outside England and Wales under common law.
>
> (3) No marriage is to be treated as valid by virtue of subsection (1) if, at the time when it purports to have been celebrated, either party was already a civil partner.'

8 See for example *MA v JA and the Attorney General* [2012] EWHC 2219 (Fam).
9 [2020] EWCA Civ 122.
10 [2013] Fam 51.

14.20 The validity of a marriage is considered in detail within **Chapter 15**. In summary, validity of the marriage is broken into two broad categories: (i) formal validity; and (ii) essential validity.

14.21 The position under private international law is that a marriage will be recognised if it would be a valid marriage and recognised as such under the requirements of the laws of the jurisdiction in which the marriage took place. This is formally referred to in its Latin form as *lex loci celebrationis*. Essential validity is generally governed by the law of either party's domicile prior to the marriage.

'At the time of the marriage either party was already lawfully married (or a civil partner)'

14.22 Under the Offences Against the Person Act 1861, s 57 bigamy is a criminal offence with for which a person convicted may be liable for penal servitude for any term not exceeding seven years.

VOIDABLE MARRIAGES

14.23 Where a marriage is voidable, in law it will be recognised to be valid until the date in which the court declares the marriage to be void. This position is different to marriages described as void ab initio which shall be treated as though they never validly existed.

14.24 The Matrimonial Causes Act 1973, s 12 provides the grounds on which a marriage is voidable:

> '(1) A marriage… shall be voidable on the following grounds only, that is to say –
>
> a. That the marriage has not been consummated owing to the incapacity of either party to consummate it;
>
> b. That the marriage has not been consummated owing to the wilful refusal of the respondent to consummate it;
>
> c. That either party to the marriage did not validly consent to it, whether in consequence of duress, mistake, unsoundness of mind or otherwise;
>
> d. That at the time of the marriage either party, though capable of giving a valid consent, was suffering (whether continuously or intermittently) from mental disorder within the meaning of the Mental Health Act 1983 of such a kind or to such an extent as to be unfitted for marriage;

e. That at the time of the marriage the respondent was suffering from venereal disease in a communicable form;

f. That at the time of the marriage the respondent was pregnant by some person other than the petitioner.

g. That an interim gender recognition certificate under the Gender Recognition Act 2004 has, after the time of the marriage, been issued to either party to the marriage;

h. That the respondent is a person whose gender at the time of the marriage had become the acquired gender under the Gender Recognition Act 2004.

(2) Paragraphs (a) and (b) above do not apply to the marriage of same sex couples.'

'Either party to the marriage did not validly consent'

14.25 As already noted, the usual petition made on behalf of the person to be protected in cases of forced marriage is in reliance of the Matrimonial Causes Act 1973, s 12(1)(c).

14.26 This is supported by the dicta of Coleridge J in *P v R (Forced Marriage: Annulment: procedure)*,[11] whereby His Lordship held:

'(a) where forced marriage is alleged, the proper course is a petition under s.12(c) of the Matrimonial Causes Act 1973 for a decree of nullity;

(b) this is in part because of the stigma that can be attached in certain communities to divorce;

(c) public funding ought to be available to spouses bringing nullity proceedings following an alleged forced marriage'.

14.27 In *NS v MI*,[12] Munby J (as he then was) set out the two 'different bases upon which a marriage can be voidable under s.12(1)(c) Matrimonial Causes Act 1973':

> '[26] 'The first is if there is 'unsoundness of mind', that is if one or other party lacks capacity to marry (as to which see *Sheffield City Council v E* [2004] EWHC 2808 (Fam), [2005] Fam 326, sub nom *Re E (an Alleged Patient); Sheffield City Council v E and S* [2005] 1 FLR 965, and *X City Council v MB* [2006] EWHC 168 (Fam), [2006] 2 FLR 968). The other is if there is some vitiating feature – 'duress' or 'mistake' – nullifying the apparent consent of someone who has capacity. It is, of course, with this latter category that I am here concerned, for there is no question of the petitioner lacking capacity to marry.'

11 [2003] 1 FLR 661.
12 [2007] 1 FLR 444.

14.28 In *NS v MI,* the case primarily concerned the ground of duress. His Lordship provided a helpful and comprehensive summary of the past authorities and essential elements required. The key points are as follows:

(a) The court must ask itself whether the threats, pressure or whatever it is, is such to destroy the reality of consent and overbear the will of the individual.[13]

(b) The source of the duress need not be the other party to the marriage.[14]

(c) There need not be force used or threatened;[15] the influence may be subtle, insidious, pervasive and powerful. In such cases, moreover, very little pressure may suffice to bring about the desired result.[16]

(d) Duress is subjective, not objective and the courts must guard against the risk of stereotyping.[17]

BARS TO RELIEF WHEN A MARRIAGE IS VOIDABLE

14.29 The Matrimonial Causes Act 1973, s 13 sets out exceptions to when the court shall not grant a decree of nullity:

> '(1) … if the respondent satisfies the court –
>
> a. That the petitioner, with knowledge that it was open to him to have the marriage avoided, so conducted himself in relation to the respondent as to lead the respondent reasonably to believe that he would not seek to do so; and
>
> b. That it would be unjust to the respondent to grant the decree.
>
> (2) Without prejudice to subsection (1) above, the court shall not grant a decree of nullity by virtue of section 12 on the grounds mentioned in paragraph (c), (d), (e), (f) or (h) of that section unless –
>
> a. it is satisfied that proceedings were instituted within the period of three years from the date of the marriage; or
>
> b. leave for the institution of proceedings after the expiration of that period has been granted under subsection (4) below.
>
> (2A) Without prejudice to subsection (1) above, the court shall not grant a decree of nullity by virtue of section 12 on the ground mentioned in paragraph (g) of that section unless it is satisfied that proceedings were instituted within the period of six months from the date of issue of the interim gender recognition certificate.

13 *Hirani v Hirani* (1983) 4 FLR 232 per Ormrod LJ at [234], *P v R (Forced Marriage: Annulment: Procedure)* [2003] 1 FLR 661 per Coleridge J at [14].
14 *Szechter (orse Karsov) v Szechter* [1971] P 286, per Sir Simon P at [297].
15 *Hall v Hall* (1868) LR 1 P&D 481, per Sir JP Wilde at [482].
16 *Re T (Adult: Refusal of Treatment)* [1993] Fam 95, [1992] 2 FLR 458, per Butler-Sloss LJ.
17 *Re K (arranged marriage)* [2005] EWHC 2956 Fam per Munby J at [93].

(3) Without prejudice to subsections (1) and (2) above, the court shall not grant a decree of nullity by virtue of section 12 above on the grounds mentioned in paragraph (e), (f) or (h) of that section unless it is satisfied that the petitioner was at the time of the marriage ignorant to the facts alleged.

(4) In the case of proceedings for the grant of a decree of nullity by virtue of section 12 above on the grounds mentioned in paragraph (c), (d), (e), (f) or (h) of that section, a judge of the court may, on an application made to him, grant leave for the institution of proceedings after the expiration of the period of three years from the date of marriage if –

a. He is satisfied that the petitioner has at some time during that period suffered from mental disorder within the meaning of the Mental Health Act 1983; and

b. He considers that in all the circumstances of the case it would be just to grant leave for the institution of proceedings.

(5) An application for leave under subsection (4) above may be made after the expiration of the period of three years from the date of the marriage.'

Leave to apply for nullity after a period of three years

14.30 The restrictive nature of the regime in the Matrimonial Causes Act 1973 has been subject to judicial comment. In *SH v NB (Marriage: Consent)*,[18] Moylan J observed:

> '[99] It can immediately be seen that, in a consent case, the grounds upon which leave can be given for the commencement of proceedings after the expiration of 3 years from the date of the marriage are very restrictive'.

14.31 However, in a number of cases the High Court has used its powers under the inherent jurisdiction to circumvent the bar created by the Matrimonial Causes Act 1973, s 13 in cases in which there had been a foreign marriage which could be held as voidable/ invalid had they been brought before the court within the three-year period.

14.32 In *SH v NB* (above) his Lordship held that in circumstances where a decree of nullity is not open to be made, the proper procedure to be followed is to seek for the marriage to be declared invalid under the inherent jurisdiction[19] applying the jurisprudence of *City of Westminster v IC (By His Friend the Official Solicitor) and KC and NN.*[20]

18 [2010] 1 FLR 1927.

19 See **Chapter 15**, declarations of non-recognition.

20 [2008] EWCA Civ 198, [2009] Fam 11, [2009] 2 WLR 185, [2008] 2 FLR 267.

14.33 The same process was followed by Baron J *in B v I (Forced Marriage)*.[21] His Lordship noted at [11] that 'the factual matrix makes it patently clear that if she had been able to apply within the relevant three-year-period for a decree of nullity, I would have had no hesitation in granting it because I am satisfied that, under the laws of this country, there was no valid consent to marriage'.[22]

14.34 Such a declaration should not be sought in cases in which it is open to the petitioner to apply for a decree of nullity on the grounds that the marriage was void.[23]

PROCEDURE FOR APPLYING FOR A DECREE OF NULLITY

Who may apply?

14.35 The spouse, be that the wife or husband who seeks the decree will be the applicant, and will be referred to within matrimonial proceedings as the 'petitioner'. For the reasons outlined within **Chapter 10**, there will often be situations where a party is placed at risk of harm or is in fear of others being informed of their contact details/address. Where the petitioner seeks to withhold such information, an application should be made to the court using Form C8 must be issued along with the petition for nullity.

14.36 In cases where the petitioner is deemed to lack capacity, the Official Solicitor may make the application on their behalf.[24]

General procedure

14.37 The relevant rules are set out within the Family Procedure Rules 2010, Part 7, PD 7A and 7B.

14.38 Proceedings for nullity are to be issued as a petition, using Form D8N.[25] Generally, the petition should be issued in the Family Court, however in cases in which a declaration is sought under the inherent jurisdiction or there are other complex features to the case, an application should be issued in the High Court Family Division.

14.39 The D8N notes make clear that it is important that the details entered into the D8N form are exactly as they are shown on the petitioner's marriage or civil partnership certificate. However, in cases involving a forced marriage there may be indeed be situations where such documentation may not be available.

21 [2010] 1 FLR 1721.
22 See also another decision of Baron J where the same principles were applied, *Re P (Forced Marriage)* [2011] 1 FLR 206.
23 See *A Local Authority v X and a Child* [2014] 2 FLR 123.
24 *XCC v AA & Ors* [2012] EWHC 2183 (COP).
25 FPR 2010, PD 5A, para 3.1.

14.40

'(a) If the applicant cannot produce –

(i) The certificate, similar document or a certified copy; and

(ii) Where necessary an authenticated translation

At the time of filing the application; and

(b) It is urgent that the application be filed.

The applicant may apply to the court without notice for permission to file the application without the certificate, document, certified copy or authenticate translation'.'[26]

14.41 In situations as above, the solicitor for the applicant must file with the application a statement explaining why: (a) the required document is not available; and (b) the application is urgent.[27] The court may give permission to file the application without the required document if the applicant gives an undertaking to file that document at the very earliest opportunity and within any time limit set by the court.[28]

14.42 Where the parties entered into a civil partnership or marriage in a foreign country and the certificate is the language of that country, the certificate should be translated into English by an authorised person (authorised for translations).[29]

14.43 In some force marriage cases the respondent will have been convicted for a criminal offence which is relevant to the petition for nullity. In such circumstances the application form must contain a statement setting out:

- the type of conviction, finding or adjudication and its date;
- the court or court-martial which made the conviction, finding or adjudication; and
- the issue in the proceedings to which it relates.[30]

Who is the respondent

14.44 The respondent will be the spouse/ civil partner to whom the petition is being bought against and any other person who is to be a party in accordance with the rules in the Family Procedure Rules 2010, Part 7.[31]

26 FPR 2010, PD 7A, para 3.2.
27 FPR 2010, PD 7A, para 3.4.
28 FPR 2010, PD 7A, para 3.3.
29 See D8N Notes available at https://assets.publishing.service.gov.uk/government/uploads/system/uploads/ attachment_data/file/688091/d8n-notes-eng.pdf.
30 FPR 2010, PD 7A para 4.1.
31 FPR 2010, r 7.10.

14.45 Upon receipt of the application, the respondent and any co-respondent must file an acknowledgment of service, using Form D10, within seven days beginning with the date on which the application for matrimonial or civil partnership order was served.[32]

14.46 However, pursuant to the Family Procedure Rules 2010, r 6.42 where the applicant served an application on a respondent in: (a) Scotland or Northern Ireland; or (b) a Member State or Hague Convention country within Europe the period for filing an acknowledgment of service is 21 days after service of the application. Where the applicant serves an application on a respondent in a Hague Convention country outside Europe the period for filing an acknowledgment of service is 31 days after service of the application.

14.47 In circumstances where the applicant serves an application on a respondent in a country not referred to above then the period for filing an acknowledgment of service or answer is set out at the Family Procedure Rules 2010, Practice Direction 6A, para 8.1 and is dependent on the country concerned.

14.48

> 'The acknowledgment of service must –
>
> (a) [….] be signed by the respondent or the respondent's legal representative or, as the case may be, the co-respondent or the co-respondent's legal representative;
>
> (b) Include the respondent, or as the case may be, co-respondent's address for service;
>
> (c) Where it is filed by the respondent, indicate whether or not the respondent intends to defend the case.'[33]

14.49 If the respondent wishes to defend the case they must file and serve an 'answer' within 21 days beginning with the date by which the acknowledgment or service is required to be filed.[34]

14.50 The answer should be filed using Form D8B. A respondent may file an answer even if the intention to do so was not indicated in the acknowledgment of service.[35]

14.51 If the application is brought on the grounds that 'at the time of the marriage either party, though capable of giving a valid consent, was suffering (whether continuously or intermittently) from mental disorder within the meaning of the Mental Health Act 1983 of such a kind or to such an extent as to

32 FPR 2010, r 7.12.
33 FPR 2010, r 7.12(3).
34 FPR 2010, r 7.12(8).
35 FPR 2010, r 7.12(10).

be unfitted for marriage[36] and the respondent filed an answer containing no more than a simple denial of the facts states in the application, the respondent must, if intending to rebut the matters stated in the application, give notice to the court of that intention when filing the answer.[37]

14.52 A respondent who wishes to make a cross application must do so within 21 days, beginning with the date by which the respondent's acknowledgment of service is required to be filed, unless the court gives permission to make the application after that time has passed. Where the respondent makes an application, that application is to be treated as an application in the same proceedings.[38]

Private or public hearings?

14.53 The general rule is that matrimonial proceedings are heard in public and do not require the court to make special arrangements for accommodating the public.[39]

14.54 However, a hearing, or any part of it, may be in private if –

- Publicity would defeat the object of the hearing;
- It involves matters relating to national security;
- It involves confidential information (including information relating to personal financial matters) and publicity would damage that confidentiality;
- It is a hearing of an application made without notice and it would be unjust to any respondent for there to be a public hearing; or
- The court considers this to be necessary, in the interests of justice.[40]

14.55 Further the court may order that the identity of ay party or witness must not be disclosed if it considers non-disclosure necessary in order to protect the interests of that party or witness.[41]

14.56 As was noted in *NS v MI*:[42]

> [38] …'There may be cases of this kind where a petitioner will be reluctant to give evidence if, for example, members of her family are present'.

In such cases:

> '[…] if special arrangements are to be sought in any particular case, the

36 Matrimonial Causes Act 1973, s 12(d).
37 FPR 2010, r 7.12(11).
38 FPR 2010, r 7.14(1), (2).
39 FPR 2010, r 7.16.
40 FPR 2010, r 7.16(3).
41 FPR 2010, r 7.16(4).
42 [2007] 1 FLR 444.

> court must be alerted to the issue in good time, and before the day of hearing, so that it can have a proper opportunity to consider whether the request should be granted and, if it is, adequate time in which to make the necessary practical arrangements.'

14.57 In *Re S (Practice: Muslim Women Giving Evidence)*,[43] a declaration of nullity was being sought by S and as such proceedings were being held in open court. S was required to give oral evidence and expressed her concerns about removing her veil to do so. The court provided a screen (a large umbrella) so that she may be shielded from her counsel, who was male, and 'careful supervision of the entrance of the court ensured that any male entering with the doors was stopped prior to being able to view S'[44]. Macur J expressed that if possible these cases should be listed before a female judge, although each case must be looked at in its own circumstances[45].

43 [2007] 2 FLR 461.
44 Ibid, at [16].
45 Ibid, at [17].

CHAPTER 15

Declarations of non-recognition

Contents at a Glance:

INTRODUCTION

15.1 A declaration of non-recognition is an order made under the inherent jurisdiction of the High Court that a marriage which may be valid under the law of a foreign jurisdiction shall not be recognised in England and Wales. A common consequence of a marriage having been found to have been contracted without the consent of both parties is that the High Court shall order the marriage not be recognised in this jurisdiction.

CHECKLIST

Key provisions for relief:	
Did one, or both parties lack capacity to consent to marriage when it was celebrated?	YES: an application may be made for a declaration of non-recognition of the marriage.
Is the marriage one that is void by virtue of s.11 Matrimonial Causes Act 1973 i.e. was the petitioner a child when the marriage was celebrated?	YES: no application should be made for a declaration of non-recognition but instead, a decree of nullity should be sought.
Procedure:	
Who can apply	Husband, wife or civil partner.
	If the petitioner lacks capacity, the Official Solicitor on their behalf.
Who is the respondent	The spouse/ civil partner whom the petition is being bought against.

To which court shall the application be made	A declaration of non-recognition is a power under the inherent jurisdiction of the High Court therefore any application must be made to the High Court and cannot be made to the Family Court or a Judge sitting in the Court of Protection.

THE EFFECT OF A DECLARATION OF NON-RECOGNITION

15.2 A declaration of non-recognition of a marriage 'performs a wider function than a nullity decree since it extends to the whole duration of the marriage.'[1] A declaration has the effect that the marriage is thereafter not considered valid under the law of the jurisdiction of England and Wales.

WHEN TO APPLY FOR A DECLARATION OF NON-RECOGNITION?

15.3 The Family Law Act 1986, s 58(5) provides that:

> 'No declaration may be made by any court whether under [part 3 of the Family Law Act 1986] or otherwise –
>
> (a) that a marriage was at its inception void…'

15.4 It follows that the only avenue through which a judicial determination may be obtained that a marriage was void at its inception is an application for a petition of nullity. Therefore, when drafting any order following a declaration of non-recognition caution must be taken not to include wording which would fall to be interpreted that the court was declaring the marriage void at inception.[2]

15.5 A person may seek a declaration of non-recognition alongside a petition for nullity on the grounds that it is voidable, however, such a declaration should not be sought in cases in which it is open to the petitioner to apply for a decree of nullity on the grounds that the marriage was void.[3]

15.6 In *A Local Authority v X & Anor (Children)*[4] X was taken to Pakistan aged 14 and was forcibly married. She subsequently became pregnant. The local authority made an application for non-recognition. Holman J held that as X was domiciled in the England and Wales at the time of the marriage, and the provisions as to minimum age are extraterritorial,[5] the marriage was void from

1 *XCC v AA and others* [2013] 2 All ER 988 at [88].
2 See *City of Westminster Social and Community Services Department v C* [2008] EWCA Civ 198).
3 See *A Local Authority v X and a Child* [2014] 2 FLR 123.
4 [2013] EWHC 3274 (Fam).
5 *Pugh v Pugh* [1951] P 482.

its inception. As the Family Law Act 1986, s 58(5) prohibits the making of a declaration that a marriage was void at inception, His Lordship felt unable to make the declaration of non-recognition, refused the application and expressed that a petition for nullity would be successful.

15.7 Such declaration is not inherently retrospective and if it is retrospective it would be equally so for void and voidable marriages. Holman J stated at paragraph [6] that he would presume that the marriage was valid under Pakistani law. This presumption was correct insomuch as the minimum age for marriage in Pakistan was 14 at the time, as it had been since 1929.[6]

15.8 It is therefore unclear how a declaration that the marriage was valid under the law of Pakistan but not recognised as a valid marriage in England and Wales amounts to a declaration that the marriage was *void ab initio* or offends the Family Law Act 1986, s 58(5). Indeed, as Holman J recognised, the only means of obtaining a declaration or decree that the marriage was void at inception is through a decree for nullity.

Foreign marriages

15.9 Declarations of non-recognition are often sought in cases involving a foreign marriage, which although would be held as valid by application of the laws of where the marriage was entered into, would not be recognised as valid in the jurisdiction of England and Wales.

15.10 For example, in *KC & Anor v City of Westminster Social & Community Services Department & Anor*,[7] a marriage entered into via telephone, whilst valid in Bangladesh, was declared as not capable of recognition in this jurisdiction.[8]

The dual domicile, intended matrimonial home tests and incapacity

Formal validity

15.11 The starting point is that any marriage entered into abroad will be recognised by the laws of England and Wales if it conformed to the requirements of a marriage under the laws of the country it was contracted into, this is 'the formal validity'.

6 It is now 18 for women and 21 for men following a 2019 amendment to the Child Marriage Restraint Act 1929.
7 [2008] EWCA Civ 198.
8 See also *El Gamal v Al Maktoum* [2012] 2 FLR 387.

15.12 There are five conditions for an overseas marriage to be considered 'formally valid'. A marriage need only satisfy one of the conditions to be valid:[9]

(a) if the marriage is celebrated in accordance with the form required or recognised as sufficient by the law of the jurisdiction[10] where the marriage was contracted;[11]

(b) if the marriage is celebrated in accordance with the requirements of the English common law in a country where the use of the local form is impossible;[12] or

(c) if the marriage is celebrated in accordance with the requirements of the English common law in a country in the belligerent occupation of military forces and one of the parties is a member of those forces or of other military forces associated with them;[13] or

(d) if the marriage is celebrated in accordance with the provisions of the Foreign Marriage Act 1892, s 22,[14] between spouses of whom at least one is a member of Her Majesty's Armed Forces serving in a foreign territory or is employed in such territory in such other capacity as may be prescribed by Order in Council; or
   (i) if the marriage, between parties of whom at least one is a British national, is celebrated outside the Commonwealth in accordance with the provisions of, and the form required by, the Foreign Marriage Acts 1892 to 1947, as amended Foreign Marriage (Amendment) Act 1988.
   (ii) The marriage need not comply with the requirements under the law of England and Wales.[15]

(e) If the local law governing marriage is based on religious principles, then those principles shall apply to whether the marriage in question is valid. In *Ismail v Choudry*,[16] the Court of Appeal held that a marriage celebrated in Pakistan was invalid because it took place within three months of the dissolution of the wife's previous marriage in contravention of the Quranic principle of Iddah.

9 See *Dicey, Morris & Collins on the Conflict of Laws* 15th Edn (Sweet and Maxwell, 2018), 17R-001.

10 The word jurisdiction is used due to the potential for the word country to cause confusion. For example, each state of the United States is likely to be considered a different 'country' for the purposes of conflict of laws. Also, in *MM v NA* [2020] EWHC 93, the High Court recognised a marriage conducted in accordance with the laws of Somaliland despite Somaliland not being a state recognised by the United Kingdom Government.

11 *Apt v Apt* [1948] 2 All ER 677, *Berthiaume v Dame Dastous* [1930] AC 79 in which Lord Dunedin held 'If a marriage is good by the laws of the country where it is effected, it is good all the world over'.

12 See *Woldenden v Wolfenden* [1946] p.61; *Penhas v Tan Soo Eng* [1953] AC 304 (PC); *In the Marriage of X* (1983) 65 F.L.R.132.

13 See for example *Merker v Merker* [1962] 3 WLR in which the parties to the marriage were both serving in the Polish Armed Forces occupying Germany in 1946 when they married.

14 As amended by the Foreign Marriage (Amendment) Act 1988.

15 See *MM v NA* [2020] EWHC 93 (Fam) at [6].

16 [2016] EWCA Civ 17.

15.13 Similarly, in *R v M*,[17] Parker J held that although the Pakistani marriage in question was valid, even though the purported marriage certificate was not valid proof of marriage.

15.14 Issues of foreign law are matters of evidence rather than questions of law for the court. It shall often be necessary to seek expert evidence as to the validity of the marriage in the country it was celebrated. This may be sought from independent counsel with specialism in that area of law and practice, from a lawyer from the named country, or from academics and professors.

Essential validity

15.15 In cases concerning the question of a party's capacity to marry ('the essential validity'), the dual domicile test is applied rather than by *the lex loci celebrationis*. The test has not been enacted into statute and instead is governed by the common law.

15.16 Therefore, the question of whether a spouse has capacity to marry will be determined under the law of the jurisdiction in which they were domiciled prior to the marriage. A marriage shall generally be invalid if either party lacks the capacity to marry the other.[18]

15.17 Capacity is meant in its broadest sense as the lawful right to enter into the marriage. It includes matters such as consent of parents, if so required.[19] Therefore, the essential validation of someone domiciled in England and Wales shall be governed by the Marriage Act 1949 wherever they are married.[20] It follows that marriages where the party concerned is under 16 or marriages within the prohibited degrees of relations shall be void.[21]

15.18 Generally, a marriage shall be invalid when either of the parties lacks, according to the law of his or her ante-nuptial domicile, the capacity to marry the other.[22] Valid consent to a marriage was held to be a matter of essential validity in *Szechter (otherwise Karsov) v Szechter* .[23]

15.19 Such approach has been confirmed and summarised by Munby J in *X City Council v MB, NB and MAB (by his Litigation Friend the Official Solicitor)* :[24]

17 [2011] EWHC 2132.
18 See further Rule 74, *Dicey, Morris & Collins on the Conflict of Laws* 15th Edn (Sweet and Maxwell, 2018), Volume 2, Part 4, Chapter 17, and *Brook v Brook* (1861) 9 HL Cas 193.
19 *Breen v Breen* (1969) 6 DLR (2d) 617 (BC).
20 *A Local Authority v X & Anor (Children)* [2013] EWHC 3274 (Fam) at [8].
21 Marriage Act 1949, ss 1, 2, Sch 1.
22 Rule 74 at *Dicey, Morris & Collins on the Conflict of Laws* 15th Edn (Sweet and Maxwell, 2018), 17R-057.
23 [1971] P 286.
24 [2006] EWHC 168 (Fam).

> '[35] The one thing which in my judgment is quite clear, and has been ever since the decisions of the House of Lords in *Brook v Brook* (1861) 9 HLC 193 and the Court of Appeal in *Sottomayor v De Barros* (1877) 3 PD 1, is that capacity to marry, in contrast with formal validity, is not governed by the *lex loci celebrationis*....The short point is that [B's] incapacity to marry in the eyes of English law means that no marriage entered into by him, either in this country or abroad, will be recognised in English law. And if it is not recognised in English law it will not be recognised by English public authorities.'

15.20 As stated in *Sottomayor v De Barros*[25] 'no country is bound to recognise the laws of a foreign State when they work injustice to its own subjects' (per Cotton LJ at [96]) and 'not every marriage valid according to the law in some friendly foreign state is entitled to recognition in this jurisdiction'.[26]

15.21 There are other cases, however, where the courts have applied an alternative test. Namely: (i) the matrimonial home test which requires the court to question whether the general presumption under the dual domicile rule could be displaced in circumstances where the marriage would be valid in the country in which the spouses intend to establish themselves; or (ii) the real and substantial connection test.

15.22 These alternatives were reviewed by Wall LJ in *City of Westminster City Council v IC*.[27] One example referred to within that judgment was the case of *Lawrence v Lawrence*[28] whereby the court held that:

> 'if the application of the criterion of real and substantial connection results in a marriage being held valid and the application of the dual domicile criterion results in an invalidation...the former should prevail' (per Lincoln J at [115]).

15.23 However, His Lordship noted in *Westminster CC* (above) that no mental or intellectual capacity was involved in *Lawrence* nor in *Perrini v Perrini*[29] and that both cases were therefore 'a very long way from the facts of the instant case'.[30] Similarly, it was held that a marriage between two competent adults in *Vervaeke v Smith*[31] was 'many miles away from a marriage entered into by an English domiciled man who lacks capacity to enter into it, and which, if celebrated in England as an English marriage would be void'.[32]

25 (1874-80) All ER Rep 94.
26 *Westminster City Council v IC* [2008] EWCA Civ 198, per Thorpe LJ at [31].
27 [2008] EWCA Civ 198 at [74]-[90].
28 [1985] Fam 106.
29 [1979] Fam 84.
30 *City of Westminster City Council v IC* [2008] EWCA Civ 198 at [76].
31 [1983] AC 145 at 148.
32 *City of Westminster City Council v IC* [2008] EWCA Civ 198 at [85].

15.24 Where one party to a marriage does not have the capacity to consent to said marriage then this will constitute a forced marriage.[33] Therefore, in such circumstances, public policy plays an important role when looking at validity.[34]

15.25 The court will consider whether 'the marriage is so offensive to the conscience of the English court that it should refuse to recognise and given effect to the proper foreign law. In deciding that question the court will seek to exercise common sense, good manners and a reasonable tolerance'.[35]

15.26 Thorpe LJ said in terms that where one party lacks capacity to marry 'it is simply inconceivable that they would be lawfully married within this jurisdiction [...] The refusal of recognition of the marriage is an essential foundation of that protection'.[36]

15.27 That being said at in *Luton Borough Council v SB & Anor*[37] Hayden J sought not to close the door to situations in which the court may, 'in the interests of justice fairness and respect for different aspects of individual autonomy', exercise their discretion not to make a declaration of non-recognition, although His Lordship considered that 'those circumstances are likely to arise very rarely indeed'.

Sham marriages

15.28 A marriage is defined as a 'sham marriage' under the Immigration and Asylum Act 1999, s.24(5) if –

'(a) either, or both, of the parties to the marriage is not a relevant national,

(b) there is no genuine relationship between the parties to the marriage, an

(c) either, or both, of the parties to the marriage enter into the marriage for one or more of these purposes:

(i) avoiding the effect of one or more provisions of United Kingdom immigration law or the immigration rules;

(ii) enabling a party to the marriage to obtain a right conferred by that law or those rules to reside in the United Kingdom.'

15.29 Sham marriages and their relationship with forced marriage are considered in **Chapter 9**. It has been held that a declaration of non-recognition is

33 *YLA v PM* [2013] EWHC 4020 (COP), *XXC v AA, BB, CC, & DD* [2012] EWHC 2183 (COP) at [30].

34 *City of Westminster Social and Community Services Department v C* [2008] EWCA Civ 198.

35 *Cheni v Cheni* [1965] P. 85 per Sir Simon P.

36 *City of Westminster Social and Community Services Department v C* [2008] EWCA Civ 198 at [32].

37 [2015] EWHC 3534 (Fam) at [52].

also an appropriate remedy for those subjected to a 'sham marriage' as was made clear by Keehan J in *A Local Authority v SY*:[38]

> 'There are also, in my judgment, compelling reasons of public policy why sham 'marriages' are declared non-marriages. It is vital that the message is clearly sent out to those who seek to exploit young and vulnerable adults that the courts will not tolerate such exploitation'.

Marriages in which the petitioner is statute barred from seeking a decree of nullity

15.30 As has been observed in **Chapter 14**, persons may seek for a marriage to be declared invalid in circumstances where they are statute barred from bringing a petition for a decree of nullity where the marriage would otherwise be voidable, e.g. where three years has lapsed since the marriage.[39]

15.31 In *B v I*,[40] Baron J considered the case of a petitioner who was 16 when forced into marriage with an 18-year-old cousin in Bangladesh. By the time the matter came before the court, more than three years had passed, and a decree of nullity was no longer available. Her Ladyship held that the ratio in *P v R (Forced Marriage: Annulment: procedure)*[41] was that the plaintiff should not be exposed to the stigma associated with divorcees in her community. As such, she should not be required to pursue divorce proceedings and accordingly was entitled to a declaration of non-recognition.

PROCEDURE FOR APPLYING FOR DECLARATIONS OF NON-RECOGNITION

15.32 An application for a declaration of non-recognition of a marriage should be made to the Family Division of the High Court. Where the case is being heard within the Court of Protection before a District or Circuit Judge an application will be required to transfer the proceedings to be heard before a High Court Judge. This is because there is no provision contained within the Mental Capacity Act 2005 to make a declaration of non-recognition of a marriage.[42]

15.33 However, it is open to High Court Judges sitting in the Court of Protection to invoke the inherent jurisdiction to make a declaration of non-recognition.[43] In *A local authority v DL*[44] the Court of Appeal confirmed that the

38 [2013] All ER (D) 199 (Nov) at [50].
39 See *SH v NB (Marriage: Consent)* [2010] 1 FLR 1927 and *in B v I (Forced Marriage)* [2010] 1 FLR 1721.
40 [2010] 1 FLR 1721.
41 [2003] 1 FLR 661.
42 *A Local Authority v SY* [2013] EWCOP 3485 at [32].
43 *A Local Authority v SY* [2013] EWCOP 3485.
44 [2012] EWCA Civ 253.

inherent jurisdiction to make declarations was not extinguished by the enactment of the Mental Capacity Act 2005:

> '[61] It would have been open to Parliament to include a similar provision, either permitting or restricting the use of the inherent jurisdiction in cases relating to the capacity to make decisions which are not within the MCA 2005. In the absence of any express provision, the clear implication is that if there are matters outside the statutory scheme to which the inherent jurisdiction applies then that jurisdiction continues to be available to continue to act as the 'great safety net'.

15.34 Further, in *XCC v AA and Others*[45] Parker J held that: '...once a matter is before the Court of Protection, the High Court may make orders of its own motion, particularly if such orders are ancillary to, or in support of, orders made on application. Since the inherent jurisdiction of the High Court in relation to adults is an aspect of the *parens patriae* jurisdiction the court has a particularly wide powers to act of its own motion'.

15.35 The above authority also reflects the position that a declaration of non-recognition of a marriage may be made of the court's own motion, a free-standing application is not necessarily required. Her Ladyship also confirmed (at [61]) 'that such declarations are not a welfare or best interests' decision'.

15.36 In circumstances where a declaration is sought in respect of marital/ civil partnership status Form D70 should be used.[46]

15.37 In cases involving a declaration sought as a result of the petitioner having lacked capacity to enter into a marriage, a capacity assessment will be required. This need not be undertaken by a medical practitioner or a psychiatrist and can be undertaken by a qualified social worker. Such approach was encouraged by Keehan J in *A Local Authority v SY*:[47]

> 'I am told by counsel that it is more usual for the assessment of capacity to be undertaken by a medical practitioner or a psychiatrist. The assessment in this case demonstrates that an appropriately qualified social worker is eminently suited to undertake such capacity assessments. I commend the practice which I hope will be followed in appropriate future cases.'

45 [2012] EWHC 2183 (COP) at [85.
46 FPR 2010, PD 5A, para 3.1.
47 [2013] EWHC 3485 (COP) at [22].

Part 3

Criminal law and procedure

CHAPTER 16

Forced marriage offences

Content at a Glance:

INTRODUCTION

16.1 The Anti-Social Behaviour, Crime and Policing Act 2014 created, for the first time, specific offences relating to forced marriage. The statute has effect from 16 June 2014.[1] The first offence under the Act is breach of a Forced Marriage Protection Order made by the Family Court or Family Division of the High Court pursuant to the Family Law Act 1996.

16.2 The second offence under the Anti-Social Behaviour, Crime and Policing Act 2014, s 121 involves the use of violence, threats or coercion for the purpose of forcing another into marriage. This offence also specifically applies to causing a person to marry who lacks capacity to consent to marriage.

16.3 The third offence is under the Anti-Social Behaviour, Crime and Policing Act 2014, s 121(3) which creates the offence of using deception with a view to luring a victim into a forced marriage abroad.

16.4 Thus far, the legislation has led to just a handful of prosecutions. The very low prosecution rate is a matter of concern in the context of many thousands of cases having been referred to the Forced Marriage Unit since the passage of the Anti-Social Behaviour, Crime and Policing Act 2014 and the fact that in

1 SI 2014/949.

2018 alone there were 324 Civil Forced Marriage Protection Orders made by the Family Court.[2]

CHECKLIST

Offences relating to Forced Marriage	**Punishment**	**Legal Principles**
Breach of a Forced Marriage Protection Order.	Up to 5 years imprisonment, a fine or both following conviction on indictment or up to 12 months' imprisonment, a fine or both following summary conviction. Breach of a Forced Marriage Protection Order is also contempt of court which can result in a custodial sentence of up to 2 years. If a person has been convicted for a breach of a Forced Marriage Protection Order they may not be punished for contempt of court and vice versa.	Family Law Act 1996, s 63CA
Using violence, threats or coercion for the purpose of forcing another into a marriage. In cases where the person lacks capacity to consent to marriage the offence is capable of being committed by any conduct carried out for the purpose of causing the victim to enter into a marriage, whether or not the conduct amounts to violence, threats or any other form of coercion.	Up to 7 years following trial on indictment, a fine or both or for a period of imprisonment not exceeding 12-months or a fine or both following summary conviction.	Anti-Social Behaviour, Crime and Policing Act 2014, 121(1)
Using deception with a view to luring a victim into a forced marriage abroad.	Up to 7 years following trial on indictment, a fine or both or for a period of imprisonment not exceeding 12 months or a fine or both following summary conviction.	Anti-Social Behaviour, Crime and Policing Act 2014, s 121(3)
Breach of a restraining order made following conviction or acquittal.	Up to 5 years' imprisonment following trial on indictment or 6 months' imprisonment following summary conviction.	Protection from Harassment Act 1997, ss 5, 5A

2 Ministry of Justice, Family Court Statistics Quarterly, England and Wales, Annual 2018 including October to December 2018.

ELEMENTS OF THE BREACH OFFENCE

16.5 The Anti-Social Behaviour, Crime and Policing Act 2014, s 121 inserted s 63CA into the Family Law Act 1996. The provision creates a freestanding offence of breaching a Forced Marriage Protection Order. Prior to the passage of the 2014 act, breach of an order would be punishable as a contempt of court thus limiting the applicable custodial sentence to two years.

16.6 It was always anticipated that the few prosecutions would be brought under the Family Law Act 1996, s 63CA, the Government Impact Assessment of the new offence having recorded that there were very few known breaches of Forced Marriage Protection Orders.[3]

16.7 The Home Affairs Select Committee found in May 2011 found that only one person had been imprisoned for a breach of a Forced Marriage Protection Order.[4] Thus, it is unclear how many, if any prosecutions have been brought under s 63CA.

16.8 The Family Law Act 1996, s 63CA provides that a person is guilty of an offence if they:

(a) Without reasonable excuse;

(b) Do anything they are prohibited from doing by a Forced Marriage Protection Order.

16.9 The Family Law Act 1996, s 63CA(3) and (4) provide if a person is convicted under the Anti-Social Behaviour, Crime and Policing Act 2014 for a breach they may not also be punished for contempt of court; conversely if somebody is held in contempt for a breach they may not also be convicted for the offence.

16.10 An offence under s 63CA is punishable by up to five years' imprisonment, a fine or both following conviction on indictment or up to 12 months' imprisonment, a fine or both following summary conviction.

OFFENCE OF FORCED MARRIAGE

16.11 The Anti-Social Behaviour, Crime and Policing Act 2014, s 121(1) created the first specific forced marriage offence in English legal history. A person commits an offence if he or she:

3 Impact Assessment, Criminalising breaches of Forced Marriage Protection Orders, Home Office, December 2011.

4 Forced Marriage, Home Affairs Select Committee, Eighth Report, Session 2010-2011, 17 May 2011.

(a) uses violence, threats or any other form of coercion for the purpose of causing another person to enter into a marriage; and

(b) believes, or ought reasonably to believe, that the conduct may cause the other person to enter into the marriage without free and full consent.

16.12 It is irrelevant whether the violence, threats or other form of coercion is directed towards the victim or any other person.

16.13 The Anti-Social Behaviour, Crime and Policing Act 2014, s 121(2) extends the scope of the offence in relation to those lacking capacity to consent to marry. If the victim lacks capacity to marry, then any conduct carried out for the purpose of causing the victim to marry shall amount to an offence. Thus, for causes involving victims who lack capacity to marry, threats, violence or coercion is not required.

16.14 The Mental Capacity Act 2005 applies when determining whether the victim lacks capacity for the purposes of the offence. As such, there is a statutory presumption that someone has capacity unless it is shown on the balance of probabilities that they do not.

16.15 It is likely that prosecutions brought in reliance of the Anti-Social Behaviour, Crime and Policing Act 2014, s 121(2) shall face arguments that the defendant was unaware of any lack of capacity and that the *mens rea* of the offence is not made out.

16.16 Marriage for the purposes of the offence is defined as any religious or ceremony of marriage whether or not that ceremony is legally binding.[5]

DECEPTION OFFENCE

16.17 Under the Anti-Social Behaviour, Crime and Policing Act 2014, s 121(3), a person commits an offence if he or she:

(a) practises any form of deception with the intention of causing another person to leave the United Kingdom; and

(b) intends the other person to be subjected to conduct outside the UK that is an offence under s 121(1) or would be an offence under that provision if the victim were in England or Wales.

16.18 The offence requires that the defendant performs a form of deception but does not require that anyone is successfully deceived. The offence could therefore be fairly characterised as a conduct crime.

5 Anti-Social Behaviour, Crime and Policing Act 2014, s 121(4).

16.19 The deceptive conduct must be directed at causing the victim to leave the United Kingdom. It matters not whether the person the defendant seeks to deceive is the victim or another person, but the deception must be with the intent that there will be a forced marriage abroad.

EXTRATERRITORIALITY

16.20 The Anti-Social Behaviour, Crime and Policing Act 2014, s 121(7) and (8) give extraterritorial effect to the offences under s 121(1) and (3). Subsection 121(7) provides that the offences shall be extraterritorial when any of the following apply:

(a) The person committing the offence or the victim or both of them are in England; or Wales;

(b) At least one of the victim or offender are habitually resident in England and Wales; or

(c) At least one of the victim or offender are a UK national.

16.21 The Anti-Social Behaviour, Crime and Policing Act 2014, s 121(8) defines a UK national as:

(a) A British Citizen, British Overseas Territories citizen, a British National (Overseas) or a British Overseas citizen;

(b) A person who under the British Nationality Act 1981 is a British subject; or

(c) A British protected person within the meaning of that Act.

ANONYMITY

16.22 The Policing and Crime Act 2017, s 173 provides lifelong anonymity for victims of forced marriage. The provision applies from the time an allegation is first made of forced marriage. Thereafter, the publication or broadcast of any information likely to result in the identification to members of the public shall amount to an offence punishable by a fine.

16.23 It is a defence to show that the defendant was not aware and did not suspect that the publication included a matter likely to lead members of the public to identify the victim or that an allegation of forced marriage had been made.[6]

16.24 A defendant shall also not be guilty of the offence if they are able to show that the victim had given written consent to the publication of material

6 Policing and Crime Act 2017, Sch 6A, para 3(2).

likely to identify them.[7] However, the defence shall not apply if the victim was under the age of 16 at the time consent was given or a person unreasonable interfered with their peace and comfort with a view to obtaining consent.[8]

SENTENCING

Offences under the Anti-Social Behaviour, Crime and Policing Act 2014, s 121

16.25 Both offences under the Anti-Social Behaviour, Crime and Policing Act 2014, s 121 of the Act are either way offences.

16.26 The maximum penalty for the offences of forced marriage under the Anti-Social Behaviour, Crime and Policing Act 2014, s 121 following trial on indictment is seven years' imprisonment or a fine or both. Following summary conviction, the maximum penalty is a term of imprisonment not exceeding 12 months[9] or a fine, or both.[10]

16.27 There are no specific sentencing guidelines for forced marriage. There have only been a handful of convictions under the Act leading to a lack of relevant appellate case law. In *R v Kayani*,[11] the Court of Appeal suggested that two years' imprisonment would be an utterly inadequate punishment for a child abduction perpetrated for the purposes of forced marriage.

16.28 The widely reported convictions that have occurred provide some guidance. In January 2020, a sentence of four years was imposed on a man who attempted to force his niece into marriage, having imprisoned her for a period a years in Pakistan.[12]

16.29 In 2015 following the first forced marriage conviction, a man was sentenced to four years imprisonment for forced marriage to run concurrently with a twelve-year sentence for rape.[13]

16.30 In 2018, a mother was sentenced to four and a half years' imprisonment for taking her daughter to Pakistan on what she told her was a family holiday, only to subsequently force her into marriage.[14]

7 Policing and Crime Act 2017, Sch 6A, para 3(3).
8 Policing and Crime Act 2017, Sch 6A, para 3(4).
9 Unless the offence was committed before the commencement of Criminal Justice Act 2003, s 154(1) in which case the maximum term of imprisonment is six months by virtue of Anti-Social Behaviour, Crime and Policing Act 2014, s 121(10).
10 Anti-Social Behaviour, Crime and Policing Act 2014, s 121(9).
11 [2011] EWCA Crim 2871.
12 Birmingham Crown Court, unreported, 24 January 2020.
13 Merthyr Tydfil Crown Court, unreported, 11 June 2015.
14 Birmingham Crown Court, unreported, 23 May 2018.

16.31 Finally, in July 2018, HHJ Simon Phillips QC sentenced a couple who had tricked their daughter into travelling to Bangladesh with the intention of forcing her into a marriage with her cousin. The father was sentenced to four and half years' imprisonment whilst the mother was sentenced to three and a half years in custody.[15]

16.32 It appears, therefore that those convicted of an offence under the Anti-Social Behaviour, Crime and Policing Act 2014, s 121 are likely to face custodial sentences in excess of four years.

16.33 The Sentencing Council's Guidelines on domestic abuse are likely to be of assistance. The guideline specifically cites the Government's definition of domestic abuse which includes forced marriage and other forms of honour-based violence as a 'useful but not statutory definition.'[16]

16.34 The guideline sets out the following principles:

(a) The domestic and familial context of offending behaviour makes the offending more serious because it represents a violation of the trust and security that normally exists between people in an intimate of family relationship and there may be an ongoing threat to the victim's safety;

(b) Domestic abuse is rarely a one-off incident and is the cumulative and it is the interlinked physical, psychological, sexual, emotional or financial abuse which has a particularly damaging effect on victims;

(c) The victim withdrawing from the prosecution does not indicate a lack of seriousness and no inference should be made from the lack of involvement of a victim in a case.

16.35 The guideline lists a number of aggravating and mitigating factors which are likely to heavily influence sentence in a forced marriage case. It also states that a sentence imposed for an offence committed in a domestic context should be determined by the seriousness of the offence, not by any expressed wishes of the victim.

16.36 The guidance states that there are a number of reasons why it may be particularly important that this principle is observed within this context:

(a) The court is sentencing on behalf of the wider public;

(b) No victim is responsible for the sentence imposed;

(c) There is a risk that a plea for mercy made by a victim will be induced by threats made by, or by a fear of, the offender; and

(d) The risk such threats will be increased if it is generally believed that the severity of the sentence may be affected by the wishes of the victim.

15 Leeds Crown Court, Indictment number T20197741, unreported, 30 July 2018.
16 Sentencing Council, Overarching Principles: Domestic Abuse, Definitive Guideline, 2018.

16.37 The guidelines also make clear that the interests of any children affected by the sentence to be imposed must be considered in the context of the likely effect on them should any further incidents of domestic abuse occur. In any event, the guideline is clear that the primary determining factor for sentence ought to be the seriousness of the offence.

16.38 Finally, the guidelines make clear that offences involving serious violence or where the emotional or psychological harm to the victim is severe will warrant a custodial sentence in the majority of cases.

Offences under the Family Law Act 1996, s 63CA

16.39 There are no specific sentencing guidelines or reported sentencing cases to provide guidance on the likely sentencing range. However, it is highly likely that the court would be guided by the Sentencing Council's definitive guidance on breach offences.[17] In particular, the guidance on breach of a protective order.

16.40 The guidance adopts the usual two stage test for assessing the seriousness of an offence, firstly the culpability of the offender and secondly the harm caused by the offence. The sentencing range is stated as a fine for the least serious of breaches up to one-four years' custody for the most serious. The guidance also lists a series of aggravating and mitigating factors practitioners ought to be aware of.

RESTRAINING ORDER

On conviction

16.41 The Protection from Harassment Act 1997, s 5 provides that where an offender is convicted of any offence, the court may make a restraining order for the purpose of protecting the victim or any other persons from harassment or conduct that will cause a fear of violence.

16.42 Orders can be made on application or on the court's own initiative. The Sentencing Council's definitive guidance on domestic abuse[18] states that whilst the court ought to consider the views of the victim, their consent is not required for the making of a restraining order.

16.43 The terms of the order may prohibit the offender from doing anything for the purpose of protecting the victim or other persons mentioned in the order from harassment or conduct which will cause a fear of violence. The order can be imposed for a specified period or until further order of the court. Prosecutors and courts shall need to carefully consider the appropriateness or necessity of making

17 Sentencing Council, Breach of Offences, Definitive Guidelines, 2018.
18 Sentencing Council, Overarching Principles: Domestic Abuse, Definitive Guideline, 2018.

or applying for restraining orders where Forced Marriage Protection Orders are already in place.

16.44 The law of evidence applicable to applications for restraining orders on conviction is the civil as opposed to criminal rules. Accordingly, parties are entitled to lead evidence which would be admissible in an application for a civil injunction.

16.45 Breach of a restraining order made under the Protection from Harassment Act 1997, s 5 is a freestanding offence. A maximum sentence of five years' imprisonment follows conviction on indictment or six months' imprisonment following summary conviction.[19]

On acquittal

16.46 The Protection from Harassment Act 1997, s 5A empowers the court to make a restraining order on acquittal if it considers it necessary to do so to protect a person form harassment by the defendant. The provisions of sub-s 5(3)–(7) apply to orders made under s 5A.

16.47 As such, orders may be for a specified period or until further notice and breach of A party may apply to have an order under either the Protection from Harassment Act 1997, s 5 or 5A to be discharged or varied. The provisions relating to breach offences are identical for ss 5 and 5A.

19 Protection from Harassment Act 1997, s 5(6).

CHAPTER 17

Human trafficking and modern slavery offences

Content at a Glance:

INTRODUCTION

17.1 The International Labour Organisation classifies forced marriage as a form of modern slavery.[1] Indeed, of the 40.3 million people estimated to be enslaved around the world, 15.4 million are in forced marriages. In 2016, the United Nations Office on Drugs and Crime estimated that 1.4 per cent of human trafficking victims globally were trafficked for the purposes of forced marriage.[2]

17.2 Human trafficking for the purposes of forced marriage takes a number of different guises. These are considered further at **Chapter 9**. A common form of human trafficking is the moving of vulnerable victims to other jurisdictions, predominantly in South Asia, to be married against their will. The National Crime Agency also identified European women being trafficked to the United Kingdom to marry Asian men not otherwise entitled to live in the United Kingdom as a form of human trafficking for forced marriage purposes.[3]

17.3 Article 3 of the UN's Palermo Protocol[4] defines human trafficking thus:

1 International Labour Organisation, Global Estimates of Modern Slavery, Geneva 2017.
2 United Nations Office on Drugs and Crime, Global Report on Trafficking in Persons, 2016.
3 The National Crime Agency, the Nature and Scale of Human Trafficking in 2014.
4 UN General Assembly, *Protocol to Prevent, Suppress and Punish Trafficking in Persons, Especially Women and Children, Supplementing the United Nations Convention against Transnational Organized Crime*, 15 November 2000.

'Trafficking in persons shall mean the recruitment, transportation, transfer, harbouring or receipt of persons, by means of the threat or use of force or other forms of coercion, of abduction, of fraud, of deception, of abuse of power or of a position of vulnerability or of the giving or receiving of payments or benefits to achieve the consent of a person having control of another person, for the purpose of exploitation. Exploitation shall include, at a minimum, the exploitation of the prostitution of others or other forms of sexual exploitation, forced labour or services, slavery or practices similar to slavery, servitude or removal of organs[5].'

17.4 Modern slavery is defined by the UK Government 'as the recruitment, movement, harbouring or receiving of children, women or men through the use of force, coercion, abuse of vulnerability, deception or other means for the purpose of exploitation.'[6]

17.5 The Modern Slavery Act 2015 created specific criminal offences of human trafficking and modern slavery. In light of the strong overlap between forced marriage, modern slavery and human trafficking and the need to disrupt multinational networks which support and facilitate forced marriages, practitioners and authorities ought to be mindful of whether investigations or prosecutions for offences under the 2015 are necessary following the discovery of individual forced marriage cases.

CHECKLIST

Key Provisions		
Other offences related to forced marriage	**Punishment**	**Legal principles**
To hold another person in slavery or servitude and in the circumstances the person knows or ought to know that the other person is held in slavery or servitude	The maximum penalty is life imprisonment or a fine, or both following trial on indictment, or 12 months' imprisonment, an unlimited fine or both following summary conviction.	Modern Slavery Act 2015, s 1(1)(a)
To require another person to perform forced or compulsory labour and the circumstances are such that the person knows or ought to know that the other person is being required to perform forced or compulsory labour.	The maximum penalty is life imprisonment or a fine, or both following trial on indictment, or 12 months' imprisonment, an unlimited fine or both following summary conviction.	Modern Slavery Act 2015, s 1(1)(b)

5 UN Protocol to Prevent, Suppress and punish Trafficking in Persons Especially Women and Children supplementing the United Nations Convention against Transnational Organized Crime.

6 Such & Salway Modern Slavery and Public Health, Research and Analysis, HMG, December 2017.

Key Provisions		
Other offences related to forced marriage	**Punishment**	**Legal principles**
To arrange or facilitate the travel of another person ('V') with a view to that person being exploited. Irrespective of whether V is an adult or a child. It is irrelevant whether V consents to the travel. This includes arranging and facilitating V's travel by recruiting, transporting, transferring, harbouring, receiving or transferring or exchanging control over V.	The maximum penalty is life imprisonment following trial on indictment, or six months' imprisonment, or an unlimited fine following summary conviction.	Modern Slavery Act 2015, s 2
Any offence committed with intent to commit an offence of Human Trafficking under Modern Slavery Act 2015, s 2 shall be a further offence.	Up to 10 years' imprisonment following trial on indictment, or up to 12 months' imprisonment, a fine or both following summary conviction. Where the offence under s 4 is committed by kidnapping or false imprisonment, a person guilty of that offence is liable, on conviction on indictment, to imprisonment for life.	Modern Slavery Act 2015, s 4
Breach of a Slavery and Trafficking Prevention Order	Up to five years' imprisonment	Modern Slavery Act 2015, ss 14–22
Breach of a Slavery and Trafficking Risk Order	Up to five years' imprisonment	Modern Slavery Act 2015, s 23

MODERN SLAVERY OFFENCES

17.6 The United Kingdom falls under an international law obligation to criminalise forced marriage through the International Labour Organisation's Conventions on Forced Labour. The state, and all emanations of it, also fall under a positive obligation to safeguard citizens' rights under Article 4 of the European Convention on Human Rights,[7] which provides that no one shall be held in slavery or required to perform forced or compulsory labour. These duties were initially discharged through the Coroners and Justice Act 2009, s 71 which created an offence of holding someone in slavery or servitude or requiring them to perform forced or compulsory labour. In 2015, s 71 was repealed and replaced with the Modern Slavery Act 2015, s 1.

7 Council of Europe, European Convention for the Protection of Human Rights and Fundamental Freedoms, 4 November 1950.

17.7 The Modern Slavery Act 2015, s 1 provides two separate offences. A person commits an offence under s 1(1)(a) if they hold another person in slavery or servitude and the circumstances are such that the person knows or ought to know that the other person is held in slavery or servitude.

17.8 An offence under s 1(1)(b) is committed where a person requires another person to perform forced or compulsory labour and the circumstances are such that the person knows or ought to know that the other person is being required to perform forced or compulsory labour.

17.9 The Modern Slavery Act 2015, s 1(2) states that references to holding a person in slavery or servitude or to a person being required to perform forced or compulsory labour are to be construed in accordance with Article 4 of the European Convention on Human Rights.[8]

17.10 In *Siliadin v France*,[9] the European Court of Human Rights described forced or compulsory labour as 'all work or service which is extracted from any person under the menace of any penalty and for which the person has not offered himself voluntarily'. This definition is largely derived from ILO Convention No 29.[10]

17.11 In *Rantsev v Cyprus and Russia*,[11] the Strasbourg Court held 'for forced or compulsory labour to arise... there must be some physical or mental constraint, as well as some overriding of the person's will'.

17.12 The Modern Slavery Act 2015, s 1(3) states that when determining whether a person is being held in slavery or servitude or required to perform forced or compulsory labour, regard may be had to all the circumstances.

17.13 In *R v Rooney*,[12] the Court of Appeal held that a jury ought to consider all the circumstances of a case when determining whether the elements have been proved.

17.14 The Modern Slavery Act 2015, s 1(4) states that regard may be had to any personal circumstances such as being a child, family relationships and mental and physical illnesses which make the person concerned more vulnerable.

17.15 Section 1(4)(b) states that the court may have regard to any work or services provided by the person, including work or services provided in circumstances which constitute exploitation within the meaning s 3(3)–(6).

8 Council of Europe, European Convention for the Protection of Human Rights and Fundamental Freedoms, 4 November 1950.
9 43 EHRR 16.
10 International Labour Organization (ILO), Convention Concerning Forced or Compulsory Labour, 28 June 1930.
11 (2010) 51 EHRR 1(1).
12 [2019] EWCA Crim 681.

17.16 The Modern Slavery Act 2015, s 1(5) provides that the consent of a person, whether adult or child to any of the acts alleged to constitute holding the person in slavery or servitude or requiring the person to perform forced or compulsory labour does not preclude a determination that the person is being held in slavery or servitude or being forced to perform forced or compulsory labour.

Sentencing

17.17 Offences under the Modern Slavery Act 2015, s 1 are triable either way. Following conviction on indictment, the maximum penalty is life imprisonment or a fine or both. Following summary conviction, the maximum sentence is twelve months imprisonment, an unlimited fine or both.[13]

17.18 Much of the case law regarding sentencing comes from the old law under the Coroners and Justice Act 2009, s 71. This has the obvious limitation that the maximum sentence was 14 years whereas the Modern Slavery Act 2015 provides for a maximum sentence on indictment of life imprisonment.

17.19 However, some assistance can be derived from *A-G's Ref (Nos 2, 3, 4 and 5 of 2013) (Connors)*.[14] The Court of Appeal held that slavery was the most serious offence followed by servitude and that forced or compulsory labour were the least serious offences.

17.20 It does not however follow that a sentence in a case of forced labour shall be lower than that for servitude or slavery. The Court of Appeal identified a host of relevant considerations including the nature and degree of the deception or coercion involved in the case, the conditions of work, the level of exploitation, the methods of control over workers, the extent of the organisation and the Defendant's role in it and the vulnerability of the victims and harm suffered by them.

HUMAN TRAFFICKING OFFENCES

17.21 The Modern Slavery Act 2015 creates an offence of Human Trafficking. The language of the Act was designed to adopt the principles of the Palermo Protocol.[15]

17.22 The Modern Slavery Act 2015, s 2 provides that a person commits an offence if he arranges or facilitates the travel of another person ('V') with a view to V being exploited. Irrespective of whether V is an adult or a child, it is irrelevant whether V consents to the travel.

13 Modern Slavery Act 2015, s 5(1).
14 [2013] EWCA Crim 234.
15 International Labour Organization (ILO), Convention Concerning Forced or Compulsory Labour, 28 June 1930.

17.23 The Modern Slavery Act 2015, s 2(3) states that a person may in particular arrange or facilitate V's travel by recruiting, transporting, transferring, harbouring, receiving or transferring or exchanging control over V.

17.24 The Modern Slavery Act 2015, s 2(4) sets out the *mens rea* of the offence and provides person arranges or facilitates V's travel with a view to V being exploited only if:

(a) The person intends to exploit V in any part of the world during or after the travel; or

(b) The person knows or ought to know that another person is likely to exploit V in any part of the work during or after the travel.

17.25 The word 'travel' is defined by the Modern Slavery Act 2015, s 2(5) as meaning arriving in or entering any country, departing from any country or travelling within any country.

17.26 It follows that it is possible to commit an offence of human trafficking through internal, domestic travelling. It is unclear on the face of the act what distance or extent of travel is required. However, in *R v Ali (Yasir)*,[16] Fulford LJ held:

> 'in our view the key factor in the present context is that travel – a journey – is contemplated and the fact that it may be short does not affect whether or not the offence is committed'.

17.27 Thus, it appears that even relatively short, local journeys can give rise to an offence under the Modern Slavery Act 2015, s 2 of the Act.

17.28 Sub-sections 2(6) and (7) function to give the offence extraterritorial effect. A person who is a UK national commits an offence regardless of whether the arranging, facilitating or travel takes place. A person who is not a UK national commits an offence under s 2 if any part of the arranging or facilitating takes place in the UK or the travel consists of arrival into, departure from or travel within the UK.

17.29 The term 'exploited' is comprehensively defined in the Modern Slavery Act 2015, s 3 insofar as it applies to s 2. A person is exploited only if one of the following apply:

(a) The person is the victim of behaviour which involves the commission of an offence under the Modern Slavery Act 2015, s 1 or which would involve the commission of such an offence if it took place in England and Wales;

(b) Something is done to or in respect of the person which involves the commission of an offence under the Protection of Children Act 1978, s 1(1)

16 [2015 EWCA Crim 1279.

(a) or the Sexual Offences Act 2003, Part 1 or would involve the commission of such an offence if it were done in England and Wales;

(c) The person is encouraged, required or expected to do anything which involves the commission of an offence under the Human Tissue Act 2004, s 32 or 33 or which would involve the commission of such an offence if it were done in England and Wales;

(d) The person is subjected to force, threats or deception designed to induce him or her to provide services of any kind, to provide another person with benefits of any kind or to enable another person to acquire benefits of any kind; or

(e) Another person uses or attempts to use the person for any of the purposes in (d) having chosen them for that purpose on the grounds that he or she is a child, mentally or physically ill or disabled or has a family relationship with a particular person and; an adult or person without the illness, disability or family relationship would be likely to refuse for that purpose.

Sentencing

17.30 The Modern Slavery Act 2015, s 2 creates an either way offence. The maximum sentence for an offence under s 2 on indictment is life imprisonment; on summary conviction, the maximum sentence is six months imprisonment and/ or an unlimited fine.[17]

17.31 In *R v Zielinski*,[18] the defendant had lured Polish nationals to the United Kingdom with promises of work. On arrival, the victims were housed in appalling conditions, subject to violence and only given a fraction of the wages they earnt. The defendant's sentence of four years was considered by the Court of Appeal to be unduly lenient and was increased to seven years.

17.32 In a different context in *R v Mohammed (Zakaria)*,[19] the defendant was sentenced for five offence of human trafficking and four offences of supplying drugs. The 21-year-old defendant had been running a 'county lines' drug dealing operation. He exploited children in furtherance of his drug dealing leading to the human trafficking conviction. The defendant appealed against consecutive sentences of eight years and six years. The Court of Appeal reduced the sentence to twelve years in total, comprising of consecutive sentences of seven years for the human trafficking offences and five years for the drug offences. The court identified (at [37]) the following sentencing considerations:

(a) Where the person whose travel was arranged with a view to exploitation was a child, the offence inevitably would be more serious than where the person was an adult;

17 Modern Slavery Act 2015, s 5(1).
18 [2017] EWCA Civ 758.
19 [2019] EWCA Crim 1881.

(b) Where the exploitation involved the commission of serious criminal offences, the exploitation offence would be especially grave;

(c) The number of children whose travel was facilitated or arranges would be of importance;

(d) The offence would be aggravated if the same child was the subject of travel with a view to exploitation more than once.

ASSOCIATED OFFENCES

17.33 Aside from an offence under the Accessories and Abettors Act 1861, s 8 in relation to the Modern Slavery Act 2015, s 2, any offence committed with intent to commit an offence of Human Trafficking under section 2 shall be a further offence under s 4. An example may include forging a passport to remove the person to be trafficked from the jurisdiction or fraudulently paying for flights, etc with the victim's money.

17.34 The Modern Slavery Act 2015, Part 2 creates two forms of injunctive civil orders. The first, created by ss 14–22, is a Slavery and Trafficking Prevention Order ('STPO'). It is open to the court to make a STPO where a defendant has:

(a) Been convicted for a slavery or human trafficking offence;

(b) Been found not guilty of slavery or human trafficking offence by way of insanity; or

(c) Been found to be under a disability and has done the act charged against the defendant in respect of a slavery or human trafficking offence.

17.35 The court may only make a STPO where it is satisfied that there is a risk that the defendant may commit a slavery or human trafficking offence; and it is necessary to make the order to protect persons generally or particular persons from the physical or psychological harm which would be likely to occur if the defendant committed such an offence.

17.36 Slavery and Trafficking Offences for the purpose of STPOs are listed in the Modern Slavery Act 2015, Sch 1 and include various offences created by eight separate statutes. Surprisingly, forced marriage and breach of a Forced Marriage Protection Order are not offences listed within Sch 1.

17.37 An STPO may be made either on conviction as part of the sentencing exercise or on application under s 15 to a magistrates' court by the Police, National Crime Agency or an Immigration Officer.

17.38 In making an order on application, the court must first be satisfied that the defendant is a relevant offender and since he was convicted of the relevant offences, has acted in a way which means that there is a risk the defendant may commit a slavery and human trafficking offence.

17.39 Secondly, the court must be satisfied that it is necessary to make the order for the purposes of protecting persons generally, or particular persons, from the physical or psychological harm which would be likely to occur if the defendant committed such an offence.

17.40 A relevant offender is a person convicted, cautioned for or found not guilty by reason of insanity of an offence of slavery or human trafficking as defined by Modern Slavery Act 2015, Sch 1. Alternatively, the defendant must have been convicted, cautioned for or found to have committed an equivalent offence

17.41 An order may make any term the court considers necessary for the purpose of protecting persons generally, or particular persons from the physical or psychological harm which would be likely to occur if the defendant committed a slavery or human trafficking offence.

17.42 A STPO may have effect for a fixed period of at least five years or until further order of the court. Individual provisions can last for longer or shorter periods than the rest of the order. Prohibitions on foreign travel, which may consist of a requirement for the defendant to surrender their passports, may last for a fixed period of not more than five years.

17.43 Breach of a STPO is punishable with up to five years' imprisonment.

CIVIL ORDERS

17.44 The Modern Slavery Act 2015, s 23 creates Slavery and Trafficking Risk Orders ('STRO'). These orders may be applied for by a chief officer of police, an immigration officer or the director general of the National Crime Agency. These orders do not require a conviction, but it is required that the court is satisfied:

(a) The defendant has acted in a way which means that there is a risk that the they shall commit a slavery or human trafficking offence listed in the Modern Slavery Act 2015, Sch 1; and

(b) It is necessary to make the order for the purpose of protecting persons generally, or particular persons, from the physical or psychological harm which would be likely to occur if the defendant committed such an offence.

17.45 STROs may prohibit a defendant from doing anything necessary to protect others from physical or psychological harm likely to occur. Orders may last for a fixed period of at least two years or until further order. Prohibitions on foreign travel may only last up to five years.

17.46 The Modern Slavery Act 2015, s 28 allows Slavery and Trafficking Risk Orders to be made on an interim basis.

17.47 Breach of a STRO is punishable with up to five years' imprisonment.

CHAPTER 18

Interplay with related proceedings

Content at a Glance:

Introduction

Disclosure to the police

Effect of a criminal conviction in civil or family proceedings

Disclosure of police material

INTRODUCTION

18.1 It is a matter of concern that despite hundreds of forced marriage protection orders being made each year and thousands of referrals to the Forced Marriage Unit, there has been only a handful of convictions for Forced Marriage Offences.[1]

18.2 An obvious way to significantly improve the conviction rate is to ensure effective partnership working on a multi-agency, cross-jurisdictional basis. Often local authorities shall be the first agencies to become aware of forced marriage situations. If the forced marriage involves a child and may consider the commission of a criminal offence, the Authority is obliged to inform the police.[2] Similarly, if the police become aware of an incident a child is involved, they must inform the responsible local authority.

18.3 The Related Family and Criminal Proceedings Guide produced by the Law Society[3] is an invaluable resource, commended by both the President of the Family Division and the President of the Queen's Bench Division.

18.4 Given that forced marriage falls under the Government definition of domestic abuse, practitioners ought also to be aware of the terms of the 2013 Protocol which relates to disclosure of information in cases of alleged child abuse.[4] The Protocol relates to inter-agency cooperation and cross jurisdictional disclosure in cases involving child abuse. The provisions in respect of disclosure

1 Ministry of Justice, Family Court Statistics Quarterly, England and Wales, Annual 2018 including October to December 2018.
2 HM Government, Working Together, to Safeguard Children Guidelines, July 2018.
3 Related Family and Criminal Proceedings, A Good Practice Guide, 2007.
4 2013 Protocol and Good Practice Model, Disclosure of information in cases of alleged child abuse and linked criminal and care directions hearings, October 2013.

of material from private proceedings and material from proceedings relating to children is considered in detail at **Chapter 12**.

DISCLOSURE TO THE POLICE

18.5 Upon the making of a forced marriage protection order, whether interim or final, a copy must be lodged with the police.[5] HM Courts and Tribunal Service guidance states that a statement should also be lodged with the police confirming that the respondents have been served with the Order and are aware of its terms.[6]

18.6 There used to be a central email hub for service of orders managed by Norfolk Police. Despite still appearing on many Court Forms and Guidance Documents, this email address no longer works, and the central hub no longer appears to operate. Thus, it appears that applicants ought to serve Orders on the local police force responsible for the area in which the person to be protected lives.

18.7 Police forces shall also be mindful of their positive obligations under Article 3 of the Convention to carry out an effective investigation when put on notice of conduct which may amount to an interference with the Article 3 rights of a citizen.[7] It may well be that service of a Forced Marriage Protection Order and related information from an applicant in a forced marriage case shall activate such a duty.

EFFECT OF A CRIMINAL CONVICTION IN FAMILY OR CIVIL PROCEEDINGS

18.8 The evidential effect of a criminal conviction is governed by the Civil Evidence Act 1968, s 11. The Act provides that:

(a) The fact that a person has been convicted of an offence by a UK Court shall be admissible in evidence for the purpose of proving that he has committed that offence;

(b) Only a subsisting conviction is admissible. In *Re U (Care Proceedings: Criminal Conviction: Refusal to give Evidence)*,[8] it was held that a conviction pending appeal is still "subsisting" for the purposes of s 11;

(c) It shall be taken that the person committed the offence for which they have been convicted unless it is proved to the contrary;

5 FPR 2010, r 11.12(3).
6 HM Courts and Tribunals Service, FL701 Guidance Form.
7 See *DSD v Commissioner of Police for the Metropolis* [2018] UKSC 11.
8 [2006] EWHC 372 (Fam).

(d) In seeking to disprove the conviction, the contents of any document which is admissible as evidence of the conviction and the contents of the information, complaint, indictment or charge sheet upon which the person was convicted shall be admissible into the family proceedings.

(e) Thus, following a conviction in the UK, a person shall be taken to have committed the offence for which they were convicted unless they can prove on the balance of probabilities that they did not commit the offence.

18.9 The Civil Evidence Act 1968, s 11 creates an exception from the general rule established in *Hollington v F Hewthorn & Co*,[9] that the findings of courts, tribunals and inquiries are not admissible in subsequent inquiries. The rationale for the rule is that one tribunal cannot be bound by the decisions made in a previous trial in which different evidence or arguments might have been advanced.

18.10 In the unusual case of *Daley v Bakiyev*,[10] the defendant was the son of the former President of the Kyrgyz Republic. The claimant sought to adduce the defendant's conviction for attempting to kill the claimant as evidence in a case concerning mining rights. Supperstone J held that applying *Hollington*, evidence of foreign convictions were not admissible into English proceedings.

18.11 It follows that foreign convictions for forced marriage, or any related offences are not admissible in applications for forced marriage protection orders or other injunctive orders.

DISCLOSURE OF POLICE MATERIAL

18.12 Evidence adduced in the course of a criminal trial is a matter of public record and can, of course, be relied upon in the court of family, civil or Court of Protection proceedings subject to the ordinary admissibility rules.

18.13 Most police forces have adopted the standard Disclosure Protocol between the Family Court and the police.[11] The protocol sets out the following principles in respect of disclosure form the police into family proceedings, including forced marriage proceedings:

(a) Parties must give very early consideration to what material held by the police might be relevant to the family proceedings. Ideally, requests ought to be made to the police prior to an application being made;

(b) If the police are unable or unwilling to release the information without a court order, it shall be for the requesting party to make the required application for disclosure to the court;

9 [1943] KB 587.
10 [2016] EWHC 1972 (QB).
11 See Law Society, Related Family and Criminal Proceedings Guide, Appendix 2.

(c) Not less than ten days before a hearing in which an application is to be made directing police disclosure, solicitors for the party requesting disclosure shall sent a written request to the Police setting out specified details of the information required;

(d) Not less than five working days before the relevant hearing, the party requesting disclosure shall obtain a response from the police setting out what information is available, timescales for information being provided, the police's views on the proposed disclosure order, the availability of any officer who may be required to give evidence and other specified information;

(e) At the disclosure hearing, the court shall consider the necessity and relevance of the information required, the wording of the proposed direction, the timescales of the disclosure and whether preparation of the order ought to be expedited.

(f) The solicitor securing the direction for disclosure shall inform the police within 24 hours of the hearing of the terms of the order made and serve the order within two days of the hearing on the police.

CHAPTER 19

Role of law enforcement organisations

Content at a Glance:

INTRODUCTION

19.1 Forced marriage is a form of criminality which cuts across the roles of many statutory bodies, agencies and organisations. From the significant differences in the number of Forced Marriage Protection Orders granted, the number of referrals to the Forced Marriage Unit and the number of prosecutions, it appears that public bodies are adopting siloed approaches to forced marriage. The government estimates that many cases of forced marriage go unreported.[1] There has been considerable statutory guidance given to try to increase detection rates of forced marriage.

19.2 The purpose of this chapter is to examine the active role that various bodies can and should play in preventing, deterring and punishing forced marriages. As shall be seen below, much of the guidance is rightly concerned with protective measures and ensuring victim's safety. Regrettably this appears to have led to a culture where prosecutions and convictions are not prioritised or very often pursued.

POLICE AND CPS

19.3 The National Police Chiefs' Council has developed a national strategy for combating forced marriage and other forms of honour- based Abuse.[2] The

1 HM Government, The Right to Choose: Multi-agency statutory guidance for dealing with forced marriage, 2014, p 5.

2 NPCC, Honour Based Abuse, Forced Marriage and Female Genital Mutilation: a Policing Strategy for England, Wales & Northern Ireland, 2015.

policy sets out an ambitious aim of the total eradication of honour-based abuse and forced marriage from all communities.

19.4 Sadly, in the years that followed the devising of the policy, only a handful of forced marriage convictions have followed. This very low conviction rate must be considered in the context of between 2014 and 2018, the Metropolitan Police alone receiving 928 reports of forced marriage.[3]

The police – multi-agency guidelines: the protective regime

19.5 Chapter 8 of HM Government, Multi-Agency Guidelines: Handling Cases of Forced Marriage ('the Guidelines)[4] provides the most useful forced marriage specific guidance for police officers. The Guidelines underline that police must have a good understanding of the issues surrounding forced marriages in order to gain the trust of victims. In particular, officers must be aware of the very significant risk of harm faced by victims that seek held. Accordingly, the Guidelines make it clear that cases of forced marriage ought to be handled by specialist officers with specific experience and training in forced marriage.

19.6 Upon being contacted by someone who fears they may be forced into marriage, officers are instructed to follow the general guidance applicable to all professionals as set out in chapters 4 and 5 of the Guidelines.

19.7 Officers should then contact the Forced Marriage Unit for advice, and make any appropriate referrals to support groups or charities that are able to support victims of forced marriage.

19.8 The Guidelines make the obvious point that police officers ought to consider whether specialist communication support is required in cases where the victim is visually impaired, deaf or has learning difficulties. Speech and language therapists, interpreters and communication aids may all need to be considered.

19.9 Officers ought to check police and social services' records for referrals of family members, including siblings. Previous reports of missing persons shall be particularly relevant as the Statutory Guidance refers to how missing persons' reports can be used to co-opt the police into returning potential victims of forced marriage to the family home. Similarly, a broader history of domestic abuse in the family home is likely to be a significant risk indicator. Officers also ought to obtain specific details of any threats, abuse or hostile actions against the victim.

19.10 The Guidelines instruct officers to create a restricted entry in the force intelligence and create a crime report if appropriate.

3 Information Rights Unit, Metropolitan Police, Offences on Crime Records flagged as Forced Marriage, January 2014 to April 2018.

4 HM Government, Multi-Agency Guidelines: Handling Cases of Forced Marriage.

19.11 The Guidelines set out very clearly that the primary consideration is the safety of the victim. Officers should not underestimate the risks that victims may face. Under the Guidelines, victims have a right to be believed and ought to be interviewed in a safe, confidential setting away from the family home.

If foreign travel with family is unavoidable

19.12 Where for some reason, foreign travel with the family becomes unavoidable, officers should take the following steps which are set out in Chapter 5 of the Guidelines[5]:

(a) Provide contact details of the agency and professional handling their case;

(b) Supply the victim or potential victim with the telephone number and email address of the nearest British Embassy or High Commission and encourage them to memorise it;

(c) If a non-British national, encourage the victim to contact the Forced Marriage Unit for details of reliable NGOs overseas and the details of the embassy of their own nationality;

(d) Advise they take a mobile phone that will work overseas and they can keep hidden;

(e) Encourage them to provide the officer with details of a trusted friend or advocate in the UK who they shall be keeping in touch with overseas who can be approached if they do not return. Contact that friend or advocate before the departure and ask them to make a written statement of their support;

(f) Advise them to take emergency cash, in case problems arise in the country of destination, together with contact details of someone there they can trust to help them;

(g) Ascertain whether they are dual nationals, as they may have two passports. Remind them about the implications of dual nationality;

(h) Advise them to contact the Forced Marriage Unit.

19.13 The police ought also to obtain all names and addresses or other geographical information of extended family members in the area the person may be staying. It is good practice to obtain details of a family tree. The Guidance states that National Police Policy also stipulates that in all cases of honour-based violence, including forced marriage, officers should obtain a photograph, fingerprints and a DNA sample from the victim with their consent for the purposes of later identification.

5 HM Government, Multi-Agency Guidelines: Handling Cases of Forced Marriage, p 23.

If someone has been taken overseas for a forced marriage

19.14 The Guidelines refer to situations where on arrival in a foreign country, a victim may have their documents removed from them, they may be drugged or otherwise subject to violent or coercive behaviour.

19.15 In circumstances where it is reported that someone has been taken overseas to be married, the Guidelines stress the importance of discretion and confidentiality when handling such cases and cautions against immediately contacting an overseas police service or organisation due to the risk that the family may move the victim to another location or expedite the forced marriage.

19.16 Instead, the Guidelines suggests a number of steps in addition to the general guidance which can be found in Chapters 4 and 5 of the Guidelines:

(a) If the victim is under 18 years old, make a referral to a Child Protection Officer;

(b) Check existing missing persons' reports;

(c) Obtain details of, and maintain contact with, the third party who reported the situation;

(d) Consider asking an Education Welfare Officer to make careful enquiries;

(e) Use existing national and local protocols for inter-agency liaison e.g. liaison with the National Crime Agency and the Forced Marriage Unit;

(f) Document a risk assessment.

19.17 The third party reporting the situation and the victim should be informed, if possible, that if the victim is a British national who wishes to return to the UK, the Foreign and Commonwealth Office may be able to repatriate the victim.[6] The Foreign Office's obligation to seek to recover the costs of the repatriation should never delay the victim being returned to safety in a forced marriage case.

19.18 Any disclosures made to overseas police services shall need to be very carefully considered. In particular, officers should be careful not to disclose any information that could place the victim at further risk. For example, if a girlfriend or boyfriend in the United Kingdom has made the report, this ought not to be disclosed to the overseas police service.

19.19 If the Forced Marriage Unit requests that officers attend a family's UK address to ask that a victim presents themselves at a British Embassy, officers should not accede to any requests to talk to the victim over the phone.

19.20 The Guidance states that officers always ought to:

6 See further **Chapter 26**.

(a) Ascertain if anyone else is aware of the situation and establish whether enquiries have already been made. Considered whether there evidence to support forced marriage and other abuses;

(b) Dissuade the third party and other agencies involved in the case from making enquiries and acting independently of the police or the Forced Marriage Unit;

(c) Find and document any evidence to confirm the threat of forced marriage and any related criminal offences;

(d) If the third party needs support, refer them to an organisation with a history of assisting in cases of forced marriage and domestic abuse.

19.21 Officers must not do any of the following:

(a) Go directly to the person's family, friends or those with influence within the community, as this will alert them to the enquiries and may place them in further danger. The only exception to this is where, exceptionally, police are requested to visit the family by the Forced Marriage Unit;

(b) Make direct contact with the British Embassy, High Commission or overseas police without first liaising with the Forced Marriage Unit;

(c) Speak to the person on the telephone in order to found out if they are being held against their will. The family may be present threatening them or it may be a different person speaking on the telephone;

(d) Make direct contact with overseas law enforcement agencies without reference to a specialist supervisor experienced in managing such bases and the Forced Marriage Unit.

Where someone has already been forced into marriage

19.22 In circumstances where a forced marriage has already taken place, officers ought to discuss the range of options open to the person and the consequences likely to flow from their choice of action.

19.23 The Guidelines particularly highlight circumstances where a victim of forced marriage may wish to prevent the person they were forcibly married to from coming to the UK on a spousal visa. The Guidelines suggest that it is not likely to be possible for a victim to prevent a successful spousal visa without all parties concerned knowing the reason for not wishing to sponsor a spousal visa.

19.24 Officers ought to take the following steps in addition to the general action set out in chapter 4 of the Guidance[7]:

(a) If the victim is under 18 years old, make a referral to a child protection officer;

7 HM Government, Multi-Agency Guidelines: Handling Cases of Forced Marriage, p 40.

(b) Record full details of the victim together with the details of the marriage including date and place;

(c) Record the name, address and date of birth of the victim's spouse together with the interview dates for their visa (if known);

(d) Refer the victim to appropriate support groups and charities;

(e) Refer the case to the Forced Marriage Unit if there is an overseas dimension to the marriage or there are concerns regarding a potential spousal visa;

(f) Suggest they contact a family panel solicitor;

(g) If they do not want to return to the family home, a strategy for leaving the home ought to be devised, personal safety advice given, and a risk assessment and management strategy should be devised;

(h) If they wish to remain at home, try to safely maintain contact and devise a risk management plan.

Where a victim has come to the UK from overseas

19.25 The Guidelines provide helpful details of what police ought to do where a victim with no previous connection to the UK is forced to marry overseas and then brought to the United Kingdom. Victims are likely to be especially vulnerable; they may not speak good English or be aware of support to which they are entitled.

19.26 Moreover, if the victim does not have indefinite leave to enter, indefinite leave to remain, humanitarian protection, discretionary leave or a right to abode in the UK then they are unlikely to have recourse to public funds. This is likely to lead to tremendous problems in fleeing the marriage. A victim is very unlikely to be able to gain access to a refuge, is ineligible for benefits, is likely to find it incredibly difficult to find alternative accommodation or means to live.

19.27 Victims brought to the United Kingdom following a forced marriage are also less likely to feel able to trust and cooperate with police or other authority figures.

19.28 The Guidelines suggests that having followed the general guidance in chapters 4 and 5 of the Guidelines police officers:

(a) If the victim is under 18 years of age, refer the matter to a Child Protection Officer;

(b) If the victim is over 18 years of age, refer them to the local community safety and domestic abuse unit;

(c) Explain the options available to the person;

(d) If they remain within the home with the perpetrator of the abuse, devise a risk assessment and management strategy;

(e) If they are leaving home, devise a risk assessment and management strategy;

(f) Ensure they are managed in a culturally sensitive way and that their wishes are recognised and respected;

(g) Arrange for the careful selection of an authorised interpreter, considering any preference the victim has in relation to the gender of the victim;

(h) Refer the victim to appropriate support groups and charities and counselling services;

(i) If immigration advice is required, refer them to an appropriate advisor, ideally one which also has family law expertise and legal aid contracts for both family and immigration;

(j) Provide the victim with written contact details of the trained/specialist officer dealing with the case to give to their solicitor together with the crime reference number, if appropriate.

(k) Record any injuries and with consent take a photograph.

(l) Arrange for a medical examination. Inform the doctor that there may be an immigration application and detailed notes will need to be taken during the examination.

(m) Create a restricted entry in the force intelligence system and submit a crime report if applicable (refer to National Crime Reporting Standards & get advice from your Force Crime Registrar if appropriate).

19.29 Officers are specifically instructed not to:

(a) Use a relative, friend, neighbour, child or those with influence in the community as an interpreter;

(b) Use an interpreter from the victim's community or cultural group;

(c) Attempt to give any immigration advice.

The police: investigatory guidance

19.30 The Protocol on the handling of 'So-called' Honour Based Violence'[8] ('the Protocol') provides guidance for the investigation and prosecution of forced marriage offences The Protocol requires that all Police Services and Crown Prosecution Service ('CPS') areas appoint a single point of contact for honour-based violence and forced marriage cases. It also highlights the importance of early consultation between the police and the CPS. It makes clear that only in exceptional cases shall simple cautions be appropriate in cases of forced marriage.

19.31 Police are required under the Protocol to explore the role and behaviour of the suspect in order to ensure a balanced consideration of the accounts provided

8 Protocol on the handling of 'so called' Honour Based Violence/Abuse and Forced Marriage Offences between the National Police Chiefs' Council and the Crown Prosecution Service, 2016.

ensuring that all available evidence is gathered. At paragraph 4.2 of the guidance officers are instructed to give particular consideration to:

(a) How plausible and consistent is the suspect's/defendant's account?

(b) What counter allegations, if any, have been made?

(c) Were there any signs of injury to the suspect upon arrest?

(d) Where there any allegations of non-violent behaviour which fall within the definition of domestic abuse?

(e) Are there any contradictions in the suspect's account?

(f) Has the suspect made no comment during interview for which an adverse inference can be drawn?

19.32 The Protocol makes clear that the safety of victims is paramount. Police should be alert to the risk to the victim, witnesses and family members. Police should establish whether a witness is in fear and inform the prosecutor. Police and prosecutors should discuss what form of protection could be applied for at the pre-charge stage. In very serious cases, witness protection may be necessary.

19.33 Police are required to carry out domestic abuse, stalking and honour-based Violence risk assessments. Officers must ask the victim about the abusers' behaviour and the risk identification process must be ongoing.

19.34 In light of the risk that abusers may remove victims from the United Kingdom to jurisdictions where there is a weak or non-existent police response to forced marriage, police officers should consider an early discussion with the CPS extradition team.

19.35 The protocol requires the police and the CPS to actively consider applying for protective orders. In particular, police ought to consider applying for a Forced Marriage Protection Order from the very start of the investigation.

19.36 Where a decision is taken not to charge, the police must inform the victim, either directly or through an interpreter or independent domestic violence advisor or other appointed person to explain the basis of the decision.

Where a victim withdraws their support for a prosecution

19.37 The Protocol at paragraph 7.3 provides that where 'a victim asks the police not to proceed or withdraws their support for a prosecution the police will take a written statement that will:

(a) explain the reasons for withdrawing support;

(b) set out whether the victim has been pressured to withdraw their complaint by any person; and

(c) confirm whether the victim is pursuing any civil action.'

19.38 The police are also required to provide a report setting out the investigator's view about the case, including the reasons for withdrawal and the impact of the withdrawal impact on the case as a whole. The report should also confirm if the victim is supported by any specialist service, an independent domestic violence advisor or supporter. If the victim is so supported, the report ought to set out the supporter's views on how the victim might react if required to attend court. Finally, the report should asses the risks to victim or any other person's safety and how the victim might react if required to attend court.

19.39 Where it is suspected that the victim has been pressured to withdraw their complaint or is frightened, further police action is required. The police should investigate the matter and consider any support that has been offered. In particular, officers should consider whether the intervention of a specialist service could make a difference. The prosecutor may ask the court to delay hearings to allow these steps to be taken.

Crown Prosecution Service

19.40 The Guidance states that it is a key principle of the regime combatting forced marriage that a victim has a choice whether to take the civil route of being provided with injunctive protection or to pursue a prosecution.

19.41 There is some tension between those overarching government guidelines and the CPS' guidelines on domestic abuse.[9] The CPS guidelines make clear that where the evidence is such that the evidence in a case is such that there is a 'realistic prospect of conviction' and the victim supports a prosecution then it shall be rare that a prosecution for domestic abuse is not deemed in the public interest. In circumstances where a victim does not support a prosecution, then it is still open to the CPS to conclude that it is in the public interest and to pursue a prosecution. The CPS' guidance on honour-based violence and forced marriage[10] states that where there is sufficient evidence to provide a realistic prospect of conviction, it will usually be in the public interest to bring a prosecution.

19.42 Prosecutors are required to actively consider and discuss with the police what protective orders might assist the victim.

19.43 Forced marriage charging decisions not taken by CPS Direct shall need to be made by prosecutors in Rape and Serious Sexual Offence Units. In circumstances where CPS Direct make the charging decision, the police must contact the local rape specialist prosecutor within three working days to make an appointment for a consultation.

9 Crown Prosecution Service, Domestic Abuse Guidelines for Prosecutors, 2020.

10 Crown Prosecution Service, Honour Based Violence and Forced Marriage available at <https://www.cps.gov.uk/publication/honour-based-violence-and-forced-marriage>.

19.44 Prosecutors are required to work closely with the police and specialist agencies to ensure that the best evidence is gathered and presented at trial. The case should have a clear narrative pre-empting and challenging any assumptions and associated myths and stereotypes.

19.45 In the event a victim withdraws their support for a prosecution but maintains the allegations were true, the CPS shall need to carefully consider the feasibility of continuing without the victim's evidence and whether it is in the public interest to do so against the victim's wishes.

19.46 The issuing of a witness summons of the victim is a last resort. Such a step should only be taken following consideration of the specific facts of the case and the impact on the complainant's safety and wellbeing. The use of a witness summons should also be discussed with the victim. Sometimes the issuing of a summons can be a useful tool to allow the victim to demonstrate to their families that they had no choice but to attend court.

19.47 Prosecutors ought to consider the use of expert evidence from those who have an understanding of forced marriage and the specific communities in which they regularly occur.

NATIONAL CRIME AGENCY

19.48 The Modern Slavery Human Trafficking Unit is a division of the National Crime Agency ('NCA'). The NCA leads its own investigations into modern slavery and human trafficking but also advises local police forces, regional organised crime units and international law enforcement on modern slavery and human trafficking investigations and victim care.

19.49 The NCA also leads the UK Protected Persons Service, a service providing protection to people judge to be at risk of serious harm and in need of specialist protection arrangements. This can include victims of crime facing significant threats. In extreme cases of forced marriage, it may be appropriate to seek the assistance of the UK Protected Persons Service.

INTERNATIONAL POLICING AGENCIES

Interpol

19.50 The International Criminal Police Organisation ('Interpol') is an international organisation, founded in 1914, which facilitates worldwide police cooperation and crime control. The role of the organisation is one of administrative liaison amongst law enforcement agencies. For example, in a forced marriage case in which a victim has been taken to Balohistan, Pakistan, a local officer in South Wales is unlikely to know how to effectively contact the local Pakistani police force. Instead, they could contact the Interpol bureaux in Islamabad who would then coordinate between the UK and Pakistani police forces.

19.51 Interpol has a dedicated global taskforce on human trafficking with considerable experience in coordinating operations targeting modern slavery and human trafficking around the world. Interpol coordinated operations have led to the liberation of thousands of modern slavery victims.

Europol

19.52 The European Union Agency for Law Enforcement Cooperation ('Europol') fulfils a similar role of Interpol on a European Union. At the time of writing, it is unclear whether the United Kingdom shall continue to have a formal relationship or partnership with Europol after its exit from the European Union.

19.53 As well as facilitating the cooperation of European law enforcement agencies, Europol also handles criminal intelligence and provides analysis of intelligence and trends in criminality. Europol also provides operational support and expertise to investigations into the trafficking of human beings.

19.54 Of particular value on a policy level is Europol's research and early warning notices which analyse and communicate trends in modern slavery, human trafficking and forced marriage. For example, in 2014, Europol released an Early Warning Notification regarding the rise in the use of human trafficking and forced marriages for immigration purposes across the European Union.

BORDER FORCE AND HOME OFFICE

19.55 Given the cross-jurisdictional nature of forced marriage and the use of forced marriage for immigration purposes, Border Force plays a vital role in the detection and prevention of forced marriage.[11] Regrettably, in 2017, when Border Force was subject to joint inspection by the UK Independent Anti-Slavery Commissioner and Her Majesty's Inspector of Constabulary, there was real concern as to victims of modern slavery being lost at UK borders. The report found significant failings in the organisation and made 12 recommendations for improvement.[12] By the re-inspection later in 2017, significant progress had been made but a number of recommendations remained open or outstanding.[13]

11 See, for example Operation Limelight in 2019.

12 Independent Chief Inspector of Borders and Immigration, an inspection of Border Force's Identification and treatment of potential victims of modern slavery, July to October 2016.

13 A re-inspection of Border Force's identification and treatment of potential victims of modern slavery, September – November 2017.

CHAPTER 20

Other offences arising in forced marriage situations

Content at a Glance:

INTRODUCTION

20.1 Often forced marriages shall involve criminality beyond the specific offences under the Anti-Social Behaviour, Crime and Policing Act 2014. The Crown Prosecution Service ('CPS') Guidance specifically invites prosecutors to consider further offences including the ones considered in this chapter.[1] This chapter shall examine some of offences which may arise in circumstances where a victim is forced to marry.

CHECKLIST

Key Provisions		
Other offences related to forced marriage	**Punishment**	**Legal principles**
Child Abduction:		
A person commits an offence of child abduction if he or she takes or sends the child out of the United Kingdom without appropriate consent.	The maximum penalty is 7 years' imprisonment on indictment, or 6 months' imprisonment and/or an unlimited fine following summary conviction.	Child Abduction Act 1984, s 1

1 Crown Prosecution Service, So-Called Honour-Based Abuse and Forced Marriage: Guidance on Identifying and Flagging cases, September 2019.

Key Provisions		
Other offences related to forced marriage	**Punishment**	**Legal principles**
Child Abduction:		
A person commits an offence if without lawful authority or reasonable excuse he takes or detains a child under the age of 16 to remove him from the: (a) the lawful control of any person having lawful control over the child; or (b) keep him out of the lawful control of any person entitled to lawful control of the child. However, this offence cannot be committed by the mother and father of the child where the parents were married to, or civil partners of each other at the time of birth; The child's mother where the parents were not married to, or civil partners of, each other when the child was born; or: (i) the guardian or special guardian of the child; (ii) a person with custody of the child or (iii) a person named in a child arrangements order as a person with whom the child is to live.	The maximum penalty is 7 years' imprisonment on indictment, or 6 months' imprisonment and/or an unlimited fine following summary conviction.	Child Abduction Act 1984, s 2
Kidnap:		
The nature of the offence is an attack on, and infringement of, the personal liberty of the victim.	The maximum penalty is life imprisonment.	Common law offence.
False imprisonment		
To unlawfully and intentionally or recklessly restrain a victim's freedom of movement from a particular place. The elements of the offence are as follows: (1) The taking or carrying away of one person by another; (2) By force or by fraud; (3) Without the consent of the person so taken or carried away; and (4) Without lawful excuse.	The maximum penalty is life imprisonment.	Common law offence.
Blackmail		
It is an offence for a person to, with a view to gain for himself or another or with intent to cause loss to another, makes any unwarranted demand with menaces and for this purpose a demand with menaces is unwarranted unless the person does so in the belief that he has reasonable grounds for making the demand; and that the use of the menaces is a proper means of reinforcing the demand.	Up to 14 years' imprisonment.	Theft Act 1968, s 21

CHILD ABDUCTION

20.2 Twenty-seven per cent of cases handled by the Forced Marriage Unit in 2019 involved children.[2] Often children are removed from the jurisdiction in order to be married. The Child Abduction Act 1984 created two offences of child abduction. Consideration may be given in the context of a live abduction, when the child is overseas with the abductor in a country with an extradition treaty with the UK as to whether an extradition request might assist in securing the return of the child.

20.3 As well as being an offence associated with forced marriage in CPS Guidance, Child Abduction for the purposes of forced marriage has been described as a form of Child Abduction at an 'extreme' in the spectrum of seriousness of offences committed under the 1984 Act.[3]

Child Abduction Act 1984, s 1 – abduction by a person connected with a child

20.4 The Child Abduction Act 1984, s 1 of the Act, applies to anyone with a connection to the child, 'a connection' being defined as someone:[4]

(a) Who is a parent of the child;

(b) Where the parents of the child were not married to one another at the time of the child's birth, there are reasonable grounds for believing that he is the father of the child;

(c) Who is the guardian of the child;

(d) Is the special guardian of the child;

(e) Is a person named in a child arrangements order as a person with whom the child is to live; or

(f) Has custody of the child.

20.5 Such a person commits an offence if he takes or sends the child out of the United Kingdom without the appropriate consent.[5] Appropriate consent means the consent of each of the following:[6]

(a) The child's mother;

(b) The child's father, if he has parental responsibility for him;

(c) Any guardian of the child;

(d) Any special guardian of the child;

2 HM Government, Forced Marriage Unit Statistics 2019, 25 June 2020.
3 *R v Kayani, R v Solomon* [2012] 1 All ER 641.
4 Child Abduction Act 1984, s 1(2).
5 Child Abduction Act 1984, s 1(1).
6 Child Abduction Act 1984, s 1(3)(a).

(e) Any person named in a child arrangements order as a person with whom the child is to live;

(f) Any person who had custody of the child;

(g) Where the child is in the care of a local authority, the consent of the authority;[7]

(h) Where the child is detained in a place of safety or remanded to local authority accommodation, the leave of any magistrates' court acting for the area in which the place of safety is located.[8]

20.6 Where a child is placed for adoption by an adoption agency under the Adoption and Children Act 2002, s 19 the leave of each person who has parental responsibility for the child or the leave of the High Court is required.[9] Where a placement order is in force in respect of the child, the leave of the court which made the placement order is required.[10] Where an application has been made for a placement or adoption order, then the leave of the court to which the application was made is required.[11] Where an order under the Adoption and Children Act 2002, s 84 has been made or an application for such an order has been made and not disposed of then the leave of the court which made the order or to which the application was made is required.[12]

20.7 Alternatively, consent can be given by the court under any provision of the Children Act 1989, Part II or by a court which awarded custody of the child to any person.[13]

20.8 Unless the removal takes place in breach of an order under the Children Act 1989, Part II, an offence is not committed under s 1, where the person taking the child out of the United Kingdom without the appropriate consent is:

(a) A person named in a child arrangements order as a person with whom the child is to live, and he takes or sends the child out of the United Kingdom for a period of less than one month; or

(b) He is a special guardian of the child and he takes or sends the child out of the United Kingdom for a period of less than three months.[14]

20.9 An offence is not committed under the Child Abduction Act 1984, s 1 by doing anything without the consent of another person whose consent is required if he does so in the belief:

(a) Has consented; or

7 Child Abduction Act 1984, s 1(8), Sch, para1(2).
8 Child Abduction Act 1984, s 1(8), Sch, para1(2)..
9 Child Abduction Act 1984, Sch para 3(2)(i).
10 Child Abduction Act 1984, Sch para 3(2)(ii).
11 Child Abduction Act 1984, Sch para 3(2)(iii).
12 Child Abduction Act 1984, Sch para 3(2)(iv).
13 Child Abduction Act 1984, s 1(3)(b), (c).
14 Child Abduction Act 1984, s 1(4), (4A).

(b) Would consent if he was aware of all the relevant circumstances.[15]

20.10 Similarly, a person shall not be guilty if they have taken all reasonable steps to communicate with the person from whom consent is required but has been unable to communicate with them.[16]

20.11 Except in cases where the person who refuses consent is: (i) named in a child arrangements order as a person with whom the child is to live; (ii) is a special guardian; (iii) has custody of the child; or (iv) in cases where the person removing the child is doing so in breach of a court order, it shall not be an offence to take or send the child out of the United Kingdom where the person who is refusing consent does so unreasonably.[17]

20.12 Once there is sufficient evidence to raise an issue as to whether: (i) consent was refused unreasonably; (ii) that the defendant believed that the person had consented; or (iii) would consent if aware of all the relevant circumstances or that the defendant had taken reasonable steps to communicate with the person but had been unable to – it shall be for the prosecution to prove that the defence is not made out.[18]

Definitions

20.13 The terms 'guardian of a child', 'special guardian' 'child arrangements' and 'parental responsibility' all have the same meanings as in the Children Act 1989.[19] A person has custody of a child for the purposes of the section where a there is an order of a court in the United Kingdom in force awarding him sole or joint custody, legal custody or care and control of the child.[20]

20.14 The Child Abduction Act 1984, s 3 defines taking, sending and detaining as follows:

(a) A person shall be regarded as taking a child if he causes or induces the child to accompany him or any other person or causes the child to be taken.

(b) A person shall be regarded as sending a child if he causes the child to be sent.

Procedure

20.15 The Director of Public Prosecutions must give their consent before a prosecution under s 1 can be brought.[21] The offence is triable either way.[22]

15 Child Abduction Act 1984, s 1(5)(a).
16 Child Abduction Act 1984, s 1(5)(b).
17 Child Abduction Act 1984, s 1(5)(c), (5A).
18 Child Abduction Act 1984, s 1(6).
19 Child Abduction Act 1984, s 1(7)(a).
20 Child Abduction Act 1984, s 1(7)(b).
21 Child Abduction Act 1984, s 4(2).
22 Child Abduction Act 1984, s 4(1).

20.16 In *R v C (Kidnapping: Abduction)*,[23] the Court of Appeal held that copies of the Child Abduction Act 1984, s 1 ought not be provided to the jury.

Defences

20.17 In circumstances where consent is given to remove a child from the jurisdiction, but the child is kept out of the country for longer than the period or agreed or not returned, an offence under the Child Abduction Act 1984, s 1 does not arise.[24] The defence of necessity is not available in relation to offences under s 1.[25]

Sentence

20.18 The maximum sentence following conviction indictment is seven years' imprisonment. Following summary conviction, the maximum sentence is six months' imprisonment and/or an unlimited fine. In *R v Kayani*,[26] the Court of Appeal held that at the most serious offences of kidnapping are akin to kidnap. The Court of Appeal underlined the need to a deterrent effect and described Child Abduction as a 'cruel' offence. Child Abduction involving forced marriage was highlighted as a particularly serious manifestation of the offence.

20.19 In *R v RH*,[27] the Court of Appeal held that the most serious cases of Child Abduction including cases involving forced marriage should attract a prison sentence of five to seven years following trial.

Child Abduction Act 1984, s 2 – Abduction by other persons

20.20 A person commits an offence under the Child Abduction Act 1984, s 2 if without lawful authority or reasonable excuse he takes or detains a child under the age of 16 so as to:

(a) Remove him from the lawful control of any person having lawful control over the child; or

(b) Keep him out of the lawful control of any person entitled to lawful control of the child.[28]

23 [1991] 2 FLR 252.
24 *R (on the application of Nicolaou) v Redbridge Magistrates' Court* [2012] EWHC 1647 (Admin), a case where a father who failed to return the child to the United Kingdom judicially reviewed the granting of an arrest warrant.
25 *R v S* [2012] EWCA Crim 389.
26 [2011] EWCA Crim 2871, 2012 2 Cr App R (S) 38.
27 [2016] EWCA Crim 1754.
28 Child Abduction Act 1984, s 2(1).

20.21 The words 'so as to' relate to the objective effect of the defendant's actions and not to his intention.[29]

20.22 An offence under the Child Abduction Act 1984, s 2 cannot be committed by:

(a) The mother and father of the child where the parents were married to, or civil partners of, each other at the time of birth;

(b) The child's mother where the parents were not married to, or civil partners of, each other when the child was born;

(c) Any other person mentioned in the Child Abduction Act 1984, s 1(2)(c)–(e).[30]

Definitions

20.23 A person shall be regarded as detaining a child if he causes the child to be detained or induces the child to remain with him or any other person.[31]

20.24 In *R v A*,[32] it was held that the offence of taking a child can be committed even where the child consents to accompany the defendant.

Procedure

20.25 Prosecutions brought under the Child Abduction Act 1984, s 2 of the Act do not require the consent of the Director of Public Prosecutions. Section 2 offences are triable either way.

Defences

20.26 It is a defence for a person to prove where the father and mother were not married to each other at the time of the child's birth:

(a) That the defendant is the child's father; or

(b) At the time of the alleged offence, he believed, on reasonable grounds, that he was the child's father; or

(c) That at the time of the alleged offence, he believed, on reasonable grounds, that the child had attained the age of 16.[33]

29 *R v Mousir* [1987] Crim LR 562 CA; *Foster v DPP* [2004] EWHC 2955 (Admin).

30 Child Abduction Act 1984, s 2(2). Any other person is as follows: (i) the guardian or special guardian of the child; (ii) a person with custody of the child; or (iii) a person named in a child arrangements order as a person with whom the child is to live.

31 Child Abduction Act 1984, s 3(d).

32 [2000] 1 Cr App R 418 CA.

33 Child Abduction Act 1984, s 2(3).

20.27 The Children Act 1989, s 51 allows the Secretary of State to grant certificates disapplying the Child Abduction Act 1984, s 2 to persons and institutions providing refuges for children at risk in particular circumstances.

Sentence

20.28 The maximum sentence following conviction on indictment is seven years imprisonment or six months, an unlimited fine or both following summary conviction.[34] The guidance summarised at **20.18–20.19** is applicable and five to seven years is the sentencing range to be expected following trial of an offence of child abduction for the purposes of forced marriage.

KIDNAPPING

20.29 Kidnapping is a common law offence with a maximum sentence of life. In *R v Kayani*,[35] the Court of Appeal suggests that in the most serious cases of child abduction, consideration may be given to bringing a charge of kidnapping. The current definition of kidnapping has been subject to criticism as containing overlapping elements, ambiguity and as creating an ill-defined relationship between kidnapping and related offences such as false imprisonment.[36]

20.30 The nature of the offence is an attack on, and infringement of, the personal liberty of the victim and it consists of four further essential elements which were summarised by Lord Brandon in *R v D*:[37]

> '(1) the taking or carrying away of one person by another; (2) by force or by fraud; (3) without the consent of the person so taken or carried away; and (4) without lawful excuse'.

20.31 In *R v Hutchins*,[38] it was held that kidnap can be committed either intentionally or recklessly as to the victim's consent.

Definitions

20.32 Force includes threats of force even where no actual violence is inflicted on the victim.[39] A victim does not have to be carried far in order for an offence

34 Child Abduction Act 1984, s 4(1).
35 [2011] EWCA Crim 2871.
36 See, for example Law Commission, Law Com 3, Simplification of Criminal Law: Kidnapping and Related Offences, November 2014.
37 [1984] 3 WLR 186.
38 [1988] Crim LR 379.
39 *R v Archer* [2011] EWCA Crim 2252.

of kidnapping to arise. For example, in *R v Wellard*,[40] it was held that tricking a victim into walking a few yards for a drug search by a man impersonating a constable was sufficient to amount to 'taking'.

20.33 Consent obtained by force or fear does not amount to true consent for the purposes of the offence.[41]

Procedure

20.34 Kidnapping is triable on indictment only. An indictment should not contain counts for both kidnaping and statutory child abduction.[42]

Sentence

20.35 The maximum sentence for kidnap is life imprisonment.[43] The Sentencing Council have not produced any definitive sentencing guidelines for the offence. In *A-G's Ref (No 92 of 2014) (Gibney)*,[44] the Court of Appeal identified the following factors which are likely to influence the seriousness of the offence for the purposes of sentencing:

(a) The length of the detention;

(b) The circumstances of the detention, including the location and any method of restraint;

(c) The extent of any violence used and the use of torture or humiliation;

(d) Any particular vulnerability of the victim whether by reason of age or otherwise;

(e) Whether weapons were used;

(f) Whether demands or threats were made of others;

(g) The effect on the victim and others;

(h) The extent of planning;

(i) The number of offenders involved; and

(j) Whether what was done arose from or was in furtherance of previous criminal behaviour.

40 [1978 3 All ER 161.
41 *R v Greenhalgh* [2001] EWCA Crim 1367.
42 *R v C* (1990) The Times, 9 November 1990.
43 Technically, being a common law offence, the maximum penalty is at large.
44 [2014] EWCA Crim 2713.

FALSE IMPRISONMENT

20.36 False Imprisonment is both a common law offence and a tortious act giving rise to civil liability. The elements of the offence were set out by the Lord Chief Justice in *R v Rahman*[45] as follows:

> 'False imprisonment consists in the unlawful and intentional or reckless restraint of a victim's freedom of movement from a particular place. In other words, it is unlawful detention which stops the victim moving away as he would wish to move.'

Definitions

20.37 The victim may be physically retrained or restrained by deliberate intimidation.[46]The imprisonment must be unlawful. In cases involving children and their parents, it shall be a question of fact in each case whether a parent has overstepped the limits of lawful restraint.[47]

Procedure

20.38 False imprisonment is triable on indictment only.

Sentence

20.39 The maximum sentence for false imprisonment is life imprisonment.[48] The sentencing factors listed at **20.35** above also apply to convictions for false imprisonment.

BLACKMAIL

20.40 Blackmail is most likely to occur in forced marriages contrived to achieve a financial advantage. The offence of blackmail is created by the Theft Act 1968, s 21 which provides:

> '(1) A person is guilty of blackmail if, with a view to gain for himself or another or with intent to cause loss to another, he makes any unwarranted demand with menaces; and for this purpose a demand with menaces is unwarranted unless the person making it does so in the belief—

45 (1985) 81 Cr App R 349.
46 *R v James* (1997) The Times, 2 October 1997.
47 In *R v Rahman* (1985) 81 Cr App R 349.
48 Technically, being a common law offence, the maximum penalty is at large.

(a) that he has reasonable grounds for making the demand; and

(b) that the use of the menaces is a proper means of reinforcing the demand.

(2) The nature of the act or omission demanded is immaterial, and it is also immaterial whether the menaces relate to action to be taken by the person making the demand.'

Definitions

20.41 The term 'view to gain for himself or another or with intent to cause loss to another' is defined by the Theft Act 1968, s 34(2)(a) which states that gain and loss are to be construed as only extending to monetary gain or loss whether temporary or permanent. In particular:

(i) Gain includes a gain by keeping what one has, as well as a gain by getting what one has not; and

(ii) Loss includes a loss by not getting what one might get, as well as a loss by parting with what one has.

20.42 The meaning of 'making a demand' has no statutory definition and has been broadly construed by the courts. In *R v Studer*,[49] it was held that a demand 'may be in language only a request'. It was held in *Treacy v DPP*[50] that the successful communication of a demand is not essential for the element of the offence to be made out.

20.43 The meaning of the term 'menaces' was considered in *R v Clear*[51] in which their Lordships held that words or conduct which would not intimidate or influence anyone to respond to the demands would not be menaces'. Instead, what is required is threats and conduct of a nature and extent that the mind of an ordinary person of normal stability and courage might be influenced or made apprehensive so as to accede unwillingly to the demand. It is not required that the threat or conduct actually does intimidate the victim.

20.44 However, in *R v Garwood*,[52] it was recognised that the victim's 'unusual timidity' could be taken into account in circumstances where the defendant knew of it.

Procedure

20.45 Blackmail is an indictable only offence.[53]

49 (1915) 85 LJ KB 1017.
50 [1971] AC 537.
51 [1968] 1 QB 670.
52 [1987] 1 All ER 1032.
53 Magistrates' Courts Act 1980, s 17, Sch 1, para 28(a).

Defences

20.46 It is a defence under the Theft Act 1968, s 21(a) and (b) if the defendant believed he has:

(a) Reasonable grounds for making the demand; and

(b) That the use of the menaces is a proper means for reinforcing the demand.

20.47 Once the issue is raised it shall be for the prosecution to prove that that the defendant did not have such belief.[54]

Sentence

20.48 The maximum sentence for blackmail is 14 years' imprisonment.[55] The offence is a serious one and in *R v Hadjou*[56] the Court of Appeal held:

> 'In the calendar of criminal offences blackmail was one of the ugliest and most vicious because it involved what one found so often, attempted murder of the soul. Deterrence was perhaps the most important part of the sentence in such a case'

20.49 There are no sentencing guidelines for blackmail.[57] In *R v Ford*,[58] the Court of Appeal identified the following relevant sentencing factors in blackmail cases:

(a) The amount of money demanded in comparison with the victim's means;

(b) The psychological harm done to the victim; and

(c) The psychological harm intended to be done.

54 *R v Ashiq* [2015] EWCA Crim 1617
55 Theft Act 1968, s 21(3).
56 [1989] 11 Cr App R (S).
57 Although following *R v Hutchinson* [2018] EWCA Crim 631, sentencing courts are entitled to take into account the sentencing guidelines for fraud.
58 [2015] EWCA Crim 561.

Part 4

Court of Protection law and procedure

CHAPTER 21

Overview of the Mental Capacity Act 2005

Content at a Glance:

Introduction

Statutory principles

Capacity to marry

Best Interests

The Court of Protection

INTRODUCTION

21.1 The National Mental Incapacity Forum estimated in 2016 that up to two million people in the UK lack capacity to make a specific decision at the specific time required.[1] The legal framework governing the welfare and interests of those lacking capacity is therefore a matter of the utmost public importance.

21.2 Prior to the commencement of the Mental Capacity Act 2005, the Court of Protection only had jurisdiction in respect of the property and financial affairs of those lacking capacity. Issues relating to welfare, care and treatment were predominantly determined by the Family Division of the High Court applying common law principles with no coherent underlying statutory regime.

21.3 This led to increasing concern about the lack of a structured decision-making process for resolving questions about how those lacking capacity ought to be cared for, what decisions ought to be made on their behalf.

21.4 In 1998, the Law Commission published a report criticising the Common Law regime as complicated, incapable and piecemeal and called for a single piece of legislation to make provision for those lacking capacity.[2]

21.5 This piece of legislation was first introduced in June 2004 as the Mental Capacity Bill, to be passed into law the following year as the Mental Capacity Act 2005. The passing of the Act was a seminal moment in the rights and protections

1 HM Government, The National Mental Incapacity Forum Report, 2016.

2 Mental Incapacity (Report) [1995] EWLC 231 (15 January 1995).

afforded to those who lack mental capacity and created a comprehensive statutory framework for decisions to be made on behalf of those who lack to capacity to make such decisions themselves.

STATUTORY PRINCIPLES

21.6 The Mental Capacity Act 2005, s 1 sets out a series of statutory principles that are at the heart of the law of mental incapacity and must be applied whenever the Act is relied upon.

The statutory principles	
As set out in the MCA 2005, s 1(1)	
1	A person must be assumed to have capacity unless it is established that they lack capacity
2	A person is not to be treated as unable to make a decision unless all practicable steps to help him to do so have been taken without success.
3	A person is not to be treated as unable to make a decision merely because he makes an unwise decision.
4	An act done, or decision made, under the Act for or on behalf of a person who lacks capacity must be done, or made, in his best interests.
5	Before the act is done, or the decision is made, regard must be had to whether the purpose for which it is needed can be as effectively achieved in a way that is less restrictive of the person's rights and freedom of action.

Presumption of capacity

21.7 The cardinal principle of the Mental Capacity Act 2005 is that it is to be presumed that a person has capacity unless it is established otherwise.[3] Capacity is decision specific, ie someone may have capacity to decide where to live, but not whether to get married. The Mental Capacity Act 2005, s 2(4) states that issues of capacity are to be determined on the balance of probabilities, the civil standard of proof.

21.8 The statutory presumption of capacity shall have to be specifically displaced by any applicant averring that they or a spouse lacked capacity to consent to marriage at the time of the wedding or lacks capacity to marry generally. Often this will be in the form of a mental capacity assessment undertaken by a social worker or other suitably qualified professional.

21.9 Within proceedings in the Court of Protection, the person said to lack capacity is referred to as 'P' and the same term is used throughout this chapter.

3 Mental Capacity Act 2005, s 1(2).

Duty to take all practicable steps to maximise capacity

21.10 Under the Mental Capacity Act 2005, s 1(3) a person is not to be treated as unable to make a decision themselves until all practicable steps have been taken to help them do so without success. In a forced marriage context, this shall often mean education relating to sexual relations and marriage. The extent of what is practicable shall always be dependent on the circumstances and it may be that the impairment leading to a lack of capacity to make the decision is such that it is obviously not practicable to even attempt to take steps to support the person to make the decision.

Unwise decision

21.11 Whilst the Mental Capacity Act 2005, s 1(4) makes clear that a person cannot be treated as lacking capacity merely because the decision they propose to make is unwise, manifestly irrational or unreasonable decisions can be treated as evidence of P lacking capacity to make those decisions. It is therefore not usually for the court to consider the merits of a prospective marriage when considering whether P has capacity to enter into it.

Duty to act in the person's best interests

21.12 The requirement that 'an act done, or decision made, under the Mental Capacity Act 2005 for or on behalf of a person who lacks capacity must be done, or made in his best interests'[4] formed part of the old common law test which required professionals 'to give the incapacitated person any treatment or care necessary to preserve their life, health or well-being which was in their best interests'.

21.13 The Mental Capacity Act 2005, s 4 provides a framework and series of considerations for determining an incapacitated person's best interests which is considered below at Part D of this Chapter.

Duty to consider less restrictive options

21.14 This requirement demands that the decision maker considers whether the necessary purpose of the act proposed can be as effectively achieved in a less restrictive way.[5]

4 Mental Capacity Act 2005, s 1(5).
5 Mental Capacity Act 2005, s 1(6).

TEST FOR CAPACITY TO MARRY

Key points on capacity

- A person lacks capacity if at the time he is unable to make a decision for himself at the material time because of an impairment or disturbance in the functioning of the mind or brain.
- It does not matter whether the impairment or disturbance is permanent or temporary.
- A lack of capacity cannot be established merely by a person's age or appearance or his condition or aspect of his appearance which might lead others to make unjustified assumptions about his capacity.
- Capacity is time specific and loss of capacity can be temporary or fluctuating.
- Capacity is decision specific and relates to the particular matter to be decided rather than a general ability to make decisions. One might have capacity to make decisions about where to live but not who to have contact with.

21.15 The Mental Capacity Act 2005, s 2 provides:

> 'for the purposes of this Act, a person lacks capacity in relation to a matter if at the material time he is unable to make a decision for himself in relation to the matter because of an impairment of, or a disturbance in the functioning of, the mind or brain.'

21.16 Thus, the test for capacity is specific to the time when a decision must be made. It is not uncommon for capacity to fluctuate and for a person to lose capacity temporarily or partially.

21.17 Capacity also relates to a specific decision. It does not follow that because a person lacks capacity to make decisions about medical treatment or finances that they shall necessarily lack capacity in respect of marriage or sex.

Who is unable to make a decision?

Inability to make a decision

A person is unable to make a decision if they are unable to:

- Understand relevant information.
- Retain that information.
- Use and weigh that information to make the decision.
- Communicate their decision.

21.18 The Mental Capacity Act 2005, s 3 sets out that a person is unable to make a decision if they are unable to:

(a) Understand the information relevant to the decision;

(b) Retain that information;

(c) Use or weigh that information as part of the process of making the decision; or

(d) Communicate their decision.

21.19 The communication of the decision could be by talking, signing, writing or any other means.

Information relevant to marriage

Relevant information in deciding to marry

A person must understand:

- Marriage is a contract formally entered into.
- The broad nature of the marriage contract.
- The duties and responsibilities that normally attach to marriage.
- Marriage confers on the parties the status of husband or wife.
- Marriage creates a relationship of mutual and reciprocal obligations.
- There may be financial consequences of the marriage and in particular a financial claim in the event of divorce.

21.20 Capacity to marry is act specific, not person specific, thus the question is not whether X has capacity to decide to marry Y, but rather, whether X has capacity to consent to marriage generally.

21.21 The test for capacity to marry was first addressed in the often-cited authority of *Durham v Durham*,[6] a case in which the Earl of Durham sought a decree of nullity on the basis his wife lacked the mental capacity to enter into a marriage. The matter came before the then President of the Probate, Divorce and Admiralty Division of the High Court, Sir James Hannen. The court held at page 81:

> 'I may say this much in the outset that it appears to me that the contract of marriage is a very simple one which does not require a high degree of intelligence to comprehend. It is an engagement between a man and a woman to live together and love one another as husband and wife to the

6 [1885] 10 PD.

exclusion of all others. This is expanded in the promises of the marriage ceremony by words having reference to the natural relations which spring from that engagement, such as protection on the part of the man and submission on behalf of the woman. I agree with the Solicitor General that a mere comprehension of the words of the promises exchanged is not sufficient. The mind of one of the parties may be capable of understanding the language used but may yet be affected by such delusions or other symptoms of insanity as may satisfy the Tribunal that there was not a real appreciation of the engagement apparently entered into.'

21.22 The 19th century references to the then gender roles of spouses have been overtaken by modern social and legal values, however, in *Mundell v Name 1*,[7] Mostyn J described the dicta in *Durham* as canonical. The position in law remains that a party is only expected to understand the essence of the 'very simple' contract of marriage to be able to understand the information relevant to the decision to wed.

21.23 In *Sheffield City Council v E and S*,[8] Munby J (as he then was) suggested that there were two parts to the test for capacity to marry:

(a) Does the person concerns understand the nature of the marriage contract; and

(b) Does he or she understand the duties and responsibilities that normally attach to the marriage?

21.24 His Lordship went on to summarise the duties and responsibilities which normally attach to a marriage as:

(a) Marriage is a contract formally entered into;

(b) It confers on the parties the status of husband and wife;

(c) The essence of the contract is an agreement between a man and a woman to live together and love one another as husband and wife to the exclusion of all others; and

(d) It creates a relationship of mutual and reciprocal obligations, typically involving the sharing of a common home and a common domestic life and the right to enjoy each other's society, comfort and assistance.

21.25 However, in *Mundell v Name 1*,[9] Mostyn J suggested that a marriage contract did not necessarily involve an agreement to live together, to love one another as husband and wife or that it would necessarily involve the sharing of a common home and a common domestic life. His Lordship also held that there is no required understanding of matters of ancillary relief other than that divorce may bring a financial claim.

7 [2019] EWCOP 50.
8 [2005] 2 WLR 953.
9 [2019] EWCOP 50.

21.26 In *Southwark LBC v KA*,[10] Parker J set out the following principles:

(a) Marriage is status-specific not person-specific;

(b) The wisdom of the marriage is irrelevant;

(c) P must understand the broad nature of the marriage contract;

(d) P must understand the duties and responsibilities that normally attach to a marriage;

(e) P must understand that there may be financial consequences of the marriage;

(f) Marriage confers the spouses with special status and connection with regard to each other;

(g) The essence of the marriage is for two people to live together and love one another; and

(h) P must not lack capacity to enter into sexual relations

The interplay between capacity to consent to sex and capacity to marry

21.27 It appears to be established law that capacity to consent to sex is a requirement for capacity to marry.[11] This rule appears incongruent with a long line of case law which makes clear that sex is not an essential ingredient of marriage and that platonic marriages are capable of being perfectly valid.[12]

Test for capacity to consent to sex

21.28 The test for capacity to consent to sex is currently subject to an application to appeal to the Supreme Court brought by the Official Solicitor. Pending the outcome of that application, the law is as set out by the Court of Appeal in *A Local Authority v JB*[13] in which their Lordships held the information relevant to the decision to consent to sex may include the following:

(a) The sexual nature and character of the act of sexual intercourse, including the mechanics of the act;

(b) The fact that the other person must have capacity to consent to the sexual activity and must in fact consent before and throughout the sexual activity;

(c) The fact that P can say yes or no to having sexual relationships and is able to decide whether to give or withhold consent;

10 [2016] EWCOP 20.

11 See *Southwark LBC v KA* [2016] EWCOP 20 and *Sheffield City Council v E and S* [2005] 2 WLR 953.

12 See *A v B* (1868) LR 1 P & D 559, 562 and *X (A Child)* [2018] EWFC 15 in which Munby J was considering a platonic marriage in which one of the spouses were homosexual.

13 [2020] EWCA Civ 735.

(d) That a reasonably foreseeable consequence of sexual intercourse between a man and a woman is that the woman will become pregnant;

(e) That there are health risks involved, particularly the acquisition sexually transmitted and transmissible infections, and that the risk of sexually transmitted infection can be reduced by the taking of precautions such as the use of a condom.

21.29 The Court of Appeal's judgment in *JB* represented a significant development of the law in that for the first time, P was required to understand the need for the other party to have capacity consent to sex, and indeed to consent.

BEST INTERESTS

21.30

The best interests considerations	
As set out in the MCA 2005, s 4.	
1	Consider all the relevant circumstances including if P will at some time have capacity in relation to the issue and if likely so, when
2	Encourage and permit the person to participate as far as is reasonably practicable in the decision making or the act to be done.
3	Consider the person's past and present wishes and feelings, in particular and relevant written statement made by him when he had capacity.
4	Consider the beliefs and values that would be likely to influence his decision if he had capacity
5	Consider the other factors that he would be likely to consider if he were able to do so
6	Take into account views of deputies, LPAs, carers or any person named as someone to be consulted.

Decisions made for a person who lacks capacity in a relevant domain must be taken in 'their best interests. The Mental Capacity Act 2005, s 4(1) makes clear that one must not determine what is in a person's best interests merely on the basis of their age, appearance, condition or an aspect of their behaviour which may lead others to make an unjustified assumption about what might be in their best interests.

21.31 The remainder of the Mental Capacity Act 2005 goes on to list a series of factors which must be taken into account when making best interests' decisions on behalf of an adult lacking capacity. The weight given to each consideration shall be dependent on the circumstances of the individual case.

21.32 In addition to the specific factors listed, the decision maker must also consider any further relevant considerations of which they are aware. No single factor has automatic precedence over the others and the weight attributed to difference considerations shall always be heavily dependent on the circumstances of the individual case.

THE COURT OF PROTECTION

21.33 The Court of Protection, as reconstituted in 2005, is a superior court of record with jurisdiction to deal with both personal welfare and property and financial affairs matters relating to those who lack mental capacity.[14]

21.34 The Mental Capacity Act 2005, s 47 stipulates that the Court of Protection has 'in connection with its jurisdiction the same powers, rights, privileges and authority as the High Court'. This includes powers in respect of contempt, witnesses, enforcement and, following *Re: SF (Injunctive Relief)* [2020] EWCOP 19, the power to grant and enforce injunctions.

21.35 Judges of the Court of Protection are split into three tiers. High Court Judges are Tier 3, Circuit Judges, Tier 2 and District Judges are classified as Tier 3. Circuit Judges and District Judges undergo specific training to become nominated judges of the Court of Protection, all High Court judges are automatically nominated to sit on the court.

Limits on the Court of Protection's jurisdiction

21.36 The Mental Capacity Act 2005, s 27 precludes the court or any other person, including those holding lasting power of attorney or deputyship to make the following decisions on behalf of a person lacking capacity:

(a) Consenting to marriage or a civil partnership.

(b) Consenting to have sexual relations.

(c) Consenting to a decree of divorce being granted on the basis of two years' separation.

(d) Consenting to a dissolution order being made in relation to a civil partnership on the basis of two years' separation;

(e) Consenting to a child's being placed for adoption by an adoption agency.

(f) Consenting to the making of an adoption order.

(g) Discharging parental responsibilities in matters not relating to a child's property.

(h) Giving a consent under the Human Fertilisation and Embryology Act 1990.

(i) Giving a consent under the Human Fertilisation and Embryology Act 2008.

14 Prior to 2005, the Court of Protection only had jurisdiction in respect of property and financial affairs.

21.37 Thus, if someone lacks capacity to consent to sex or marriage, it is not open to their deputy, legal power of attorney or the court to decide on their behalf to get married or to consent to sexual relations.

21.38 The Mental Capacity Act 2005, s 28 prevents the Court of Protection from making decisions in respect of treatment of those suffering from a mental disorder as such treatment is governed by the Mental Health Act 1983.

21.39 The Mental Capacity Act 2005, s 29 prevents the court or any other person making a decision on voting in elections or referendums on behalf of a person lacking capacity.

CHAPTER 22

Circumstances in which Court of Protection proceedings may be necessary

Content at a Glance:

INTRODUCTION

22.1 Often proceedings relating to forced marriage shall be started in the family jurisdiction and parties shall need to consider whether simultaneous proceedings in the Court of Protection are required or would be helpful. Commonly, if such proceedings are instigated, the case ought to be allocated to a judge authorised to sit both in the Family Division of the High Court and the Court of Protection. This is because whilst judges can simultaneously sit in the High Court and the Court of Protection, it does not appear that a judge may sit in both the Family Court and the Court of Protection at the same time.[1] The rationale for this approach is presumably that under the Mental Capacity Act 2005, s 47, a judge in the Court of Protection is exercising the rights and privileges of the High Court in respect of their jurisdiction whereas a family court judge has a much more limited jurisdiction as defined by statute.[2]

22.2 There is, to some extent a conflict between the statutory principles of the Mental Capacity Act 2005 and Family Law Act 1996. Both require the court to consider P's wishes and feelings.[3] The Mental Capacity Act 2005 places a primary focus on P's best interests and the Family Law Act 1996 requires the Court to consider P's welfare.

1 Munby P, President's Guidance: Jurisdiction of the family court: allocation of cases within the family court to High Court judge level and transfer of cases from the family court to the High Court, 2018.
2 The Family Court was established by Crime and Courts Act 2013, s 31A.
3 Family Law Act 1996, s 63A(3) and Mental Capacity Act 2005, s 4(4).

22.3 However, the Family Law Act 1996 contains no requirement that injunctions made are in P's best interests. Indeed, in *Re K (Forced Marriage: Passport Order)*,[4] the Court of Appeal specifically endorsed the Southall Black Sisters' submission that:

> 'Cases of forced marriage do not just involve private individuals, but they involve the State undertaking an active and positive role in the protecting of an individual from themselves and, normally their community'.

22.4 Further, there is nothing to suggest that 'well-being' within the meaning of the Family Law Act 1996, s 63 has the same meaning as 'best interests' under the Mental Capacity Act 2005.

22.5 It shall therefore be essential that practitioners engaged in parallel proceedings are mindful of what jurisdiction orders are being made under and therefore which statutory tests are applicable.

22.6 Local authorities, when dealing with adults lacking capacity, ought to actively consider whether further steps are required to safeguard the person to be protected than simply obtaining a forced marriage protection order.

22.7 The Care Act 2014 requires authorities to make whatever enquiries it thinks necessary to decide whether any action should be taken in circumstances where an adult in its area has needs for care and support, is experiencing or is at risk of abuse and neglect and cannot protect themselves due to their care needs. Forced marriage shall often form part of wider abuse of the person to be protected and local authorities must always consider whether further orders or intervention is required.

APPLICATIONS AND ORDERS WHICH MAY BE MADE

- Declarations
- Orders pursuant to the Mental Capacity Act 2005, s 16
- The appointment of deputies pursuant to the Mental Capacity Act 2005, s 16
- Orders in relation to Lasting Powers of Attorney
- Orders in relation to Enduring Powers of Attorney
- International protection of adults
- Interim orders

4 [2020] EWCA Civ 190.

Declarations

22.8 A common application to the Court of Protection during forced marriage proceedings is an application that the person to be protected lacks capacity to marry or consent to sexual relations. Such applications are brought under the Mental Capacity Act 2005, s 15 which states the court may make declarations as to:

(a) Whether a person has or lacks capacity to make a decision specified in the declaration;

(b) Whether a person has or lacks capacity to make decisions on such matters as are described in the declaration;

(c) The lawfulness or otherwise of any act done, or yet to be done, in relation to that person.

22.9 An application the Mental Capacity Act 2005, s 15 is most likely to be appropriate in circumstances where an application for a forced marriage protection order has been made on the basis that the party to be protected lacks capacity to consent to marry or have sex. The appropriate jurisdiction for resolving disputes about capacity is the Court of Protection: in circumstances where there is any dispute or question regarding the issue of capacity, an application ought to be brought for a declaration under the Mental Capacity Act 2005, s 15 to resolve the issue.

22.10 In almost all such cases it shall be appropriate for the applications under the Mental Capacity Act 2005 and the Family Law Act 1996 to be heard together by the same judge.

Orders pursuant to the Mental Capacity Act 2005, s 16

22.11 The Mental Capacity Act 2005, s 16 provides that where P lacks capacity in relation to a matter or matters relating to P's personal welfare or property and affairs, the court may make decisions on P's behalf in relation to the matters P lacks capacity. Section 16(3) provides that the court's powers under s 16 must be exercised in accordance with the principles contained in s 1 and in particular, that an order made under s 16 must be in P's best interests as defined by s 4.

22.12 The Mental Capacity Act 2005, s 17(1) provides that the court may, in particular, make orders under s 16:

(a) Deciding where P is to live;

(b) Decided what contact if any, P is to have with any specified persons;

(c) Making an order prohibiting a names person from having contact with P;

(d) Giving or refusing consent to the carrying out or continuation of a treatment by a person providing health care for P;

(e) Giving a direction that a person responsible for P's health care allow a different person to take over that responsibility.

22.13 Following *Re SF (Injunctive Relief)*,[5] it is now established law that the Court of Protection may impose injunctions with penal notices attached in order to enforce orders made pursuant to the Mental Capacity Act 2005, s 16.

22.14 Section 16 applications are most likely to be required in a forced marriage context when P has been under the care of those involved in an attempt to force them to marry. Typically, this would involve a situation in which an adult lacking capacity lives with family members who have been engaged in an attempt to force P into marriage. Local authorities or others may well reach the conclusion that it is no longer in P's best interests to live with or be subject to the control of their family members. Accordingly, if P lacks capacity to make decisions about residence and care, an application under s.16 may be made to remove P from the family home to a more appropriate and safer placement. Where there is a particular concern about particular individuals, the court may order a prohibition on contact with those individuals under the Mental Capacity Act 2005, s 16.

22.15 Similarly, the court can make decisions regarding P's property and financial affairs under s.16 if they lack capacity to make such decisions themselves. The Mental Capacity Act 2005, s 18 stipulates that the court's powers in respect to financial matters under s 16 in particularly extend to:

(a) the control and management of their property;

(b) the sale, exchange, charging, gift or other disposition of their property;

(c) the acquisition of property in their name or on their behalf;

(d) the carrying on, on their behalf, of any profession, trade or business;

(e) the taking of a decision which will have the effect of dissolving a partnership of which the person is a member;

(f) the carrying out of any contract entered into by the person;

(g) the discharge of the person's debts and any of their obligations whether legally enforceable or not;

(h) the settlement of any of their property, whether for their benefit or for the benefit of others;

(i) the execution for them of a will;

(j) the exercise of any power vested in the person whether beneficially or as a trustee or otherwise;

(k) the conduct of legal proceedings in the person's name or on their behalf.

22.16 There are two common issues in forced marriage cases which may be resolved through an application under the Mental Capacity Act 2005, s 16.

5 [2020] EWCOP 19.

22.17 First, if the family of the person to be protected control their finances and are not taking any steps to allow P to be represented in proceedings, the court may be asked either to order that P's financial information is provided to the Legal Aid Agency or if they don't qualify for legal aid, that their funds are used to pay for representation if such steps are held to be in P's best interests.

22.18 Secondly, due to financial requirements for spousal visas into the United Kingdom, it is not uncommon for significant sums of money to be transferred into the accounts of those at risk of forced marriage. When protective orders are imposed and the proposed marriage is prevented, this can leave P with significant sums of money in their account. It may well be necessary to apply to the Court of Protection to determine how this money ought to be dealt with.

The appointment of deputies pursuant to the Mental Capacity Act 2005, s 16

22.19 The Mental Capacity Act 2005, s 16 empowers the court to appoint a deputy to make decisions on a person's behalf either in respect of personal welfare or property and financial affairs. The Act provides that if the court can make the decision in question, then that preferable over the appointment of a deputy.

22.20 It is more likely, in a forced marriage context, that the court is concerned that a deputy who was previously appointed has behaved in such a way that they ought no longer to continue as deputy. The court may, under the Mental Capacity Act 2005, s 16(8) revoke the appointment of a deputy or vary their powers when it is satisfied that the deputy:

(a) Has behaved, or is behaving, in a way that contravenes the authority conferred on them by the court or is not in P's best interests; or

(b) Proposes to behave in a way that would contravene that authority or would not be in P's best interests.

22.21 If the court is of the view that P would benefit from a deputy but there is no one known to P who is appropriate to act, it may decide to appoint a panel deputy who shall generally be an independent solicitor. The Court of Protection Rules, SI 2017/1035, r 19.13(2) allows the court to make order remunerating professional deputies out of P's estate.

Orders in relation to Lasting Powers of Attorney

22.22 The Mental Capacity Act 2005, ss 22 and 23 set out the court's powers in respect of lasting powers of attorney. Section 22 stipulates that ss 22 and 23 will apply where:

(a) P has executed or purported to execute an instrument with a view to creating a lasting power of attorney; or

(b) an instrument has been registered as a lasting power of attorney conferred by P.

22.23 The court may consider pursuant to the Mental Capacity Act 2005, s 22 whether the requirements for the formation of a lasting power of attorney have been met or whether the power has otherwise been revoked or ended.

22.24 Of greater relevance to forced marriage is the provisions of the Mental Capacity Act 2005, s 22(4) which applies if the court is satisfied:

(a) That fraud or undue pressure was used to induce P to execute an instrument for the purpose of creating a lasting power of attorney or to create a lasting power of attorney; or

(b) That the donee of a lasting power of attorney has behaved, is behaving or proposes to behave in way that would contravene his authority or is not in P's best interests.[6]

22.25 If the court is so satisfied then it may:

(a) Direct that an instrument purporting to create a lasting power of attorney is not to be registered; or

(b) If the person lacks capacity to do so, revoke the instrument or the lasting power of attorney.

Orders in relation to enduring powers of attorney

22.26 The Mental Capacity Act 2005, Sch 4 sets out the court's powers in respect of enduring powers of attorney. The court may direct that enduring powers of attorney are revoked or give directions as to how P's affairs ought to be managed by the donee of the enduring power of attorney.

International protection of adults

22.27 The Hague Conference on International Law[7] has 80 members including 79 states and the European Union. The purpose of the conference is 'to work for the progressive unification of rules of private international law'.[8]

22.28 In 2000 the Conference devised the Convention of 13 January 2000 on the International Protection of Adults.[9] There are currently 19 contracting states to the Convention, including the United Kingdom. The purpose of the Convention

6 Mental Capacity Act 2005, s 22(3).
7 Statute of the Hague Conference on Private International Law, 15 July 1955.
8 Article 1, Statute of the Hague Conference on Private International Law, 15 July 1955.
9 Hague Convention on the International Protection of Adults, 13 January 2000.

is to manage and resolve conflicts of laws in the field of mental incapacity and to promote the recognition and enforcement of protective orders.

22.29 The Mental Capacity Act 2005, s 63 relates to the Convention on the International Protection of Adults 2000 (the Hague Convention). Section 63 provides that Schedule 3 to the Act gives effect to the Convention and makes provisions as to the private international law of England and Wales.

22.30 The Mental Capacity Act 2005, Sch 3 provides that the Court of Protection has jurisdiction in respect of:

(a) An adult habitually resident in England and Wales;

(b) an adult's property in England and Wales;

(c) an adult present in England and Wales or who has property there, if the matter is urgent, or;

(d) an adult present in England and Wales, if a protective which is temporary and limited in its effect to England and Wales is proposed in relation to him.

22.31 The Mental Capacity Act 2005, Sch 3, Part 4 allows for the Court of Protection to recognise and enforce protective measures imposed by other Convention countries in respect of adults habitually resident in that country. The applicability of these provisions to cases of forced marriage shall be obvious.

22.32 There are however a number of circumstances in which the court may decline to recognise or enforce a measure taken by the courts of another Convention country, these are:

(a) The case in which the measure was taken was not urgent;

(b) The adult was not given an opportunity to be heard and that omission amounted to a breach of natural justice;

(c) Recognition of the measure would be manifestly contrary to public policy;

(d) The measure would be inconsistent with a mandatory provision of the law of England and Wales; or

(e) The measure is inconsistent with one subsequently taken, or recognised, in England and Wales in relation to the adult.

22.33 The Mental Capacity Act 2005, Sch 3, Part 4, para 22 allows an interested party to apply to the Court of Protection for a declaration that a protective measure under the law of another Convention country is enforceable or is to be registered in England and Wales. If such a declaration is granted then the measure in question is enforceable as though it were an order made by the court in England and Wales.

Interim orders

22.34 Forced marriage cases shall often be brought before the court on a matter of urgency. Accordingly, it may well be that whilst urgent orders are required, there is not yet sufficient expert evidence to rebut the presumption of capacity on the balance of probabilities. As such, it shall be necessary to consider an application for interim orders to safeguard P.

22.35 The Mental Capacity Act 2005, s 48 empowers the court to make interim orders and directions if it has reason to believe that P lacks capacity in relation to the relevant matter and it is in the best interests of P to do so.

22.36 The level of evidence required to satisfy the court that it has jurisdiction to exercise its powers under s 48 was considered by HHJ Hazel Marshall QC in *Re F*.[10] The court held what was required was reasonable belief P lacks capacity:

> '[44] 'The proper test for the engagement of s 48 in the first instance is whether there is evidence giving good cause for concern that P may lack capacity in some relevant regard. Once that is raised as a serious possibility, the court then moves on to the second stage to decide what action, if any, it is in P's best interests to take before a final determination of his capacity can be made.'

22.37 In *Wandsworth LBC v M & ors*,[11] the now Vice President of the Court of Protection considered the test for the Mental Capacity Act 2005, s 48 and applied a more rigorous approach to the test for interim orders under s 48. His Lordship held:

> 'There can be no doubt that the cogency of quality of evidence required to justify a declaration of incapacity, pursuant to Section 15, will be greater than that required to establish the interim test. However, it is important to emphasise that the presumption of capacity is omnipresent in the framework of this legislation and there must be reason to believe that it has been rebutted, even at the interim stage. I do not consider, as the authors of the 'Mental Capacity Assessment' did that a 'possibility', even a 'serious one' that P might lack capacity does justification to the rigour of the interim test. Neither do I consider 'an unclear situation' which might be thought to suggest a serious possibility that P lacks capacity' meets that which is contemplated either by Section 48 itself or the underpinning philosophy of the Act.'

22.38 In *DP v Hillingdon LBC*,[12] Hayden J considered a string of authorities on the meaning of the Mental Capacity Act 2005, s 48 which in some respects

10 [2010] 2 FLR 28.
11 [2017] EWHC 2435.
12 [2020] EWCOP 45.

were difficult to reconcile with one another. His Lordship provided the following guidance:

> '(a) The words of the Statute in section 48 require no gloss;
>
> (b) The question for the Court is "is there reason to believe P lacks capacity?"
>
> (c) In answering that question, the Court shall scrutinise all the evidence in the case;
>
> (d) Section 48 is a permissive provision in the context of an emergency jurisdiction which can only be used where it is identifiably in P's best interests;
>
> (e) The presumption of capacity applies to an application for an interim order under S.48 as strongly as it does in other situations;
>
> (f) The Court shall consider in s.48 applications whether the evidence establishes reasonable grounds to believe P may lack capacity, this is a different exercise from a determination under s.15 where the question is whether P does in fact lack capacity; and
>
> (g) The objective of s.48 is not restrictive, requiring a high level of proof, nor facilitative as a perfunctory gateway to a protective regime.'

22.39 Best interests shall always be considered with reference to the Mental Capacity Act 2005, s 4.

ORDERS THE COURT IS PRECLUDED FROM MAKING

22.40 The Mental Capacity Act 2005, s 27 provides that nothing in the Act allows a person to make decisions on behalf of P relating to certain family matters.

22.41 In particular, the court may not consent to a marriage or civil partnership or consent to P having sexual relations. Thus, if P lacks capacity to marry, there is no legal means by which any person or tribunal can consent on their behalf.

COSTS AND OTHER MISCELLANEOUS CONSIDERATIONS

22.42 The default position in the Court of Protection is that there is no order as to costs for proceedings relating to P's personal welfare. In proceedings relating to property and financial affairs, the general rule is that the costs are ordered to be paid from P's estate. In proceedings relating to both personal welfare and property, the Court shall apportion costs between the respective issues.

22.43 The Court of Protection Rules, SI 2017/1035, r 19.5(1) allows the court to depart from the general rule if the circumstances so justify. When considering whether to depart from the general rule, the court shall consider all the circumstances including:

(a) The conduct of the parties;

(b) whether a party has succeeded on part of that party's case, even if not wholly successful; and

(c) the role of any public body involved in the proceedings.

22.44 The Mental Capacity Act 2005, s 49 allows for the court to call for reports. In particular, the court may require a local authority or NHS body to arrange for a report to be made. Given there is no cost to the parties, this provision can be extremely useful in resolving issues of capacity to marry in forced marriage cases.

CHAPTER 23

Interplay with related proceedings

Content at a Glance:

INTRODUCTION

23.1 In a forced marriage context, Court of Protection proceedings shall often take place alongside other proceedings whether criminal or family. It is therefore important that practitioners are mindful of the confidentiality provisions which govern disclosure of material from Court of Protection and the relevant provisions which might limit disclosure of material from past family applications into the Court of Protection proceedings.

23.2 There shall also be circumstances where a judge is sitting simultaneously in the Court of Protection and the Family Division of the High Court. Whilst this is permissible, it does not appear that a judge may sit in both the Family Court and the Court of Protection simultaneously.[1]

DISCLOSURE OF MATERIAL FROM COURT OF PROTECTION PROCEEDINGS

23.3 The disclosure of material from Court of Protection proceedings is governed by the terms of the standard transparency order made under the Court of Protection Rules, r.4.2 and PD 4C. In particular it is not permitted for any material or information which might identify P, where they live, are being cared for, their contact details or the identity of P's family members to be communicated outside the proceedings.

1 President's Guidance, Jurisdiction of the Family Court: Allocation of Cases within the Family Court to the High Court Judge Level and Transfer of Cases within the Family Court to High Court Judge Level and Transfer of Cases from The Family Court to the High Court, 2018.

23.4 Therefore, in order to rely upon information generated in the course of Court of Protection proceedings, either for the purposes of a prosecution or for use in family proceedings, an application is required.

23.5 Such applications are made under the Court of Protection Rules, Part 10 and as a rule, ought to be made on notice with each party having an opportunity to make representations. It may be appropriate, in exceptional circumstances, to dispense with notice if, for example, the disclosure is for the purposes of an application for an urgent injunctive order.

DISCLOSURE INTO COURT PROTECTION PROCEEDINGS

23.6 Similar rules exist in respect of disclosure from Family Proceedings into Court of Protection proceedings. This is considered in full in **Chapter 14**.

23.7 Where Family proceedings have been concluded, the usual confidentiality provisions of the Family Procedure Rules 2010 shall apply and an application under Part 18 shall be necessary. Generally, such applications ought to be made to the judge that heard the proceedings and ought to be on notice to the other parties.

JURISDICTIONAL ISSUES

23.8 In forced marriage cases involving adults, Family and Court of Protection proceedings shall often run alongside one another being hearing by the same judge in the course of the same hearings. This can lead to confusion and the conflation of two very separate statutory regimes and a further common law set of principles relating to the exercise of the inherent jurisdiction.

23.9 In *XCC v AA & Ors*,[2] Parker J considered the interplay between the Mental Capacity Act 2005 and the inherent jurisdiction of the Family Division of the High Court to grant a declaration of non-recognition.

23.10 Her Ladyship, having expressly stated that the principles of the Mental Capacity Act 2005, Part I are not imported into the High Court's decision making under the inherent jurisdiction, held:

> 'I consider that I am entitled to grant a non-recognition declaration in this case on the specific ground that DD's consent has not been given, as did Baron J in *B v I*; irrespective of capacity. That is not a welfare or best interests' decision.'

2 [2012] EWHC 2183 (COP).

23.11 Similarly, practitioners shall be mindful of the differences in the statutory regime contained in the Family Law Act 1996, s 63A and the principles of the Mental Capacity Act 2005. Judges considering applications for forced marriage protection orders must consider all the circumstances of the case and in particular the need to secure the health, safety and well-being of the person to be protected. They are not, however required to undertake a best interest's analysis within the meaning of the Mental Capacity Act 2005, s 4 or to apply any of the principles of s 1 except that they must presume a person has capacity until that presumption is displaced on the balance of probabilities.

23.12 Whereas, any orders made pursuant to the Mental Capacity Act 2005 must of course be made in accordance with P's best interests and the principles in ss 1 and 4. This can create a perceived tension when a judge is considering one situation through two different statutory lenses.

Part 5

Best practice

CHAPTER 24

International cooperation

Content at a Glance:

INTRODUCTION

24.1 Forced marriage is a global phenomenon with many, if not the majority of, forced marriages in the UK having an international dimension. International cooperation in the enforcement of protective measures is therefore essential in combatting forced marriages and protecting victims. Cooperation and coordination between law enforcement agencies is considered at **21.48** *et seq.*

24.2 The enforceability of protective orders are generally governed by the rules of private international law. Chapters 19 and 21 of *Dicey, Morris & Collins on the Conflict of Laws* (15th Edn) provide comprehensive treatment of the rules applicable to children and adults lacking capacity. A full analysis of the enforceability and recognition of orders is beyond the scope of this book. What follows is therefore intended simply as a general guide as to international cooperation, recognition and enforcement of orders relating to forced marriage.

INTERNATIONAL COOPERATION IN THE PROTECTION OF ADULTS

24.3 The rules in relation to protective measures taken for the benefit of adults lacking capacity is set out in Rule 125 of *Dicey and Morris*:[1]

(a) Where a measure is taken to protect and adult under the law of a foreign country, the measure shall be recognised in England if the measure was taken on the ground that the protected adult was habitually resident in the foreign country;

1 *Dicey, Morris & Collins on the Conflict of Laws* 15th Edn (Sweet and Maxwell, 2018), Chapter 21, Section 3.

(b) a measure taken to protect and adult under the law of a foreign Convention country will be recognised in England if taken on a ground set out in Chapter 2 of the Hague Convention of 2000 (see **26.14** *et seq)*;

(c) a foreign protective order made under the law of a foreign jurisdiction and enforceable in that jurisdiction shall be enforceable in England as though it had been an order of the English Court if the Court of Protection makes a declaration to that effect under paragraph 22 of Schedule 3 of the Mental Capacity Act 2005.

24.4 The principles as above are subject to the exceptions in the Mental Capacity Act 2005, Sch 3, para 19 namely:

> '(3) But the court may disapply this paragraph in relation to a measure if it thinks that—
>
> (a) the case in which the measure was taken was not urgent,
>
> (b) the adult was not given an opportunity to be heard, and
>
> (c) that omission amounted to a breach of natural justice.
>
> (4) It may also disapply this paragraph in relation to a measure if it thinks that—
>
> (a) recognition of the measure would be manifestly contrary to public policy,
>
> (b) the measure would be inconsistent with a mandatory provision of the law of England and Wales, or
>
> (c) the measure is inconsistent with one subsequently taken, or recognised, in England and Wales in relation to the adult.
>
> (5) And the court may disapply this paragraph in relation to a measure taken under the law of a Convention country in a matter to which Article 33 applies, if the court thinks that that Article has not been complied with in connection with that matter.'

24.5 Article 33 of the Convention requires that if an authority with jurisdiction contemplates the placement of an adult in a placement in another contracting state, the state with jurisdiction shall first consult the state where the placement shall be located. If the state where the placement is located indicates its opposition within a reasonable time then the decision on the placement may not be made in the requesting state.

Hague Convention on the International Protection of Adults 2000

24.6 The Hague Convention on the International Protection of Adults ('the 2000 Convention') Convention applies to the protection in international situations of adults who, by reason of an impairment of insufficiency of their personal faculties, are not in a position to protect their interests'.[2]

24.7 The currently Contracting States are: Austria, Belgium, Cyprus, Czech Republic, Estonia, Finland, France, Germany, Greece, Ireland, Italy, Latvia, Luxembourg, Monaco, Netherlands, Poland, Portugal, Switzerland; and the United Kingdom of Great Britain and Northern Ireland.[3]

24.8 The Mental Capacity Act 2005, s 63 provides that Sch 3 to the Act gives effect in England and Wales to the Convention on the International Protection of Adults signed at The Hague on 13 January 2000 and makes related provision as to the private international law of England and Wales.

24.9 Article 4 provides that the 2000 Convention does not apply to the formation, annulment and dissolution of a marriage or any similar relationship, as well as legal separation.

Jurisdiction

General Principle

24.10 As a primary position, jurisdiction falls to the Contracting State of the habitual residence of the adult.[4] Habitual residence is not defined and remains a question of fact.[5] This falls in line with the domestic jurisprudence.[6]

24.11 When exercising jurisdiction, the authorities of the Contracting State shall apply their own laws.[7] However, States may exceptionally apply or take into consideration the law of another State with which the situation has a substantial connection.[8]

Those whose habitual residence cannot be established

24.12 For adults who are refugees and those who, due to disturbance occurring in their country, are internationally displaced, and those who unable to have their habitual residence established, the authorities of the Contracting State of the territory of which these adults are present have jurisdiction as if the adult was habitually resident there.[9] In cases where the adult's habitual residence cannot be established, this jurisdiction with cease if, at the time when the adult's habitual residence is established, this is elsewhere.[10]

2 Article 1 HC 2000,
3 https://www.hcch.net/en/instruments/conventions/status-table/?cid=71.
4 HC 2000, Article 5.
5 P Lagarde, Explanatory Report on the 2000 Hague Protection of Adults Convention 2017.
6 *Reg v Barnett LBC, exp Shah* [1983] 1 All ER 226, HL.
7 HC 2000, Article 13(1).
8) HC 2000, Article 13(2).
9 HC 2000, Article 6(1), (2).
10 P Lagarde, Explanatory Report on the 2000 Hague Protection of Adults Convention 2017, para 55.

Jurisdiction of the state of the adult's nationality

24.13 The authorities of the Contracting State of which the adult is a national have jurisdiction to take measures for the protection of the person or property of the adult if they consider that they are in a better position to assess the interests of the adult, and after advising the authorities having jurisdiction by reason of habitual residence of the adult, or in cases where habitual residence cannot be established, as a result of the adult being present in the territory.[11] This does not apply to adults who are refugees or adults who, due to disturbance occurring in their country, are internationally displaced as such State would be ill placed to exercise over the protection of an adult who has been forced to leave that State'.[12]

24.14 However, the authorities of the Contracting State which the adult is a national shall not exercise their jurisdiction if they have been informed by the authorities of another Contracting States having jurisdiction by virtue of –

'(i) the adult being habitually resident in their territory,[13] or

(ii) the adult is present in the territory and their habitual residence cannot be established,[14] or

(iii) another Contracting State having requested the authorities take measures for the protection of the person or property of the adult –[15]

that they have taken measures required by the situation or have decided that no measures should be taken or that proceedings are pending before them.[16] In such cases the national authorities 'must decline their jurisdiction and, if they were seized first, must even close the case if they learn that proceedings have started before one of the authorities mentioned above'.[17]

24.15 Where the authorities of a Contracting State have jurisdiction by virtue of the adult: (i) being habitually resident; or, (ii) present within the territory (in the case of adult refugees, or those who, due to disturbances occurring in their State of nationality, are internationally displaced, or adults who cannot have their habitual residence established) they may, of their own motion or on application by the authority of another Contracting State, request the authorities of one of the following Contracting States take measures for the protection of the person or property of the adult:

(a) A State of which the adult is a national;

(b) The State of the preceding habitual residence of the adult;

11 HC 2000, Article 7.
12 P Lagarde, Explanatory Report on the 2000 Hague Protection of Adults Convention 2017, para 58.
13 HC 2000, Article 5.
14 HC 2000, Article 6(2).
15 HC 2000, Article 8(1)-(2).
16 HC 2000, Article 7.
17 P Lagarde, Explanatory Report on the 2000 Hague Protection of Adults Convention 2017, para 61.

(c) A State in which property of the adult is located;

(d) The State whose authorities have been chosen in writing by the adult to take measures directed to his or her protection;

(e) The State of the habitual residence of a person close to the adult prepared to undertake his or her protection;

(f) The State in whose territory the adult is present, with regard to the protection of the person of the adult.[18]

24.16 Where one of the above Contracting States does not accept jurisdiction following such request, the authorities in the Contracting State where the adult is habitually resident or present in the territory (in the case of adult refugees, or those who, due to disturbances occurring in their State of nationality, are internationally displaced) retain jurisdiction.[19]

Presence of an adult's property

24.17 Where property of the adult is situated in a Contracting State, that State has jurisdiction to take measures of protection concerning that property, to the extent that such measures are compatible with those taken by the authorities who have jurisdiction by reason of: (i) the adult's habitual residence; or (ii) as a result of another Contracting State having requested the authorities take measures for the protection of the person or property of the adult.[20]

Cases of urgency

24.18 As noted throughout this book, forced marriage protection orders or other injunctive relief are often sought where there is an imminent risk of harm to the person to be protected.

24.19 In cases of urgency, the authorities of any Contracting State in whose territory the adult or property belonging to the adult is present have jurisdiction to take any necessary measures for protection. The Contracting State exercising jurisdiction as a matter of urgency shall, if possible, inform the authorities of the state of the adult's habitual residence.[21]

24.20 Any measures taken with regard to an adult within the territory of a Contracting State as a result of urgency shall lapse as soon as any of the following authorities have taken measures required by the situation:

(i) the State in which the adult is habitually resident in their territory;

(ii) the State in which the adult is present (in the case of adult refugees, or those who, due to disturbances occurring in their State of nationality, are

18 HC 2000, Article 8(2).
19 HC 2000, Article 8(3).
20 HC 2000, Article 9.
21 HC 2000, Article 10(4).

internationally displaced, or adults who cannot have their habitual residence established);

(iii) the State which has taken measures for protection of the person or property of the adult following another Contracting State having requested they do so; or

(iv) the State in which the property of an adult is present[22].

24.21 Where measures have been taken as a matter of urgency and the adult is habitually resident in a non-Contracting State, the measures shall lapse in each Contracting State, as soon as measures required by the situation and taken by the authorities of a State are recognised in the Contracting State in question.[23]

Temporary measures

24.22 The Contracting State in whose territory the adult is present has jurisdiction to take temporary measures of a temporary character for the protection of the adult which have a territorial effect limited to the State in question, in so far as those measures are compatible with those already taken by the authorities which have jurisdiction by reason of:

(i) the adult being habitually resident;

(ii) the adult being present within the territory (in the case of adult refugees, or those who, due to disturbances occurring in their State of nationality, are internationally displaced, or adults who cannot have their habitual residence established);

(iii as a result of another Contracting State having requested the authorities take measures for the protection of the person or property of the adult. In such circumstances, the authorities of the State in which the adult is habitually resident are to be notified of measures being taken.[24]

24.23 Once the authorities who have jurisdiction by reason of –

(i) the adult being habitually resident;

(ii) the adult being present within the territory (in the case of adult refugees, or those who, due to disturbances occurring in their State of nationality, are internationally displaced, or adults who cannot have their habitual residence established);

(iii) another Contracting State having requested the authorities take measures for the protection of the person or property of the adult;

Have taken a decision in respect of the measure of protection which may be required by the situation, the measures taken as a temporary measure shall lapse immediately.[25]

22 HC 2000, Article 10(2).
23 HC 2000, Article 10(3).
24 HC 2000, Article 11(1) with Articles 5–8.
25 HC 2000, Article 11(2) with Articles 5–8.

Jurisdiction checklist

(1) Is the adult habitually resident in the jurisdiction?	YES: the court has jurisdiction. NO: consider (2).
(2) Is the adult a refugee, or due to a disturbance occurring in their country, internationally displaced so that their habitual residence is unestablished?	(i) YES: are they currently present within the territory? YES to (i): the court has jurisdiction until the adult's habitual residence is established, if this is elsewhere. NO to (2) or (i): the court does not have jurisdiction.
(3) Is the adult a national of the jurisdiction but measures are not urgent?	(i) YES: have the authorities in which the adult is currently present taken any measures required or, decided that no measures should be taken? YES to (i): the court does not have jurisdiction. NO to (i): the court has jurisdiction if they consider they are in a better position to assess the interests of the adult. The authorities having jurisdiction as a result of habitual residence or, as a result of the adult being present in the territory (in the case of adult refugees, or those who, due to disturbances occurring in their State of nationality, are internationally displaced) are to be advised of this position.
(4) Has another authority in a Contracting State sought to delegate jurisdiction?	(i) YES: has jurisdiction been accepted? YES to (i): the court has jurisdiction. NO to (ii): The authorities having jurisdiction as a result of habitual residence or, as a result of the adult being present in the territory (in the case of adult refugees, or those who, due to disturbances occurring in their State of nationality, are internationally displaced) retain jurisdiction.
(5) Is there an urgent need to take measures?	(i) YES: Is the adult present within the territory? YES to (i): the court has jurisdiction to take measures necessary for protection. (ii) NO to (i): the court does not have jurisdiction.

(6) Are temporary measures which have limited territorial effect required?	(i) YES: is the adult present within the territory? (ii) YES to (i): the court has jurisdiction. NB: the measures to be take must be compatible with those already taken by the authorities which have jurisdiction by reason of (i) the adult being habitually resident (ii) the adult being present within the territory (in the case of adult refugees, or those who, due to disturbances occurring in their State of nationality, are internationally displaced, or adults who cannot have their habitual residence established); (iii) as a result of another Contracting State having requested the authorities take measures for the protection of the person or property of the adult. (iii) NO to (i): the court does not have jurisdiction.

Enforceability of orders in other Contracting States to the Hague Convention on the International Protection of Adults 2000

24.24 Where a measure taken in one Contracting State is implemented in another Contracting State, the conditions of its implementation are governed by the law of the Implementing State.[26]

24.25 In circumstances where a protective measure has been taken in relation to an adult under the law of a Convention Country other than England and Wales it shall be recognised in England and Wales if it was taken on a ground mentioned in Chapter II of the Convention (jurisdiction – above) (Mental Capacity Act 2005, Sch 3, Part 4).

24.26 'Protective measure' is defined broadly under Mental Capacity Act 2005, Sch 3, Part 1, para 5(1) as being 'a measure directed to the protection of the person or property of an adult; and it may deal in particular with any of the following:

(a) the determination of incapacity and the institution of a protective regime,

(b) placing the adult under the protection of an appropriate authority,

(c) guardianship, curatorship or any corresponding system,

(d) the designation and functions of a person having charge of the adult's person or property, or representing or otherwise helping him,

(e) placing the adult in a place where protection can be provided,

(f) administering, conserving or disposing of the adult's property,

(g) authorising a specific intervention for the protection of the person or property of the adult.

26 HC 2000, Article 14.

24.27 This is a non-exhaustive list and may encompass circumstances in which a person who has been made subject to an order in another Contracting State protecting them from a forced marriage. If so, then the Mental Capacity Act 2005, Sch 3 provides a mechanism for recognition of such order and the protections it brings within this jurisdiction.

24.28 The measures taken by the authorities of a Contracting State shall be recognised by operation of law in all other Contracting States.[27] However, recognition may be refused:

(a) If the measure was taken by an authority who did not have jurisdiction;

(b) If the measure was taken, except in a case of urgency, in the context of judicial or administrative proceedings, without the adult having been provided the opportunity to be heard, in violation of fundamental principles of procedure of the requested State;

(c) If such recognition is manifestly contrary to public policy of the requested State, or conflicts with a provision of the law of that State which is mandatory whether law would otherwise be applicable;

(d) If the measure is incompatible with a later measure taken in a non-Contracting State which would have had jurisdiction by reason of the adult being habitually resident or as a result of the adult's property being within the jurisdiction, where this later measure fulfils the requirements for recognition in the requested State;

(e) If an authority has not consulted the Central Authority or other competent authority of another Contracting State in circumstances where the Contracting State having jurisdiction as set out within the Convention under Articles 5–8 contemplates the placement of the adult in an establishment or other place where protection could be provided and such placement is the other Contracting State, nor transmitted a report to the adult together with the reasons for the proposed placement as required by Article 33.[28]

24.29 Any interested person may request from the competent authorities of a Contracting State that they decide on the recognition or non-recognition of a measure taken in another Contracting State.[29]

24.30 The authority of the requested State is bound by the findings of fact on which the authority of the State where the measure was taken based its jurisdiction.[30]

24.31 If measures taken in one Contracting State and enforceable there require enforcement in another Contracting State, they shall, upon request by an interested party, be declared enforceable or registered for the purpose of

27 HC 2000 Article 22.
28 HC 2000, Article 33.
29 HC 2000, Article 23.
30 HC 2000, Article 24.

enforcement in that other State according to the procedure provided in the law of the latter State.[31] Each Contracting State shall apply to the declaration of enforceability or registration a simple and rapid procedure.[32] The declaration of enforceability or registration may be refused only for one of the reasons set out in Article 22, paragraph 2.[33]

24.32 Measures taken in one Contracting State and declared enforceable, or registered for the purpose of enforcement, in another Contracting State shall be enforced in the latter State as if they had been taken by the authorities of that State.

24.33 Enforcement takes place in accordance with the law of the requested State to the extent provided by such law.[34]

INTERNATIONAL RECOGNITION AND ENFORCEMENT OF ORDERS CONCERNING CHILDREN

24.34 International recognition and enforcement of orders relating to children is of fundamental importance in combatting forced marriage. In 2019, 27 per cent of cases dealt with by the Forced Marriage Unit involved children.[35]

24.35 The regime governing the recognition and enforcement of English and Welsh orders concerning children is dependent on the country in which recognition is sought.

Within the European Union

24.36 At the time of writing, the future of the applicability within the UK of the regime governing the recognition of Family Orders within the European Union is unclear. Until the end of the Implementation Period on 31 December 2020, the position remains unchanged and Brussels IIa takes precedence in cases involving two member states. After this date, the Brussels IIa Regulation, which governs recognition and enforcement within the European Union is retained EU Law under the European (Withdrawal) Act 2018 and shall continue to have domestic effect. However, the United Kingdom cannot legislate for reciprocity and absent a separate agreement between the EU and UK, parties shall not be able to rely on the Regulation to enforce UK Orders in European Courts.[36]

31 HC 2000, Article 25(1).
32 HC 2000, Article 25(2).
33 HC 2000, Article 25(3).
34 HC 2000, Article 27.
35 HMG, Forced Marriage Unit Statistics 2019, 25 June 2020.
36 Thompson, Ministry of Justice Impact Assessment, For the Jurisdictions and Judgments (Family) Regulations 2018, 2019.

24.37 At present the United Kingdom has proposed an agreement for criminal judicial cooperation but no equivalent Civil or Family proposed agreement.[37] It currently appears, based on both the United Kingdom's and European Union's position that at the expiry of the implementation period, the default position shall fall back to the principles of Civil Judicial Co-operation codified in the Hague Convention on Private International Law.[38]

24.38 As such, the provisions and rules of the Brussels IIa Regulation are not explored here, however, the cessation of the reciprocity of Brussels IIa Regulation shall have the following consequences for pan-European judicial cooperation in cases involving the protection of children:

(a) Article 9 of Brussels IIa provides that for the first three months of a child's relocation to another member state, their habitual residence shall remain in their former state. The Hague Convention 1996 does not adopt this rule;

(b) Articles 11(6) to 11(8) of the Regulation provides a procedure whereby following a Court making a 'non-return order' under the 1980 Hague Convention, that is an order that a child is not to be returned to the country they were habitually resident immediately before their wrongful removal or retention, the parties may make further submissions. This allows parties to effectively have a second attempt at obtaining the return of a child. There shall be no equivalent provision following the Regulation ceasing to have effect;

(c) Under the1980 Hague Convention, Contracting States may refuse to return a child subject to a return order if it considers that there is a grave risk that the return of that child would expose them to *'physical or psychological harm or otherwise place the child in an intolerable situation'*. The Brussels IIa Regulation includes a sensible provision removing a Court's discretion to refuse to order the return of the child if there are adequate protective measures in place to rectify the identified risk. This proviso shall not apply after 31 December 2020;

24.39 Overall, it appears that Brexit is likely to bring about a considerable reduction in judicial cooperation between the United Kingdom and European jurisdictions.

The 1996 Hague Conventions

24.40 The Hague Convention 1996 is an international convention intended to improve the protection of children internationally and avoid conflicts between legal systems relating to jurisdiction, applicable law, recognition and enforcement

37 HMG, Draft working text for an agreement on law enforcement and judicial cooperation in criminal matters, 2020.

38 HMG, 'The Future Relationship with the EU: The UK's Approach to Negotiation' CP211, February 2020; The European Council, 'Directives for the Negotiation of a New Partnership With the United Kingdom of Great Britain and Northern Ireland'.

of measures for the protection of children.[39] The Convention came into force in the United Kingdom in 2012.[40] The Convention has 52 signatories including all members of the European Union. The Convention was specified as a Treaty within the meaning of the European Communities Act 1972 and as such was implemented by way of Statutory Instrument under the Act. It is not expected that the Convention should be affected by the United Kingdom's exit from the European Union.[41]

24.41 The Convention's Contracting States at the time of writing were:[42]

(1) The United Kingdom;

(2) The European Union's 27 member states;

(3) Albania;

(4) Armenia;

(5) Australia;

(6) Barbados;

(7) Cuba;

(8) Dominican Republic;

(9) Ecuador;

(10) Fiji;

(11) Guyana;

(12) Honduras;

(13) Lesotho;

(14) Monaco;

(15) Montenegro;

(16) Morocco;

(17) Nicaragua;

(18) Norway;

(19) Paraguay;

39 Convention of 19 October 1996 on Jurisdiction, Applicable Law, Recognition, Enforcement and Co-Operation in Respect of Parental Responsibility and Measures for the Protection of Children, preamble.

40 Convention of 19 October 1996 on Jurisdiction, Applicable Law, Recognition, Enforcement and Co-Operation in Respect of Parental Responsibility and Measures for the Protection of Children.

41 See *Butterworths Family Law Service*, Issue 223, 2020, Chapter 4A; Nigel Lowe 'What are the implications of the Brexit vote for the law on international child abduction?' *Child and Family Law Quarterly* [2017] CFLQ 253.

42 https://www.hcch.net/en/instruments/conventions/status-table/?cid=70 accessed 02 October 2020.

(20) The Russian Federation;

(21) Serbia;

(22) Switzerland;

(23) Turkey;

(24) Ukraine; and

(25) Uruguay.

24.42 The Convention is yet to be ratified in:

(1) Argentina;

(2) Canada;

(3) Republic of North Macedonia; and

(4) The United States of America

Jurisdiction under the 1996 Hague Convention

24.43 The grounds upon which Contracting States can acquire jurisdiction in respect of children are set out at Articles 5 to 10 of the Convention:

> '(a) The court of a Contracting State in which the child is habitually resident has jurisdiction to take measures directed to the protection of the child's person or property.[43] Where the child changes habitual residence, the authorities of the new State shall have jurisdiction,[44]
>
> (b) Contracting States shall have jurisdiction for displaced and refugee children or children whose habitual residence cannot be established, if the child is present in the State,[45]
>
> (c) Where a child is wrongfully removed or retained, the Contracting State in which the child was habitually resident immediately before their arrival or retention shall have jurisdiction until the child has acquired a habitual residence in another state,[46] and
>
> i. Each person, institution or other body having rights of custody has acquiesced in the removal or retention; or
>
> ii. The child has resided in that other state for a person of at least one year after the person, institution or other body having rights of custody has or should have had knowledge of the whereabouts of the child, no request for return lodged within that period is still pending and the child is settled in their new environment.[47]

43 HC 1996, Article 5 (1).
44 HC 1996, Article 5 (2).
45 HC 1996, Article 6.
46 See HC 1996, Article 7(2) for definition of wrongful removal or retention.
47 HC 1996, Article 7.

(d) A Contracting State with jurisdiction under Articles 5 or 6 may, if it considers that the Authority of another Contracting State would be better placed in the particular case to assess the best interests of the child may either:[48]

i. Request that the other Authority assumes jurisdiction to take such measures of protection as it considered necessary; or

ii. Suspend consideration of the case and invite the parties to introduce such a request before the authority of the other state.[49]

The Contracting State being requested to exercise jurisdiction may do so if it considers doing to be in the child's best interests.

(e) Conversely, a Contracting State of which the child is a national, in which the child's property is located, in which matrimonial proceedings relating to the child's parents are underway or a state with which the child has a substantial connection does not have jurisdiction it may either:[50]

i. Request the Contracting state of the habitual residence of the child authorises it to exercise jurisdiction to take measures of protection which it considers necessary; or

ii. Invite the parties to introduce such a request such a request before the Authority in the Contracting State in which the Child is habitually resident.[51]

(f) If the authorities of a Contracting State are exercising jurisdiction to determine matrimonial proceedings relating to the parents of a child habitually resident in another Contracting State, the State handling the matrimonial proceedings may, if their domestic law so provides, take measures directs to the protection of the person or property of such a child if:

i. At the time of the commencement of the proceedings, one of his or her parents habitually resides in that State and one of them has parental responsibility in relation to the child; and

ii. The jurisdiction of these authorities to take such measures has been accepted by the parents, as well as by any other person who has parental responsibility in relation to the child, and it is in the best interests of the child.

48 HC 1996, Article 8.

49 See HC 1996, Article 8 (2), (3) and (4) for further requirements including that the Contracting States concerned must be states of which the child is a national, in which the child's property is located, in which matrimonial proceedings relating to the child's parents are underway or a state with which the child has a substantial connection.

50 HC 1996, Article 9.

51 See HC 1996, Article 9(2) and (3) for further provisions, in particular, the requesting State may only exercise jurisdiction once authorised by the State in which the child is habitually resident.

This jurisdiction ceases as soon as the decision allowing or refusing the application for divorce, legal separation or annulment of the marriage has become final or the proceedings have ended for another reason.'

24.44 Article 11 of the Convention allows in cases of urgency for any Contracting State in whose territory the child or property belonging to the child is present to take any necessary measures of protection. Such measures shall lapse immediately once a Contracting State with jurisdiction under Articles 5–10 have taken the necessary measures. Where the child is habitually resident in a non-contracting state, the measures taken under Article 11 shall lapse as soon as the measures required are taken by the Non-Contracting State and those measures have been recognised in the Contracting State in question.

Recognition and enforcement of orders relating to parental responsibility under the 1996 Hague Convention

24.45 Article 23(1) of the Hague Convention 1996 creates a presumption that 'measures taken by the authorities of a Contracting State shall be recognised by operation of law in all other Contracting States'. Article 24 allows for any interested party to seek a decision on the recognition or non-recognition of a measure taken in another Contracting State. This provision provides an avenue through which pre-emptive applications for recognition could be make. For example, if a child is to be places overseas with a family member, clarity can be obtained on whether any associated orders are to be recognised and enforced in the country before the child travels there.

24.46 Where enforcement of an order made in one Contracting State is applied for in another Contracting State, the relevant interested party is required by Article 26(1) to obtain a declaration of enforceability/registration for enforcement. Courts are not entitled to review the merits of the measures concerned.[52] Recognition may only be refused for the following reasons.[53]

(a) If the measure was taken, except in a case of urgency in the context of a judicial or administrative proceeding without the child having been provided the opportunity to be heard, in violation of fundamental principles of procedure of the State in which enforcement or recognition is sought;[54]

(b) Where the court is requested to refuse recognition by a person claiming that the measure infringes his or her parental responsibility, if such a measure was taken, except in a case of urgency, without the person claiming parental responsibility haven been given an opportunity to be heard;

52 HC 1996, Article 27.

53 HC 1996, Article 23.

54 In a UK context see *NG v OG* [2014] EWHC 4182 (Fam), [2015] All ER (D) 59 (Jan) where the High Court refused to recognise a Russian Order on the basis that one of the children concerned had not been given an opportunity to be heard.

(c) Such recognition is manifestly contrary to the public policy of the State in which recognition is sought, taking into account the best interests of the child;[55]

(d) The measure is incompatible with a later measure taken in a non-contracting state in which the child is habitually resident, where the later measure fulfils the requirements for recognition in the requested state; and

(e) Where the procedure in Article 33 of the Convention has not been complied with.

24.47 Article 33 of the Convention requires that where a Contracting State is considering placing a child in a another Contracting State with a foster family in institutional care or for care by kafala or an analogous institution it is necessary to first obtain the consent of the requested state.

Procedure in England and Wales for the registration of orders pursuant to Article 24 of the Convention

24.48 The Family Procedure Rule 2010, r 31.5, supplemented by PD 31A sets out the procedure for obtaining recognition of orders made by another Contracting State in the UK under the Hague Convention 1996.

24.49 Applications are to be made to a District Judge of the Principal Registry of the Family Division of the High Court.[56] Applications are made using the Part 19 procedure on form FP1.[57] The further procedural requirements are set out below:

Evidence required in support of all applications for registration, recognition of non-recognition under the Hague Convention 1996	• Sworn statement or affidavit which exhibits the judgment or verified, certified or otherwise authenticated copy of the judgment of which recognition or registration is sought;[58] • A translation of the judgment;[59] • Other documents required depending on the type of application, as set out below, must be translated into English certified by a notary public or a person qualified for the purpose or accompanied by a witness statement or affidavit confirming that the translation is accurate.[60]

55 In *LAB v KB* [2009] EWHC 2243 (Fam), [2010 Fam Law 933, the High Court held that refusal of recognition on the grounds of public policy shall be 'extremely rare'.
56 FPR 2010, r 31.4.
57 FPR 2010, PD 31A, para 1.1.
58 FRR 2010, PD 31A, para 2.2.
59 FRR 2010, PD 31A, para 2.2.
60 FPR 2010, PD 31A para 2.3.

Material required in support of an application for registration or recognition	• Those documents necessary to show that the judgment is enforceable according to the law of the Contracting State in which it was given[61] • A description of the opportunities provided by the authority which gave the judgment in question for the child to be heard, except where the judgment was given in a case of urgency;[62] • Where the judgment was given in a case of urgency, a statement as to the circumstances of the urgency that led to the child not having the opportunity to be heard;[63] • details of any measures taken in the non-Contracting State of the habitual residence of the child, if applicable, specifying the nature and effect of the measure, and the date on which it was taken;[64] • In as far as not apparent from the copy of the judgment provided, a statement of the grounds on which the authority which gave the judgment based its jurisdiction, together with any documentary evidence in support of that statement;[65] • Where appropriate, a statement regarding whether Article 33 of the 1996 Hague Convention has been complied with, and the identity and address of the authority or authorities from which consent has been obtained, together with evidence of that consent;[66] and • Whether the judgment provides for the payment of a sum or sums of money;[67] • Whether interest is recoverable on the judgment or part of the judgment in accordance with the law of the State in which the judgment was given, and if that is the case, the rate of interest, the date from which interest is recoverable, and the date on which interest ceases to accrue;[68]and • An address within the jurisdiction of the court for service of process on the party making the application and stating, in so far as is known to the applicant, the name and usual or last known address or place of business of the person against whom judgment was given.[69]

61 FPR 2010, PD 31A, para 4.2(a).
62 FPR 2010, PD 31A, para 4.2(b).
63 FPR 2010, PD 31A, para 4.2(c).
64 FPR 2010, PD 31A, para 4.2(d).
65 FPR 2010, PD 31A, para 4.2(e).
66 FPR 2010, PD 31A, para 4.2(f).
67 FPR 2010, PD 31A, para 3.2(c).
68 FPR 2010, PD 31A, para 3.2(d).
69 FPR 2010, PD 31A, para 3.2(e).

Material required in support of an application for non-recognition	• A statement of the ground or grounds under Article 23 of the 1996 Hague Convention on which it is requested that the judgment be not recognised, the reasons why the applicant asserts that such ground or grounds is or are made out, and any documentary evidence on which the Applicant relies; and; • An address within the jurisdiction of the court for service of process on the applicant and stating, in so far as is known to the applicant, the name and usual or last known address or place of business of the person in whose favour judgment was given.

24.50 The Court has broad case management powers. Where a party making an application does not produce the required documents the court may fix a time within which the documents are to be produced, accept equivalent documents or dispense with the need to produce the documents if the court considers it has sufficient information. Under the Family Procedure Rules 2010, r 31.6(1), the court may direct:

‘(g) That service of the application may be dispensed with;

(h) That part or all of the proceedings be expedited;

(i) The steps to be taking in proceedings and the time by which each step shall be taken;

(j) The service of documents; and

(k) The filing of evidence;’

24.51 Rule 31.8 requires that where an application is made for the registration or non-recognition of a judgment given in another Contracting State, that the court will serve the application on the person against whom registration is sought.[70] The court shall not hear submissions either from the person against whom registrations is sought or any child in relation to whom the judgment was given.[71]

24.52 Where an application is made that a judgment should not be recognised, the court officer will serve the application on the person in whose favour judgment was given.[72]The beneficiary of the judgement must then file answer to the application within one month if resident in the UK or two months if resident in another Contracting State although the court may extend this time limit on account of distance.[73] In their answer, the person who the judgment benefits may request recognition of the judgment and in doing so much comply with the requirements as set out above.[74]

70 FPR 2010, r 31.8(2)(a).
71 FPR 2010, r 31.8(2)(b).
72 FPR 2010, r 31.8 (3)(a).
73 FPR 2010, r 31.8 (3) (b) (i), (ii), (4).
74 FPR 2010, r 31.8 (5).

24.53 If the person in whose favour the judgment was given fails to file an answer to an application of non-recognition, the following consequences may follow:[75]

(a) If the 1965 Hague Convention applies[76] then Article 15 of that Convention ought to be applied, in particular judgment will not be given unless it is established that:[77]
   (i) The document was served by a method prescribed the internal law of the state address for the service of documents in domestic actions upon people within its own territory; or
   (ii) The document was actually delivered to the party or their residence by another method provided for in the Convention in sufficient time to allow the party to defend that application.
   (iii) Notwithstanding the above, the court may give judgement if the document was transmitted by one of the methods provided for in the Convention; a period of not less than six months and considered adequate by the judge has elapsed since the transmission of the judgment; and no certificate of any kind has been received even though reasonable efforts have been made to obtain it from the state addressed.

(b) In all other cases, the court shall not consider the application unless it is proved to the satisfaction of the court that the person in whose favour judgment was given was served with the application within a reasonable time to arrange for his response; or the court is satisfied that the circumstances of the case justify proceeding with consideration of the application.

24.54 If an application for non-recognition is refused the court may direct that the decision to refuse the application is to be treated as a decision that the judgment is to be recognised.[78]

24.55 A route of appeal to a High Court judge exists from orders relating to the recognition or non-recognition of judgments under the Hague Convention.[79] The time limit for the bringing of an appeal is one month if resident in the UK or two months if habitually resident in another Contracting State, although the court may extend time limits due to distance.[80] Under the Family Procedure Rules 2010, r 31.16 the court may stay the enforcement of judgments pending appeal.

24.56 The court shall not enforce a judgment registered until the time limit for bringing an appeal has expired or the stay ordered pursuant to the Family Procedure Rules 2010, r 31.16 has expired.[81] However, this is subject to an

75 FPR 2010, r 31.8(7), (8).
76 Convention of 15 November 1965 on the Service Abroad of Judicial and Extrajudicial Documents In Civil or Commercial Documents.
77 Convention of 15 November 1965 on the Service Abroad of Judicial and Extrajudicial Documents In Civil or Commercial Documents, Article 15.
78 FPR 2010, r 31.10(a).
79 FPR 2010, r 31.15.
80 FPR 2010, r 31.15(2).
81 FPR 2010, r 31.17(1).

exception whereby a court may enforce a judgment which has been registered before the expiration of the appeal time limit where the urgent enforcement of the judgment is necessary to secure the welfare of the child to whom the judgment relates.[82]

Procedure for seeking the recognition or enforcement of English or Welsh orders in other countries under the 1996 Hague Convention

24.57 The steps required to obtain recognition or enforcement of orders abroad shall be subject to the national law of the state concerned. However, there are steps which can be taken in England and Wales to ease the obtaining of recognition abroad. Parties ought to request that the Court provides certified copies of orders and judgments in circumstances where an application overseas under the Hague Convention 1996 may be required. The court should state on the certified copy of the order the basis upon which it has jurisdiction for the purposes of Article 23(2)(a) of the 1996 Hague Convention.[83]

24.58 Where a party requires a certified copy of a judgment previously made, an application under the Family Procedure Rules 2010, r 31.18 may be made.

International recognition and enforcement in jurisdictions without reciprocal arrangements with the UK

24.59 If there is no international framework to achieve reciprocal recognition of orders and judgments between the United Kingdom and another state, then the only recourse is through the domestic law of the country concerned. Mirror Orders are order which mirror the terms of orders made in another jurisdiction. In English Law, Mirror Orders are made pursuant to the inherent jurisdiction.[84] Local legal advice shall have to be sought in each case.

INTERNATIONAL COOPERATION IN CASES OF CHILD ABDUCTION

24.60 In a case of child abduction involving two states of the European Union, the provisions of Brussels IIa provide effective remedies to secure the return of children and the recognition and enforcement of orders. Due to the uncertainty about the future of Brussels IIa's applicability to the United Kingdom, as set out at **26.36** *et seq*, the Regulation is not considered in detail in this Chapter. However, practitioners should be aware that there has been authority that as long as the Regulation is available, it ought to be pursued in preference to remedies available under the 1980 Hague Convention.[85]

82 FPR 2010, r 31.17(1A).
83 FPR 2010, r 31.18(4).
84 See *Re P (A Child: Mirror Orders)* [2000] 1 FLR 435.
85 *JRG v EV (Abduction: Brussels II Revisited)* [2013] 1 FLR 203 at para 17.

24.61 The Hague Convention on the Civil Aspects of International Child Abduction ('1980 Hague Convention) was adopted on 25 October 1980 and came into force in the United Kingdom through the Child Abduction and Custody Act 1985. There are currently 101 Contracting States to the Convention.

24.62 The following states have not acceded to the Convention or their ratification has not been accepted by England:

(1) Barbados;

(2) Bolivia;

(3) Cuba;

(4) Dominican Republic;

(5) Gabon;

(6) Guatemala;

(7) Guinea;

(8) Guyana;

(9) Iraq;

(10) Jamaica;

(11) Lesotho;

(12) Nicaragua;

(13) Pakistan;

(14) Thailand;

(15) Trinidad and Tobago.

Pakistani cases

24.63 Pakistan has a particularly strong association with UK related cases of Forced Marriage. Pakistan is not a Contracting State to the 1980 Hague Convention. The UK-Pakistan Protocol on Children Matters was signed in 2003 by the Chief Justice of Pakistan and the then President of the Family Division, Dame Butler-Sloss DBE. The protocol provides that:

> '(1) In normal circumstances the welfare of a child is best determined by the courts of the country of the child's habitual/ordinary residence
>
> (2) If a child is removed from the UK to Pakistan, or from Pakistan to the UK, without the consent of the parent with a custody/residence order or a restraint/interdict order from the court of the child's habitual/ ordinary residence, the judge of the court of the country to which the child has been removed shall not ordinarily exercise jurisdiction over

the child, save in so far as it is necessary for the court to order the return of the child to the country of the child's habitual/ordinary residence.

(3) If a child is taken from the UK to Pakistan, or from Pakistan to the UK, by a parent with visitation/access/contact rights with the consent of the parent with a custody/residence order or a restraint/interdict order from the court of the child's habitual/ordinary residence or in consequence of an order from that court permitting the visit, and the child is retained in that country after the end of the visit without consent or in breach of the court order, the judge of the court of the country in which the child has been retained shall not ordinarily exercise jurisdiction over the child, save in so far as it is necessary for the court to order the return of the child to the country of the child's habitual/ordinary residence.

(4) The above principles shall apply without regard to the nationality, culture or religion of the parents or either parent and shall apply to children of mixed marriages

(5) In cases where the habitual/ordinary residence of the child is in dispute the court to which an application is made should decide the issue of habitual/ordinary residence before making any decision on the return or on the general welfare of the child, and upon determination of the preliminary issue as to habitual/ordinary residence should then apply the general principles set out above.

(6) These applications should be lodged by the applicant, listed by the court and decided expeditiously.

(7) It is recommended that the respective governments of the UK and Pakistan give urgent consideration to identifying or establishing an administrative service to facilitate or oversee the resolution of child abduction cases (not covered by the 1980 Hague Convention on the Civil Aspects of International Child Abduction).

(8) It is further recommended that the judiciaries, the legal practitioners and the non-governmental organisations in the UK and Pakistan use their best endeavours to advance the objects of this protocol.

(9) It is agreed that the UK and Pakistan shall each nominate a judge of the superior court to work in liaison with each other to advance the objects of this protocol.'

24.64 The Protocol has been described as having questionable utility, dependent on the Pakistani region and court involved.[86] However, the Protocol continues to have weight in UK cases where the protocol applies and heavily influenced Francis J's decision in *Y v S*.[87]

86 *Butterworths Family Law Service*, Issue 223, 2020, Chapter 4A, para 2004.
87 [2017] EWHC 1020 (Fam).

The Hague Convention 1980

24.65 The objects of the Convention are to secure the prompt return of children wrongfully removed or retained in any contracting state and to ensure that rights of custody and access under the law of one Contracting State are effectively respect in other Contracting States.[88] The Convention applies to any child who was habitually resident in a Contracting State immediately before any breach of custody or access rights and ceases to apply when a child reaches the age of 16.[89]

24.66 Under the Convention, each Contracting State must establish a central authority responsible for matters relating to the convention and in particularly for cooperating with other competent authorities to secure the prompt return of children and achieve the other objects of the Convention.[90]

24.67 Nationals of Contracting States are entitled to legal aid for bringing applications related to the Convention in any other Contracting State.[91]

24.68 Article 3 of the Convention provides that the removal or retention of a child is considered to be wrongful where:

(a) It is in breach of rights of custody attributed to a person, an institution or any other body, either jointly or alone, under the law of the State in which the child was habitually resident immediately before the removal or retention; and

(b) At the time of the removal or retention those rights were actually exercised, either jointly or alone or would have been so exercised but for the removal or retention.[92]

24.69 In *Re J (A Minor) (Abduction: Custody Rights), Re*,[93] it was confirmed that Wardship amounts to custody for the purposes of Article 3 of the Convention. In *Re C (Child Abduction) (Unmarried Father: Rights of Custody)*,[94] Munby J held that the court would be invested with rights of custody if the case had come before a judge who had given directions powers even if no substantive order had been made. A solely administrative step was not enough to give rise to rights of custody being invested in the court.

24.70 Article 8 of the Convention confers the right on any person, institution or body claimant that a child has been removed or retained in breach of custody rights to apply either to the central authority of the child's habitual residence or

88 HC 1980, Article 1.
89 HC 1980, Article 4.
90 HC 1980, Article 6.
91 HC 1980, Article 25.
92 The rights of custody referred to may arise in particular by operation of law or by reason of judicial or administrative decision, or by reason of an agreement having legal effect under the law of the state: 1980 Hague Convention Article 3.
93 [1990] 2 FLR 442.
94 [2003] 1 FLR 252.

to the central authority of any other Contracting State for assistance in securing the return of the child. The application must contain:

(a) information concerning the identity of the applicant, of the child and of the person alleged to have removed or retained the child;

(b) where available, the date of birth of the child;

(c) the grounds on which the applicant's claim for return of the child is based;

(d) all available information relating to the whereabouts of the child and the identity of the person with whom the child is presumed to be.[95]

24.71 Where the central authority receiving an application under Article 8 has reason to believe the child concerned is in another Contracting State, it shall immediately inform that state's Central Authority.[96]

24.72 Article 10 requires that the central authority of the state in which the child is shall take all appropriate measures to secure the voluntary return of the child. The Family Division of the High Court has adopted a Child Abduction Mediation Scheme.[97] The Family Division's Guidance requires that a direction at the first on notice hearing is made that both the applicant and the respondent have the opportunity to speak separately with a mediator to discuss the possibility of mediation under the scheme.[98]

24.73 Judicial and administrative authorities are required to act expeditiously and where a decision has not been reached within six weeks of the start of proceedings, the state requesting the child's return shall be entitled to request an explanation for the delay.[99] In the course of those proceedings, where a child has been wrongfully removed or retained[100] and at the start of the proceedings it had been less than a year since the removal or retention, the return of the child must be ordered forthwith.[101]

24.74 If more than a year has elapsed since the wrongful removal or retention at the start of proceedings, the child's return must still be ordered unless it is

95 The application may also contain an authenticated copy of any relevant decision or agreement; a certificate or an affidavit emanating from a Central Authority, or other competent authority of the state of the child's habitual residence, or from a qualified person, concerning the relevant law of that state and any other relevant document.

96 HC 1980, Article 9.

97 Run by the charity Reunite, contactable at reunite@dircon.co.uk or 01162555345.

98 Sir James Munby P, Practice Guidance, Case Management and Medication of International Child Abudction Proceedings, 2018 accessible at https://www.judiciary.uk/wp-content/uploads/2018/03/presidents-practice-guidance-case-management-mediation-of-international-child-abduction-proceedings-20180227-1.pdf.

99 HC 1980, Article 11.

100 Within the meaning of Article 3 of the Convention.

101 HC 1980, Article 12, para 1.

demonstrated that the child is not settled in their new environment.[102] If the child has been taken to another state, the court may stay or dismiss the proceedings.[103]

24.75 The court shall not be obliged to order the return of the child if, having taken account of information provided relating to the child's social background, it finds:[104]

(a) the person, institution or other body having the care of the person of the child was not actually exercising the custody rights at the time of removal or retention, or had consented to or subsequently acquiesced in the removal or retention;

(b) there is a grave risk that his or her return would expose the child to physical or psychological harm or otherwise place the child in an intolerable situation; or

(c) The child objects to being returned and has attained an age and degree of maturity at which it is appropriate to take account of their views.

24.76 A court may, prior to making a return order request that the applicant obtain a decision or other determination that the removal or retention was wrongful[105] from the country of the child's habitual residence.[106] The court may not decide on the merits of rights of custody until it has been determined that the child shall not be returned under the Convention or until an application under the Convention has not been lodged within a reasonable time following receipt of notice.[107]

24.77 A decision or entitlement in respect of custody in the requested state is not in and of itself a ground for refusing to return a child under the Convention.[108] It is however a factor that may be taken into account in applying the Convention.

24.78 An order for the return of a child may be refused if it would not be permitted by the fundamental principles of the requested state related to human rights and fundamental freedoms.

Habitual residence

24.79 Habitual residence is a question of fact and reflects some degree of integration by the child in a social and family environment.[109] In *Re B (a minor)*

102 HC 1980, Article 12, para 2.
103 HC 1980, Article 12, para 3.
104 HC 1980, Article 13.
105 Within the meaning of Article 3 of the Convention.
106 HC 1980, Article 14.
107 HC 1980, Article 16.
108 HC 1980, Article 17.
109 *A v A and another (Children: Habitual Residence) (Reunite International Child Abduction Centre and others intervening)* [2013] UKSC 60, [2014] AC 1.

(habitual residence),[110] Hayden J comprehensively summarised the principles of the concept of habitual residence (at [17]):

> 'i) The habitual residence of a child corresponds to the place which reflects some degree of integration by the child in a social and family environment (*A v A*[111], adopting the European test).
>
> ii) The test is essentially a factual one which should not be overlaid with legal sub-rules or glosses. It must be emphasised that the factual enquiry must be centred throughout on the circumstances of the child's life that is most likely to illuminate his habitual residence *(A v A, Re KL*[112]*)*.
>
> iii) In common with the other rules of jurisdiction in Brussels IIR its meaning is 'shaped in the light of the best interests of the child, in particular on the criterion of proximity'. Proximity in this context means 'the practical connection between the child and the country concerned': *A v A* (para 80(ii)); Re B[113] (para 42) applying *Mercredi v Chaffe*[114] at para 46).
>
> iv) It is possible for a parent unilaterally to cause a child to change habitual residence by removing the child to another jurisdiction without the consent of the other parent (*Re R*[115]).
>
> v) A child will usually but not necessarily have the same habitual residence as the parent(s) who care for him or her (*Re LC*[116]). The younger the child the more likely the proposition, however, this is not to eclipse the fact that the investigation is child focused. It is the child's habitual residence which is in question and, it follows the child's integration which is under consideration.
>
> vi) Parental intention is relevant to the assessment, but not determinative (*Re KL, Re R* and *Re B*).
>
> vii) It will be highly unusual for a child to have no habitual residence. Usually a child lose a pre-existing habitual residence at the same time as gaining a new one (*Re B*); (emphasis added).
>
> viii) In assessing whether a child has lost a pre-existing habitual residence and gained a new one, the court must weigh up the degree of connection which the child had with the state in which he resided before the move (*Re B* – see in particular the guidance at para 46).
>
> ix) It is the *stability* of a child's residence as opposed to its *permanence* which is relevant, though this is qualitative and not quantitative, in the sense

110 [2016] EWHC 2174 (Fam).
111 [2013] UKSC 60.
112 [2013] UKSC 75.
113 [2016] UKSC 4.
114 [2011] EWCA Civ 272.
115 [2015] UKSC 35.
116 [2014] UKSC 1.

that it is the integration of the child into the environment rather than a mere measurement of the time a child spends there (*Re R* and earlier in *Re KL* and *Mercredi*).

x) The relevant question is whether a child has achieved *some degree of* integration in social and family environment; it is not necessary for a child to be *fully* integrated before becoming habitually resident (*Re R)* (emphasis added).

xi) The requisite degree of integration can, in certain circumstances, develop quite quickly (Art 9 of BIIR envisages within 3 months). It is possible to acquire a new habitual residence in a single day (*A v A; Re B)*. In the latter case Lord Wilson referred (para 45) those '*first roots*' which represent the requisite degree of integration and which a child will '*probably*' put down '*quite quickly*' following a move.

xii) Habitual residence was a question of fact focused upon the situation of the child, with the purposes and intentions of the parents being merely among the relevant factors. It was the stability of the residence that was important, not whether it was of a permanent character. There was no requirement that the child should have been resident in the country in question for a particular period of time, let alone that there should be an intention on the part of one or both parents to reside there permanently or indefinitely (*Re R*).

xiii) The structure of Brussels IIa, and particularly Recital 12 to the Regulation, demonstrates that it is in a child's best interests to have an habitual residence and accordingly that it would be highly unlikely, albeit possible (or, to use the term adopted in certain parts of the judgment, exceptional), for a child to have no habitual residence; As such, "if interpretation of the concept of habitual residence can reasonably yield both a conclusion that a child has an habitual residence and, alternatively, a conclusion that he lacks any habitual residence, the court should adopt the former" (*Re B* supra).'

How to make an application under the Hague Convention 1980

24.80 In all cases, an application shall have to be made in the domestic courts of the country in which the child is located. Legal aid shall be available in accordance with Article 25 of the Convention. The United Kingdom's Central Authority established in compliance with Article 6 of the Convention is the International Child Abduction and Contact Unit ('ICACU').

24.81 In cases of child abduction overseas to a Hague Convention state, practitioners have a choice of pursuing an application via ICACU or directly with the Central Authority in the state concerned. Details of how to contact ICACU and alternative emergency telephone numbers are set out in the Family Procedure Rules 2010, PD 12F.

Domestic applications

24.82 Prompt consideration of domestic applications ought to be made in all cases of international child abduction. The court shall only have jurisdiction whilst the child remains habitually resident in England and Wales.

24.83 Even where the child's removal from the jurisdiction was lawful, the obtaining of an order for the immediate return of the child shall have the effect of rendering the retention wrongful for the purposes of Article 3 of the Hague Convention. However, in *Re S (abduction: Hague Convention)*,[117] the Court of Appeal held that the best course was to allow an application under the Convention in the other state to be determined before the making of a return order.

24.84 In circumstances where it is unclear whether a child has yet been removed from the jurisdiction, the issuing of wardship proceedings are likely to be the most effective remedy. Such order imposes and immediate prohibition on the removal of the child from the jurisdiction. Of equal significance is the ability to invoke the assistance of the High Court Tipstaff. Common standard form orders available in cases of child abduction include:

(a) Location orders;

(b) Passport orders; and

(c) Collection orders

24.85 The standard terms for location and collection orders include port alerts which notify all police forces and immigration officers of the child's details which are placed on the Child Abduction Warning List for 28 days.

24.86 If a child has successfully been brought to a non-Hague Convention country, an application for the summary return of the child shall have to be pursued under the inherent or wardship jurisdictions of the High Court. In *Re J (A Child) (Custody Rights: Jurisdiction)*,[118] it was held that whether or not to grant a summary return order was a welfare question and that the child's welfare was the primary consideration. At [32] it was held that the starting point is whether 'it is likely to be better for a child to return to his home country for any disputes about his future to be decided there. A case against his doing so has to be made'. At paragraphs [33]–[41], their Lordships set out the following relevant considerations:

(a) The degree of connection between the child and each country;

(b) The length of time spent in each country;

(c) The law in the foreign jurisdiction; and

(d) The effect of the decision on the child's primary carer.

117 [2018] 4 All ER 806.
118 [2006] 1 AC 80.

Other remedies

24.87 If there is an extradition treaty between the United Kingdom and the country to which the child has been abducted, it may be possible to secure the return of the abductor by making a criminal complaint of child abduction and a subsequent extradition request being pursued.[119]

THE ROLE OF BRITISH DIPLOMATIC MISSIONS OVERSEAS

In cases where the person to be protected is abroad the court in England and Wales the court may wish to invoke diplomatic assistance, especially in circumstances where the views of the person to be protected may not be directly known as a result of family, influence or fear.

24.88 For example, *in Re SK*,[120] SK was a British citizen and there was evidence before the court (albeit untested) to suggest that SK may be being kept by her friends and relatives, contrary to her will and her return to the country may have been frustrated by an attempt to marry her forcibly. Singer J noted (at [5]) that:

> 'the English courts have over recent years demonstrated their capacity to act in concert with, amongst others, the Foreign and Commonwealth Office in this country and abroad, a number of NGO's in this country and aboard and humanitarian and committed judges and lawyers abroad to attempt to prevent such gross transgressions of an individual's integrity and, wherever possible, to remedy their consequences'.

24.89 His Lordship went on to make orders that SK was to be interviewed by the British High Commission in Dhaka and requested the assistance of all judicial and administrative bodies and police authorities in the People's Republic of Bangladesh to render assistance in establishing her whereabouts and arranging for her to be placed in contact with the British High Commission. The purpose of such orders was to establish SK's true wishes in an environment where she would, it was hoped, feel able to express them.

24.90 Such orders can be made directly against the person to be protected and/or the relevant family members, friends or other persons they are known to be residing with.

24.91 However, difficulties can arise where either there is no diplomatic presence in the country that the person to be protected is residing and/or where their whereabouts is unknown.[121]

119 Child Abduction Act 1984, ss 1 and 2 create offences of child abduction.

120 [2004] EWHC 3202 (Fam).

121 See for example, *KBH & Others (Forced Marriage Protection Order – Persons to be protected permanently resident abroad)* [2018] EWHC 2611 [at 4].

24.92 The Forced Marriage Unit offers advice to anyone within the United Kingdom, their nationality is irrelevant. However, British Embassies and High Commissions can only offer consular assistance to British nationals and, in some circumstances European Union or Commonwealth nationals whose country does not have a local Embassy or Consulate in the country concerned. Nor can they offer assistance to European Union or Commonwealth nationals in the country of their own nationality.[122]

24.93 If a person is a dual national, depending on their nationality and principles of that country, the British High Commission or Embassy may not be recognised as having any right to offer assistance to them. However, 'in cases where there is special humanitarian reason to do so, the Foreign and Commonwealth Office will consider offering assistance to dual nationals in the country of their other nationality. Forced marriage is one of those circumstances where such an exception may be made'.[123]

24.94 A British national overseas can seek the assistance of the British Embassy or High Commission directly. For example, *A v SM and HB (Forced Marriage Protection Orders)*[124] in which the person to be protected contacted the British High Commission following her arrival in Bangladesh and was subsequently returned to the jurisdiction of England and Wales and *SH v NB (Marriage: Consent)*[125] whereby the person to be protected was assisted by the High Commission in Islamabad and the Pakistani courts. The High Commission assisted in preparing a habeas corpus petition, based on an assertion that the respondent was being kept in Pakistan, against her will, by her family. The petition was heard by the Honourable Chief Justice of Pakistan who ordered the police to ensure that the respondent boarded a flight to the UK.

24.95 The Foreign and Commonwealth Office can thereafter try and repatriate the person to be protected to the UK from overseas. Repatriation can be facilitated by the Forced Marriage Unit through issuing temporary travel documents, arranging flights and/or arranging temporary accommodation whilst the person to be protected is overseas. In exceptional circumstances the Forced Marriage Unit may provide a loan from public funds to allow the person to be protected to return to the UK.[126]

122 Multi-agency statutory guidance for dealing with forced marriage (HM Government June 2014), at page 16.

123 Multi-agency statutory guidance for dealing with forced marriage (HM Government June 2014), at 3.15 page 15.

124 [2012] 2 FLR 1077.

125 [2010] 1 FLR 1927 [at 28].

126 Multi-agency statutory guidance for dealing with forced marriage (HM Government June 2014), at 13.14.

24.96 Such assistance can also be sought from the relevant British Embassy and High Commission via the Foreign and Commonwealth Office in London. Guidance was given by Munby P (as he then was) on the liaison between courts in England and Wales and British Embassies and High Commissions Abroad, 2016[127] which should be read prior to such assistance being sought.

127 Guidance from the Presidents' Office, 'Liaison between Courts in England and Wales and British Embassies and High Commissions Abroad' April 2016.

CHAPTER 25

Role of organisations

Content at a Glance:

Introduction

Schools, colleges and universities

NHS bodies

Local housing authorities

Adult social care

Children's social care

INTRODUCTION

25.1 At the heart of government guidance on forced marriage is the 'the one chance rule'; the principle that there may only be one opportunity for professionals to speak to a potential victim and 'thus … may only have one chance to save a life'.[1] This principle underlines the crucial need for professionals from all relevant bodies and organisations being alive to the risk of forced marriage and aware of the steps that can be taken to help a victim. All practitioners, public bodies and professionals should have regard to:

(a) The Multi-Agency Practice Guidelines: Handling Cases of Forced Marriage[2] ('Multi-Agency Guidelines'); and

(b) The Statutory Guidance on Forced Marriage[3] ('the Statutory Guidance').

25.2 The role and best practices of law enforcement agencies is considered in detail within Chapter 21. This chapter focuses on organisations most likely to come into contact with vulnerable potential victims of forced marriage.

25.3 The need for multi-agency, cross-departmental cooperation in the protection vulnerable adults and children has been underlined by the courts. In the very different context of *Tower Hamlets LBC v M* ,[4] a case concerning the welfare of children said to be at risk of leaving the country to travel to territory

1 HM Government, Multi-agency statutory guidance for dealing with forced marriage, 2014.
2 HM Government, Multi-agency practice guidelines: handling cases of forced marriage, 2014.
3 HM Government, Multi-agency statutory guidance for dealing with forced marriage, 2014.
4 [2015] EWHC 869 (Fam).

held by ISIS, Hayden J highlighted 'the importance of coordinated strategy, predicated on open and respectful cooperation between all safeguarding agencies involved'.

25.4 His Lordship continued at [51]:

> '…only open dialogue, appropriate sharing of information, mutual respect for the differing roles involved and inter-agency cooperation is going to provide the kind of protection that I am satisfied that the children subject to these applications truly require'.

25.5 The spirit of the judgment of Hayden J in *M* is reflected in the statutory and best practice guidance relating to forced marriage. This chapter seeks to draw together the key provisions, proposed protective steps and actions to be taken by public bodies when dealing cases of force marriage that are contained within the Multi-Agency Guidelines and Statutory Guidance.

SCHOOLS, COLLEGES AND UNIVERSITIES

25.6 In addition to Statutory Guidance and Multi-Agency Guidelines, lecturers, teachers and senior managers should have regard to:

(a) Statutory Guidance – Keeping Children Safe in Education;[5]

(b) NASUWT's useful Forced Marriage Guidance, England.[6]

25.7 The Multi-Agency Guidelines require senior managers to ensure that their organisation has a lead person with overall responsibility for safeguarding children, protecting adults with support needs, or, victims of domestic abuse. This person shall also have responsibility for forced marriage issues.

25.8 There is a particular emphasis on the need for vigilance. For example, a student presenting as anxious, depressed and emotionally withdrawn, with low esteem ought to give rise to further inquiries.

25.9 Chapter 7 of both the Statutory Guidance and the Multi-Agency Guidelines provides both practical and preventative steps that may be taken by staff and managers in educational establishments in cases of forced marriage. There is a considerable overlap, and therefore the key provisions are as follows[7]:

(a) Those at risk of forced marriage may have mental health disorders and display behaviours such as self-harming, self-cutting or anorexia. They may also come to the attention of the police through drug taking, alcohol misuse

5 Keeping Children Safe in Education – For Schools and Colleges, 2015.

6 NASUWT Teacher's Union Guidance on Forced Marriage.

7 Pp 32–33, HM Government, Multi-agency practice guidelines: handling cases of forced marriage, 2014.

or shoplifting. Often such symptoms may be exacerbated in the lead up to the holiday period, a time which staff ought to be particularly vigilant.

(b) A sudden decline in performance, aspirations or motivations ought to give rise to particular cause for concern. Students may feel studying is pointless if they are going to be forced to be marry and therefore deprived of the opportunity to continue with their education.

(c) Students facing forced marriage may be subject to excessive restrictions and control at home amounting to virtual imprisonment. Particular risk indicators are:
   (i) Not being allowed to attend extra-curricular or after school activities;
   (ii) Girls and young women being accompanied to and from school or college, even during lunch breaks;
   (iii) A student abruptly stopping attending school;
   (iv) A decline in punctuality in circumstances where the student is having to negotiate their way out of the house; and
   (v) Homework that has been done late at night without the knowledge of the family due to the family discouraging the student from engaging in education.

(d) Teachers may become aware of a conflict between the student and their parents about whether the student shall be allowed to continue in education. In particular, disputes over whether the student shall be allowed to go to university or college and the distance of the institution from the family home.

(e) A family history of older siblings leaving education and marrying early is also a warning sign. This may be indicative of their parents' view that it is their duty to ensure that their children are married soon after puberty in order to protect them from extramarital sex. These cases may involve a history of lengthy absences authorised by the student's parents.

(f) Students may directly seek assistance from a teacher or lecturer, or their friends may report concerns to staff. Educational establishments should aim to create an 'open environment' where students feel comfortable and safe to discuss the problems they are facing. In particular, forced marriage should be discussed openly within the curriculum and support and counselling should be routinely provided.

(g) Staff in special schools ought to be particularly aware of the potential warning signs of forced marriage and appropriately trained in issued relating to forced marriage.

25.10 Both the Statutory Guidance and the Multi-Agency Guidelines outline a 'checklist' of what educational establishments ought to be doing:

(a) Signpost and encourage young people to access appropriate further support and advice;

(b) Display the Department for Children Schools and Families (DCSF) and Forced Marriage Unit posters on forced marriage;

(c) Display relevant information such as details of the NSPCC Helpline, Child Line and appropriate forced marriage support groups;

(d) Ensure a private telephone is available for students to seek help discreetly;

(e) Educate staff about the issues surrounding forced marriage and the presenting symptoms;

(f) Refer students to an education welfare officer, pastoral tutor, learning mentor or school counsellor as appropriate; and

(g) Encourage young people to access appropriate advice, information and support;

(h) Discuss different types of marriage within classes[8].

25.11 The Statutory Guidance sets out that where staff believe a student is being forced into marriage, they ought to:[9]

(a) Talk to the student regarding their concerns;

(b) Contact and seek advice from the Forced Marriage Unit;

(c) Carry out the general steps in Chapters 4 and 5 of the Statutory and Multi-Agency Practice Guidelines;

(d) Liaise with senior colleagues as appropriate;

(e) If the student is under 18 years old, activate child safeguarding procedures and use existing national and local protocols for multi-agency liaison with police and children's social care; and

(f) Establish if the student has dual nationality and/or more than one passport.

25.12 In addition, the Multi-Agency Guidelines add that staff should:[10]

(a) Liaise with local police and adult or children's social care to establish if any incidents have been reported;

(b) Activate local child safeguarding procedures and use national and local protocols for multi-agency liaison.

(c) Establish if there is a family history of forced marriage, domestic-violence, self-harm, family disputes, unreasonable restrictions.

25.13 Both the Multi-Agency Guidelines and the Statutory Guidance stress that staff should not:[11]

8 See p 33, HM Government, Multi-agency practice guidelines: handling cases of forced marriage, 2014.

9 See pp 33–34 HM Government, Multi-agency practice guidelines: handling cases of forced marriage, 2014.

10 See no 10.

11 P 34, HM Government, Multi-agency practice guidelines: handling cases of forced marriage, 2014.

(a) Treat allegations merely as a domestic issue and send the student back to the family home;

(b) Ignore what the student has told them or dismiss the need for immediate protection;

(c) Decide it is not their responsibility to follow-up the allegation;

(d) Approach the student's family or those with influence within the community without the express consent of the student;

(e) Contact the family in advance of any enquiries by the Police, Forced Marriage Unity or social services;

(f) Share information outside the information sharing protocols without the student's consent;

(g) Attempt to mediate or encourage mediation, reconciliation, arbitration or family counselling.

Where a student stops attending school

25.14 If staff have a suspicion that a student has stopped attending school due to a forced marriage, then the Statutory Guidance provides that the following steps ought to be taken:

(a) A referral should be made to the local authority's children or adult social care team and to the police;

(b) The Forced Marriage Unit ought to be contacted;

(c) The educational establishment ought to liaise with the local police domestic abuse unit;

(d) As must information as possible ought to be obtained about the student;

(e) It should be established if there is a history of siblings being forced to marry;

(f) Staff should consider speaking with the student's friends.

(g) An Educational Welfare Officer or teacher may visit the family in the UK to find out why the student is not attending school. The family may claim the student is being educated overseas. In the event the family suggest the Officer or a teacher speak to the student on the phone, they ought to refuse. Instead, if the student is a British National they should insist that the student is produced at the nearest British Embassy or High Commission.[12]

12 Pp 34–35, HM Government, Multi-agency practice guidelines: handling cases of forced marriage, 2014.

Making referrals

25.15 It is not the role of education staff to investigate safeguarding concerns or allegations of abuse. Therefore, all referrals should be made in accordance with Government Statutory Guidance, Working Together to Safeguard Children: A Guide to agencies working to safeguard and promote the welfare of children, or in cases of children with disabilities, in accordance with the local Multi-Agency Adult Protection Committee procedures and protocols to protect vulnerable adults from abuse. All cases of a suspected forced marriage ought also to be reported to the Forced Marriage Unit by schools or universities.

NHS BODIES

25.17 Chapter 6 of both the Multi-Agency Guidelines and Statutory Guidance relates to Health Professionals, the key provisions from both documents are as follows:

(a) NHS Trusts should:
   i. Display relevant information such as the contact details of the National Domestic Violence Helpline, NSPCC, Child Line and other forced marriage support groups;
   ii. Circulate and display copies of the Forced Marriage Unit's leaflets and posters;
   iii. Educate health professionals about the issues surrounding forced marriage;
   iv. Include forced marriage and honour-based violence issues within training for health professionals, including safety planning, risk assessment and management.

(b) Health professionals should be vigilant for signs that a patient may be a victim of forced marriage, warning signs include unexplained injuries, depression, anxiety, self-harm or substance misuse.

(c) Particular considerations arise when a person presents who may not have capacity but mentions that they are married or, for example, that they are trying to get pregnant. Practitioners ought to carefully consider whether it is likely the patient lacks capacity to consent to marriage or sex.

(d) As stated in the Statutory Guidance, an interview with a health professional may be the only opportunity some victims have to tell anyone what is happening to them. To prevent this type of abuse, professionals must be willing to use these limited opportunities to openly discuss issues of forced marriage. Health professionals ought to adopt a proactive role to establish whether forced marriage is an issue. Consideration should be given to whether questions about forced marriage could be incorporated into standard questions asked of patients in the same way that domestic abuse questions are incorporated into various questionnaires for taking patients' details. Both the Statutory Guidance and Multi-Agency Guidelines provide some helpful examples of lines of questions that could be used.

(e) It is important to try to speak to patients on their own, even if they are accompanied. If they require an interpreter, family members, friends or prominent members of the community should not be used. Accredited interpreters should always be used and it may be that a telephone interpreting service gives the victim a greater sense of anonymity and as such allows them to speak more freely. Some people may not wish to speak to a health professional who is male or from their own community.[13]

Confidentiality

25.18 As emphasised in both the Multi-Agency Guidelines and the Statutory Guidance, Victims shall often be reluctant to allow information to be shared with other statutory services.

25.19 Accordingly, difficulties can often arise for health practitioners who want to help victims but are unable to obtain consent to make a referral or report. In those circumstances both documents require the following steps to be taken:[14]

(a) For cases involving a child or an adult who has children that does not want a referral to be made, the health professional shall need to consider what is in the best interests of the child concerned. In particular, whether their wishes should be respected or whether their safety or the safety of their child requires further action to be made. If the health practitioner goes against the person's wishes, they must inform them of this.

(b) A referral to the local police child protection unit should be made if there is any suspicion that a crime has been or may be committed.

(c) In cases involving adults, health practitioners should carefully consult the detailed guidance at Chapter 6.4 of the Statutory Guidance and Chapter 6.10 of the Multi-Agency Guidelines.

LOCAL HOUSING AUTHORITIES

25.20 When a person flees a forced marriage, they also generally flee their only source of support and accommodation and may be rendered homeless. Therefore, local housing authorities are essential in ensuring that victims are able to escape abuse and not forced to return to the family home.

25.21 The Multi-Agency Guidelines underline that it is essential front-line housing officers are aware of the risk of harm facing those who have been or may be forced to marry.

13 Page 24, HM Government, Multi-agency practice guidelines: handling cases of forced marriage, 2014.

14 See pp 27–31, HM Government, Multi agency practice guidelines: handling cases of forced marriage, 2014 for helpful and comprehensive guidance.

25.22 Chapter 11 of the Multi-Agency Guidelines and Chapter 12 of the Statutory Guidance set out what steps housing authorities should take (over and above taking the general action as set out at chapter 4 of the Statutory Guidance) in cases of forced marriage which can be summarised as follows:

(a) Particular vigilance is urged in considering requests for information about a person's whereabouts. Granting such requests can put victims at significant risk. Therefore, housing authorities should not inform family members or friends of victims' whereabouts.

(b) Authorities are also discouraged from using a relative, friend, community leader or neighbour as an interpreter.

(c) When considering whether an applicant who has been forced to marry or is at risk of forced marriage is vulnerable and therefore in priority need under the Housing Act 1996, s 189, the Authority ought to have regard to the Multi-Agency Practice Guidelines and Statutory Guidance.

25.23 It is hard to contemplate a situation where a victim of forced marriage would not be 'significantly more vulnerable than an ordinary person would be if they became homeless'.[15]

ADULT SOCIAL CARE

25.24 Adults with disabilities and care needs may be particularly vulnerable to forced marriage. They may lack capacity to decide whether to marry and in circumstances where their family cares for them, shall be particularly vulnerable to decisions to marry them without their free and full and consent, which they have capacity to give.

25.25 Local authorities have a statutory duty under the Care Act 2014, s 42 in circumstances where it has reason to believe that an adult in its area:

(a) Has needs for care and support (whether or not the Authority is meeting those needs;

(b) Is experiencing, or is at risk of, abuse or neglect, and

(c) As a result of those needs is unable to protect himself or herself against the abuse or neglect or the risk of it.

25.26 In such circumstances, an authority must make whatever enquiries it thinks necessary to decide whether any action should be taken in the adult's case and if so, what any by whom.

25.27 Authorities should not assume that an adult with support needs is at risk of being forced into marriage simply on the basis they are being taken on

15 *Hotak v Southwark LBC* [2015] UKSC 30.

an extended family holiday. Such assumptions and stereotyping can, of course, cause great distress to the family.

25.28 However, in circumstances where it is feared that an adult with support needs may be forced into marriage, Chapter 10 of the Multi-Agency Guidelines and Chapter 11 of the Statutory Guidance deals with forced marriages cases that have a cross over with adult social care provides that the following steps ought to be taken:

(a) All efforts should be made to establish the full facts of the case at the earliest opportunity;

(b) The matter ought to be discussed with the Forced Marriage Unit;

(c) Seek advice from the local authority legal department;

(d) If the risk of forced marriage is immediate, it may be necessary to take emergency action to remove them from the home in order to protect them.

(e) If there is a question as to the person's capacity to consent to marriage or sex, a capacity assessment ought to be undertaken;

(f) Consider the need for a communication specialist if the person is deaf, visually impaired or has learning difficulties;

(g) Check police and social care records for past referrals of family members, including siblings;

(h) Establish if there is a family history of forced marriage;

(i) Consensual referrals to forced marriage support groups ought to be made;

(j) Follow the Multi-Agency Guidelines and Statutory Guidance's general guidance.[16]

25.29 Particular consideration ought to be given to whether an urgent application for a Forced Marriage Protection Order is necessary. In circumstances where the person lacks capacity as to residence and care, an urgent application to the Court of Protection may also be necessary to remove the person from the family home.

Where a forced marriage has already happened

25.30 Sometimes, cases shall only come to the attention of social services after a forced marriage has taken place. The remedies available to an Authority in such circumstances are considered in **Chapter 5**.

16 Page 55, HM Government, Multi-agency practice guidelines: handling cases of forced marriage, 2014.

25.31 However, both the Multi-Agency Guidelines and Statutory Guidelines suggest the authorities take the following steps upon being notified that an adult with support needs has been forcibly married:

(a) Follow the general guidance of the Multi-Agency Guidelines and Statutory Guidance;

(b) Refer them to the Forced Marriage Unit;

(c) Refer the adult with support needs to the local police domestic abuse unit;

(d) Record full details of the adult together with details of the marriage including the time and date;

(e) Record the name, address and date of birth of the spouse as well as interview dates for their visa;

(f) Refer to a family panel solicitor for legal advice;

(g) If the person does not want to return to the family home, then devise a strategy for leaving the home and give personal safety advice;

(h) Consensually refer to forced marriage support groups and/or counselling;

(i) If the adult wants to remain at the family home, consider maintaining contract without placing them at risk; and

(j) Consider maintaining contact using community workers or health workers.

Assisting in repatriations

25.32 The Forced Marriage Unit may ask adult social services for assistance with an adult with support needs who is being repatriated to the United Kingdom. The Statutory Guidance and Multi-Agency Guidelines, suggest what authorities ought and ought not to do.

25.33 They should:

(a) Arrange for someone to meet the returning person at the airport – for example a social worker, police officer or other sympathetic adult;

(b) Inform the police in case family members seek to intercept and abduct them at the airport;

(c) Organise safe and secure accommodation;

(d) Explain the options available; and

(e) Inform the police that the person's family may attempt to locate them;

(f) If consent is given, accommodate or relocate them to a different local authority;

(g) Consensually refer to forced marriage support groups and/or counselling;

(h) Assess the risk for any other younger family members;

(i) Ensure confidentiality, which may include witness protection schemes[17].

25.34 Adult social services should not meet the adult at their new address, refuge or accommodation as social workers may be followed. Professionals ought to be careful to ensure they do not put themselves or the victim at risk of harm. In particular, the victim should not be sent back to the family home against their wishes and family members or friends should not be informed of the victim's whereabouts. Professionals should not seek to facilitate mediation or reconciliation.

Where a forced marriage victim comes to the UK

25.35 The Multi-Agency Guidelines and Statutory Guidance highlights that victims with support needs who come to the UK from overseas, having been forced to marry, have a number of specific vulnerabilities including[18]:

(a) They may be suffering domestic abuse or may have run away;

(b) They may not speak English;

(c) They may be unaware of the support to which they may be entitled;

(d) They may not be eligible for recourse to public funds, meaning they have little or no means to live independently of their abuser; and

(e) They may feel unable to co-operate with social care services or others perceived to be in a position of authority.

25.36 In such cases, the documents suggest that social care services ought to follow the general guidance in Chapters 4 and 5 of the Guidelines and then[19]:

(a) Ensure the victim is dealt with in a culturally sensitive way and their wishes are recognised and respected;

(b) Arrange for an authorised interpret who speaks the dialect of the person, if necessary obtain consent form the victim through language line and establish any preferences regarding the gender of the interpreter;

(c) Explain all the options available and consensually refer them to forced marriage support groups;

(d) If necessary, refer them to an appropriate solicitor or law centre, ideally with both Family and Immigration Law expertise and legal aid contracts near where they live;

17 Page 57, HM Government, Multi-agency practice guidelines: handling cases of forced marriage, 2014.

18 Page 58, HM Government, Multi-agency practice guidelines: handling cases of forced marriage, 2014.

19 See no 22.

(e) Provide written contact details of the social worker dealing with the case to give to the solicitor;

(f) With the person's consent, notify the local police domestic abuse unit; and

(g) Record any injuries and arrange a medical examination. The doctor ought to be informed that there may be an immigration application and that detailed notes shall need to be taken.

25.37 Although not stated in the Multi-Agency Guidelines, if a social worker suspects the victim may lack capacity in any relevant domain and in particular in respect of capacity to consent to marriage or sex, capacity to make decisions about contact with others or capacity to decide where to live or what care to receive, they ought to undertake a mental capacity assessment.

25.38 Both the Multi-Agency Guidelines and Statutory Guidance make clear that adult social care workers must not use a relative, friend, community leader or neighbour as an interpreter; or attempt to give any immigration advice;

CHILDREN'S SOCIAL CARE

25.39 Children's social services play a pivotal role in protecting and supporting children affected by forced marriage. Children's social services are under a duty pursuant to the Children Act 1989, s 47 to make enquiries when they have reasonable cause to suspect that a child is suffering, or likely to suffer, significant harm. Forced marriage is child abuse which puts children at risk of physical, emotional and sexual abuse. In all cases, the personal safety of the child is paramount.

25.40 Cases which involve the risk of forced marriage may include fast paced litigation and the need to urgent steps to be taken. Social services should be aware that it is possible and indeed often necessary to seek orders out of normal business hours on an extremely urgent basis. Munby P (as he then was) held in *Re M* :[20]

> '…it is important that the public should be able to understand, and I trust appreciate, just how quickly, effectively and flexibly the family courts are able to respond, if need be outside normal court hours, in urgent cases and where events may, as here, be changing 'on the ground' very rapidly but far away. There is always, every minute of every day and night throughout the year, a judge of the Family Division on duty, 'out of hours', to deal with cases so urgent that they cannot wait. This case, I believe, shows the system working well. The court became involved in the early morning of Tuesday 5 May. The children had returned to this country by the middle of the afternoon of Thursday 7 May. For another example of the family

20 [2015] EWHC 1433 (Fam) at [25].

court system working as it should and reacting promptly to rapidly changing circumstances see *Re Ashya King (A Child)* [2014] EWHC 2964 (Fam)'

25.41 In addition to the Multi-Agency Guidelines and Statutory Guidance, children's social workers should also have regard to the following statutes and Government Guidance:

(a) HM Government, Safeguarding Disabled Children, Practice Guidance, 2009

(b) HM Government, Working Together to Safeguard Children, 2018

(c) BASW, Safeguarding Children: Working Together Under the Children Act 2004, 2006

(d) HM Government, what to do if you are worried a child is being abused, 2006

(e) Children Act 1989

(f) Children Act 2004

(g) Homelessness Act 2002

(h) Sexual Offences Act 2003

25.42 Each Local Safeguarding Children Board ought to have multi-agency policies and procedures that include handling cases where forced marriage is alleged or known about.[21]

Where a child fears they may be forced into marriage

25.43 The Multi-Agency Guidelines and Statutory Guidance recommend that in circumstances where there is real and warranted concern that a child may be forced to marry, not based on assumption of stereotyping, then the following steps should be taken:[22]

(a) Seek advice from the Authority's legal department and the Forced Marriage Unit;

(b) Consider obtaining a court order such as wardship and a Forced Marriage Protection Order to protect the child or young person and prevent hem being taken overseas;

(c) Refer the child to appropriate support groups;

(d) Check police reports and social services' records for past referrals of family members;

(e) Establish whether there is a family history of forced marriage;

21 Page 45, HM Government, Multi-agency practice guidelines: handling cases of forced marriage, 2014.

22 Page 46, HM Government, Multi-agency practice guidelines: handling cases of forced marriage, 2014.

(f) Consider liaising with the school to identify any concerns they may have;

(g) Talk to the child about whether they can avoid going overseas and discus the difficulties they may face;

(h) Discuss the implications of dual nationality;

(i) If their consent if given, refer them to forced marriage support groups and counselling;

(j) Follow the general guidance in the Statutory Guidance and Multi-Agency Guidelines.[23]

25.44 In all cases, the social worker needs to discuss the range of options available with the child or young person and the consequences of those actions. Chapter 5 of both the Statutory Guidance and Multi-Agency Guidelines set out that in circumstances where it is unavoidable that the child shall be taken overseas the following steps ought to be taken:[24]

(a) Provide contact details of the agency and professional handling their case;

(b) Supply the child with the telephone number and email address of the nearest British Embassy or High Commission and encourage them to memorise it;

(c) If a foreign national, encourage the child to contact the Forced Marriage Unit for details of reliable NGO's overseas and the details of the Embassy of their own country;

(d) Advise the child to take a mobile phone that will work overseas, and that they can keep it hidden;

(e) Encourage them to provide the social worker with details of a trusted friend or advocate in the UK who they shall be keeping in touch with overseas who can be approached if they do not return. Contact that friend or advocate before the departure and ask them to make a written statement of their support;

(f) Advise them to take emergency cash, in case problems arise in the country of destination, together with contact details of someone there they can trust to help them;

(g) Ascertain whether they are dual nationals, as they may have two passports. Remind them about the implications of dual nationality;

(h) Advise them to contact the Forced Marriage Unit.

25.45 Social workers ought also to obtain all names and addresses or other geographical information of extended family members in the area the person may be staying.

23 Page 46, HM Government, Multi-agency practice guidelines: handling cases of forced marriage, 2014.

24 Page 21, HM Government, Multi-agency practice guidelines: handling cases of forced marriage, 2014.

Where a third-party reports that a child or young person has been taken overseas for a forced marriage

25.46 In circumstances where a third party reports that a child has been taken overseas to be married, both the Statutory Guidance and the Multi-Agency Guidelines emphasise the need for confidentiality and discretion. Social workers are discouraged from immediately contacting overseas organisations or authorities due to the risk the family may become aware and move the child.

25.47 As well as completing the general guidance in Chapter 4 of the Guidelines, both documents recommend that social workers:

(a) Seek advice from the Authority's legal department;

(b) Consider asking an Education Welfare Officer to make enquiries;

(c) Liaise with the police to check existing missing person reports;

(d) Obtain details of, and seek to maintain contact with, the third party in case the young person contacts them whilst overseas or on their return.

(e) Use existing national and local protocols for inter-agency liaison.

(f) Extreme care should be taken not to disclose information to the overseas police or any other overseas organisation that could place the young person in further danger. For example, it the third party reporting the situation is the victim's boyfriend or girlfriend, this must not be disclosed;

(g) Inform the third party that if the child or young person being held overseas wishes to return to the UK and they are a British National, the Foreign & Commonwealth Office can try to repatriate them as soon as possible.

(h) Ascertain if anyone else is aware of the situation and establish whether enquiries have already been made. Consider whether there is evidence to support forced marriage and other abuses.

(i) Dissuade the third party and others from making enquiries or acting independently of children's social care and the police.

(j) Find and document any evidence to confirm the threat of a forced marriage and any related abuse.

(k) Consider referring the third party to appropriate support groups.

25.48 Social workers should not go directly to the young person's family, friends or those with influence in the community as this may alert the family that the authorities are aware and place the child at greater danger.

Where a child or young person has already been forced into marriage

25.49 When social services become aware of a child or young person who has been forcibly married, the Multi-Agency Guidelines and the Statutory Guidance provides that they ought to follow the general guidance in Chapters 4 and 5, have regard to any specific warning signs and then[25]:

(a) Consider the use of legal remedies to protect the child or young person from family members if they wish to leave the family home or wish the spouse to leave;

(b) Contact the Forced Marriage Unit if the marriage has an overseas dimension or there are concerns about the spouse obtaining a visa;

(c) Record full details of the young person as well as details of the marriage including date and place;

(d) Make a referral to a police officer with responsibility for safeguarding children.

(e) Record the name, address and date of birth of the spouse as well as with interview dates for their visa;

(f) If they require legal advice suggest they consult a family panel solicitor.

(g) If the child or young person does not want to return to the family home, then a strategy for leaving home should be devised and personal safety advice discussed.

(h) If the child or young person wishes to remain at the family home, try to maintain contact without placing them at risk.

(i) Make a referral to an appropriate support group.

Where a child or young person is repatriated

25.50 In circumstances where a young person has been repatriated due to concerns about forced marriage, the Forced Marriage Unit may ask children's social care services for assistance. Professionals should be mindful of and sensitive to the distress that children may have faced as a result of their experiences.

25.51 The Foreign Office shall always try to repatriate a child who contacts a British Embassy or High Commission as quickly as possible: this may mean that children's services have little notice of a child's return to the United Kingdom.[26]

25.52 Remarkably, the Foreign, Commonwealth and Development Office ('FCDO') shall seek to recover or avoid the costs of repatriation, even in cases involving children who have been forced to marry. This means that the FCDO may ask the victim, their friends and their school or college if they are able to cover the costs of repatriation. Government policy is that this ought never to delay the process of getting a child to safety.[27]

25 Pages 46–47, HM Government, Multi-agency practice guidelines: handling cases of forced marriage, 2014.

26 Page 48, HM Government, Multi-agency practice guidelines: handling cases of forced marriage, 2014.

27 Page 45, HM Government, Multi-agency practice guidelines: handling cases of forced marriage, 2014.

25.53 Both the Multi-Agency Guidelines the Statutory Guidance provide that in cases where children's social services are asked to assist with a repatriation, they ought to:[28]

(a) Arrange for someone to meet the child at the airport such as a social worker, police officer or reliable, sympathetic adult. There is a child protection officer based at Heathrow airport;

(b) Consider contacting an appropriate national support agency for further advice on assisting repatriated victims of forced marriage;

(c) Where the child is arriving at Heathrow or Gatwick airports, contact "Travel Care";

(d) Inform the police in case family members try to abduct the young person at the airport;

(e) Explain the options available to the child or young person;

(f) Consider applying for an emergency protection order or an interim care order;

(g) Organise safe and secure accommodation;

(h) If the child is less than 17 years old and it is not appropriate to apply for a care order, inform the police that the young person's family may attempt to locate them.

(i) Consider whether specific support under the Children Act 1989, s 17 ought to be provided in the form of cash, clothes and toiletries. The local authority in which the child's last permanent address was should provide funding.

(j) Consider accommodating or relocating the child with a different local authority if the child consents. This may require a transition period and the negotiating of funding and support with the receiving authority;

(k) Refer the child or young person, with their consent to appropriate support groups;

(l) Take active steps to ensure that the child's identity together with their records are kept confidential. This may require liaison with witness protection schemes such as the UK Protected Person Service. It may be appropriate to seek legal advice for the child in respect of changing their name and National Insurance Number; and

(m) Assess the risk to any other siblings, now and in the future. Younger siblings may be at particular risk of being forced to marry and it may be appropriate to talk to them about forced marriage and the help available.

25.54 It is recommended that social workers ought not to meet the child or young person at their new accommodation in case they are followed. Particular care must be taken not to put the child or professionals at risk. In particular,

28 Page 48–29, HM Government, Multi-agency practice guidelines: handling cases of forced marriage, 2014.

friends and family members should not be informed of the child's whereabouts. The child or young person should not be sent back to the family home. It is also not appropriate for social workers to attempt to mediate or encourage medication, reconciliation or family counselling.

25.55 Specific considerations then arise as to how to accommodate and care for the child or young person. Both documents emphasise that arranging a foster family from the same community may not be appropriate and may give rise to a risk of harm. Children should be encouraged to be accommodated outside the immediate geographical area.

Where a spouse has come to the UK from overseas

25.56 A young person forced to marry and brought to the United Kingdom is likely to be particularly vulnerable. The Statutory Guidance notes that they may not speak English and may not be aware of the support to which they are entitled. A child who is married is entitled to support and should be treated as an unaccompanied child.

25.57 The Multi-Agency Guidelines and Statutory Guidance recommend that the following steps are taken by social services in such circumstances:

(a) Discuss the options available with the child;

(b) Ensure the child or young person is treated in a culturally sensitive way and that their wishes are recognised and respected;

(c) Arrange for an authorised interpreter who speaks the language or dialect of the child or young person. It may be necessary to obtain consent from the child or young person through Language Line. Social workers should establish any preferences regarding the gender of the interpreter;

(d) Refer the child or young person, with their consent, to appropriate support and counselling groups;

(e) If immigration advice may be required, the child or young person should be referred to an appropriate solicitor ideally with an immigration and family law legal aid certificate near to where they live;

(f) Provide the child or young person with written contact details of the social worker handling their case to give to their solicitor.

(g) With the child or young person's consent, contact the local police specialist unit dealing with domestic abuse and forced marriage;

(h) Carefully record any injuries and arrange a medical examination. The doctor should be informed that there may be an immigration application and detailed notes will need to be taken during the examination;

(i) Follow the general guidance within the Statutory Guidance and Multi-Agency Guidelines;

(j) If the child or young person has a disability they will be entitled to an assessment of their needs.

(k) If the young person is under the age of 18 years old, is present in United Kingdom without their family, and states that they were forced into marriage and does not wish to remain with their spouse; children's social care should treat the child or young person in the same manner as an unaccompanied asylum-seeking minor, and should accommodate them pursuant to s.20 Children Act 1989. Where the victim is under 18 and has children, she should still be treated as an unaccompanied child.[29]

25.58 Just as with adult social care, children's social services should not use a friend, community leader or neighbour as an interpreter. In light of the fact that providing unqualified immigration advice is a criminal offence, social workers should also avoid giving any immigration advice to the victim.[30]

Duties to accommodate

25.59 The Children Act 1989, s 17 places a duty on local authorities to make provision for children in their area who are 'in need'. Section 17 grants the authority the power to provide accommodation to a child or young person. Authorities should carefully consider whether other support under s 17 is required, whether that be financial support, providing food, clothes and toiletries or covering travel expenses.

25.60 The Children Act 1989, s 20 contains a mandatory duty rather than being merely a power of local authorities. Authorities must provide accommodation for any child 'in need' within their area who appears to them to require accommodation. This can be as a result of the person who has been caring for the child being prevented from providing them with suitable accommodation or care, no person having parental responsibility for the child or the as a result of the child having been lost or abandoned.

25.61 The Children Act 1989, s 20(3) requires that every local authority shall provide accommodation for any child in need within their area who has reached the age of sixteen and whose welfare the authority consider is likely to be seriously prejudiced if they do not provide them with accommodation. The Multi-Agency Guidelines and Statutory Guidance make clear that a child who has been forcibly married or is at risk of forced marriage is highly likely to fall within this definition.

25.62 The Children Act 1989, s 20 does not allow the local authority to share parental responsibility for the child in question, therefore in cases where the

29 Pages 50–51, HM Government, Multi-agency practice guidelines: handling cases of forced marriage, 2014.

30 Immigration and Asylum Act 1999, s 91.

child is under 16, should their s 20 consent be revoked, the local authority shall return the child to their care or take further steps to apply for public law or other injunctive orders. As a result, where there may be cases involving familial conflict or involvement then s 20 is likely to not be able to provide the necessary protections for the child.

Safeguarding disabled children

25.63 It is not uncommon for both children and adults who are forced to marry to have mental ill health, learning difficulties or physical disabilities. Such marriages may be motivated by a desire to ensure that the victim shall have someone to care for them after their parents have died. Whilst children under 16 cannot have capacity to marry, those who are 16–18 are presumed to have capacity to decide to marry with parental consent.[31] Social workers shall therefore need to carefully consider whether 16 and 17-year olds may lack capacity and carry out a capacity assessment if necessary.

25.64 As noted within the Statutory Guidance and Multi-Agency Guidelines, disabled children and young people are particularly vulnerable to forced marriage because as they may be reliant on their families for care. They may also have communication difficulties which limit their opportunities to tell anyone outside the family about what is happening to them. It is therefore good practice to:

(a) Listen to disabled children and young people and ensure they know how to raise concerns;

(b) Consider whether a communication specialist is needed if a child or young person is deaf, visually impaired or has another communication impairment;

(c) Make sure disabled children and young people have access to adults outside the family who they can turn to for help;

(d) Provide training and raise awareness about forced marriage amongst staff who care for disabled children and young people.

Further considerations

25.65 Local authorities shall be familiar with the range of remedies available in forced marriage cases. In particular, the Statutory Guidance makes clear that authorities ought to consider and make children aware of:

(a) Forced Marriage Protection Orders;

(b) Non-molestation orders;

31 Mental Capacity Act 2005, s 1.

(c) Occupation Order;

(d) Injunctions against harassment;

(e) Police protection;

(f) Emergency protection orders;

(g) Care and supervision orders.

25.66 In circumstances where a forced marriage has already taken place, local authorities ought to consider the remedies available in as set out in **Chapter 5** of the Guidelines.

CHAPTER 26

Possible civil liability arising from failures to protect

Content at a Glance:

INTRODUCTION

26.1 Local authorities, the police and other public bodies have clearly defined roles and duties in detecting, preventing and remedying forced marriages. Failure to fulfil these roles can cause immeasurable harm to victims and give rise to liability on the part of public authority concerned.

26.2 There are a number of leading texts which explore different aspects of potential liability for public authorities.[1] Thus, this chapter is simply intended as an introductory guide to the type of actions which can be brought for a failure to protect a victim of forced marriage.

CHECKLIST

Key Provisions

Forced marriage engages a person's human rights and the protections under the Human Rights Act 1998 and European Convention on Human Rights.

Public bodies have defined roles and duties in detecting, preventing and remedying forced marriages.

1 See Clayton and Tomlinson, *Civil Actions Against the Police* (Sweet and Maxwell), the 4th Edn of which is due for publication in 2021, Karon Monaghan, Monaghan on Equality Law 2nd Edn (Oxford University Press, 2013) and *Clerk and Lindsell on Torts*, 23rd Edn (Sweet and Maxwell, 2020).

It is unlawful for a public authority to act in a manner incompatible with a Convention Right.

The Human Rights Act 1998, s 7 provides a right to either bring proceedings against the authority which has violated the victims Convention rights or to rely on the violated Convention rights in the course of any legal proceedings.

In circumstances where a public body has failed to discharge their positive obligations under the European Convention on Human Rights a person may bring freestanding proceedings under the Human Rights Act 1998, ss 7 and 8 for damages.

A claim may be brought against the police and/or children's services for negligence however, it is particularly challenging and if possible, consideration should be given to bringing a claim under the Human Rights Act 1998 instead.

HUMAN RIGHTS

26.3 An analysis of the human rights implications of forced marriage is set out at **Chapter 6**. It is unlikely to be disputed that a forced marriage engages and violates the human rights of the victim.[2] In particular, it is highly likely that a forced marriage shall amount to a violation of a person's rights under Article 3 of the Convention.[3] As a result of this, the UK State and all emanations of it are likely to fall under a number of positive obligations when made aware of an actual or potential forced marriage.

Positive obligations

26.4 The European Convention of Human Rights and, by extension, the Human Rights Act 1998 only have vertical application. This means that whilst any public body can violate your rights under the Convention, individuals, in law, cannot. Thus, as a starting point, the duty on public bodies to act in a manner which is compatible with the Convention imposes a duty not to actively violate the convention rights of individuals.

26.5 However, the Convention goes a step further and imposes positive obligations on states which require public bodies to do positive certain acts. The

2 See for example Singer J's comment that 'forced marriage is simply an abuse of human rights… it dehumanises people' in *Re SK (An Adult) (Forced Marriage: Appropriate Relief)* [2004] EWHC 3202 (Fam).

3 See paragraph 25 of *Re K (Forced Marriage: Passport Order)* [2020] EWCA Civ 190 and *Volodina v Russia (Application No 41261/17)* read with Practice Direction 12J of the Family Procedure Rules 2010.

ambit of the State's positive obligations is expanding, however, some of the key positive obligations relevant to forced marriage are:

(a) When the State is on notice of a specific and immediate threat to someone's life, it is bound to take effective protective steps;[4]

(b) The law must provide effective and adequate protection against rape a sexual abuse;[5]

(c) Conduct effective investigations into allegations of rape or other conduct which amounts to an interference with Article 3;[6]

26.6 In *Re K (Forced Marriage: Passport Order)*,[7] in submissions, the Secretary of State identified the following positive obligations in respect of forced marriage cases:

(a) Preventing a breach of the right to marry under ECHR, Article 12;[8]

(b) Discharging the UK's positive obligation under ECHR Article 8 (the right to a private and family life) with regard to the right to respect for private life and the protection of the moral and physical integrity of individuals by enhancing or liberating the autonomy of a vulnerable adult;

(c) Discharging the UK's positive obligations under ECHR, Article 3 (prohibition on torture, cruel and degrading treatment) in cases where forced marriage may give rise to a real risk of behaviour sufficient to engage Article 3. In cases in which the Article 3 threshold has been crossed, the UK has an obligation to take reasonable steps to prevent a real risk of inhuman or degrading treatment at the hands of non-State actors, which includes treatment which may be imposed outside the jurisdiction;

(d) Discharging the UK's positive obligation under ECHR Article 5 with respect to deprivation of liberty;

(e) In particularly serious cases, discharging the UK's positive obligations under ECHR Article 2 (the right to life).

Remedies following breach

26.7 The effect of the Human Rights Act 1998, s 6 is that it is unlawful for a public authority to act in a manner incompatible with a Convention Right.[9] Section 6(3) defines a public body as either a court or tribunal or any person carrying out a public function. As such, local authorities, police forces and courts

4 *Osman v United Kingdom* (Application No 23452/94) (2000) 29 EHHR 245.

5 *MC v Bulgaria* [2005] 40 EHRR 20).

6 *Commissioner of Police of the Metropolis v DSD* [2018] UKSC 11.

7 [2020] EWCA Civ 190.

8 See *R (Quila) v Secretary of State for the Home Department* [2011] 3 WLR 836.

9 Council of Europe, *European Convention for the Protection of Human Rights and Fundamental Freedoms,* 4 November 1950.

all have a duty to give effect to the Convention when making decisions about forced marriage.

26.8 If a party is, or would be, a victim of an unlawful act under the Human Rights Act 1998, s 6, ie an act of a public body acting in a manner incompatible with the Convention, then s 7 comes into play. Section 7 provides a right either to bring proceedings against the authority which has violated the victims Convention rights or to rely on the violated Convention rights in the course of any legal proceedings.

26.9 It follows that if the applicant for a forced marriage protection order is the person to be protected, it is open to them to rely on Articles 3 and 8 during the course of those proceedings if they aver that they are at risk of those rights being breached.

26.10 Victims who claim that a public body has failed to discharge their positive obligations under the Convention may bring freestanding proceedings under the Human Rights Act 1998, ss 7 and 8 for damages.

NEGLIGENCE

26.11 Tortious liability for negligence has four essential elements:

(a) Duty of care;

(b) Breach of duty;

(c) Damage caused by the breach; and

(d) Foreseeability of the damage.

The police

26.12 Establishing a successful claim for negligence against the police is particularly challenging and if possible, victims ought to consider bringing a claim under the Human Rights Act 1998 instead.

26.13 The Courts have consistently proved reluctant to impose a duty of care on police services. In *Hill v Chief Constable of West Yorkshire*,[10] the court was concerned with Jacqueline Hill, the last victim of Peter Sutcliffe, commonly known as the Yorkshire Ripper. Over a five-year period, Sutcliffe had committed 13 murders and 8 attempted murders. Ms Hill's mother brought an action in negligence against West Yorkshire Police on the basis that the defendant had negligently failed to catch the murderer. The House of Lords held that there was insufficient proximity to give rise to a duty of care; Ms Hill was merely one of a large number of women at risk.

10 [1988] 2 WLR 1049.

26.14 This general approach was followed in *Alexandrou v Oxford*.[11] The case concerned a shop owner who had installed an alarm which would notify the police in the event of a burglary. The shop was burgled, the alarm automatically dialled 999 and relayed a recorded message. The police failed to take steps to secure the shop. The Court of Appeal held that there was no special relationship between a member of the public making an emergency call and the police. Similarly, in *Michael v Chief Constable of South Wales*,[12] a victim having called 999 shortly before being murdered was not sufficient to give rise to a duty of care. Therefore, it appears that even a forced marriage victim who specifically makes the police aware of a risk shall not have the benefit of a duty of care on the part of the police.

26.15 In *Smith v Chief Constable of Sussex Police*,[13] Lord Phillips held:

> '...so it seems to me, that in the absence of special circumstances the police owe no common law duty of care to protect individuals against harm caused by criminals.'

26.16 In *Smith,* Lord Brown posed the question as whether a duty of care 'should be found to exist when the police, without having assumed any particular responsibility towards the eventual victim, are engaged rather in discharging their more general duty of combatting and investigating crime'.

26.17 The exception to the rule is set out in *Robinson v Chief Constable of West Yorkshire Police*.[14] Officers acted carelessly when arresting a suspect in circumstances where it was foreseeable that said carelessness would result in injury. The Supreme Court held that as the police failures involved a positive act and there was foreseeable harm that flowed from that act, a duty of care did arise. Thus, in circumstances where a positive act by the police, as opposed to an omission, cause foreseeable harm, a duty of care is likely to be found. It follows that should officers, in breach of the Multi-Agency Practice Guidance commit a positive act causing foreseeable damage to a victim of forced marriage, such an act may be actionable in negligence. Examples may include inappropriately disclosing information to family members which subsequently causes the victim harm or notifying a foreign police force without first liaising with the Forced Marriage Unit.

Children or adult social services

26.18 The courts have taken a similarly restrictive approach to imposing private law duties of care on public bodies discharging social care duties. In *X v Bedfordshire CC*,[15] the House of Lords held that in cases involving Acts of Parliament which establish frameworks for the promotion of the social

11 [1993] 4 All ER 328.
12 [2015] AC 1732.
13 [2009] 1 AC 225.
14 [2018] AC 736.
15 [1995] 2 AC 633.

welfare of the community, it would require exceptionally clear language to show a parliamentary intention that those responsible for carrying through that framework shall be liable in damages if they fail to fulfil their statutory duties.

26.19 In *Poole BC v GN*,[16] the Supreme Court considered the when a duty of care shall arise in the context of a local authority exercising functions under the Children Act 1989. The case concerned a family housed by social services under the Children Act 1989, s 17 next door to anti-social neighbours. The family were subject to abuse, harassment, criminal damage and physical assault over several years. One of the children became suicidal and ran away from home.

26.20 In respect of when a duty of care shall be owed, the Supreme Court held:

(a) Public authorities may owe a duty of care in circumstances where the principles applicable to private individuals impose such a duty unless such a duty would be incompatible with the legislation under which the Authority is exercising its powers;

(b) Public authorities do not owe a common law duty of care simply on the basis that they had statutory powers or duties to act in a certain way, even if by exercising their functions that could have prevented the claimant suffering harm;

(c) Authorities could fall under a common law duty to protect from a person harm in if principles applicable to private individuals or bodies would impose such a duty, for example where if the authority had created the source of danger or had assumed a responsibility to protect the claimant from harm, unless the imposition of such a duty would be inconsistent with the relevant legislation.

26.21 However, on the facts of the case, the Supreme Court held that the local authority had not accepted responsibility for the family's safety and the local authority had not taken the children into care and accepted responsibility for their welfare. The Supreme Court held that the nature of statutory functions relied upon did not involve an acceptance of responsibility towards the children to discharge those functions with reasonable care. Therefore, the action failed.

26.22 It follows therefore that as with the police, there are significant hurdles to bringing actions against local authorities following failures to protect in forced marriage cases or failures to adequately investigate. A breach of statutory duty is unlikely, in and of itself, to be sufficient.

16 [2019] 2 WLR 1478.

Index

[All references are to paragraph numbers.]

H

P

www.ingramcontent.com/pod-product-compliance
Ingram Content Group UK Ltd.
Pitfield, Milton Keynes, MK11 3LW, UK
UKHW051955040526
470653UK00002B/12

9 781526 515957